Subject to Colonialism

Subject to Colonialism

African Self-Fashioning and the Colonial Library

GAURAV DESAI

DUKE UNIVERSITY PRESS   Durham and London   2001

© 2001 Duke University Press
All rights reserved
Printed in the United States of
America on acid-free paper ∞
Designed by Amy Ruth Buchanan
Typeset in Carter & Cone Galliard by
Wilsted & Taylor Publishing Services
Library of Congress Cataloging-in-
Publication Data appear on the last
printed page of this book.

For Papa and Aai

Lovely things, I thought much about you in childhood.

Before I had you I wanted you dearly

For you are so beautiful and have all my love.

Oh! How beautiful you are and perfectly shaped,

How clean you are and well kept,

I marvel you shine with such brightness . . .

I would never have thought you could cause me so much pain.

A poem written by a Ugandan schoolboy addressing his shoes, circa 1950. Quoted
in F. Musgrove, "A Uganda Secondary School as a Field of Cultural Change"

Contents

Acknowledgments

Completing one's first book project is perhaps one of the most awe-inspiring moments of an academic's career. One spends many years looking forward to its completion, and yet when it is done, one cannot help but feel nostalgic over the many trials and tribulations it has posed and the many persons in many places that have sometimes unknowingly provided encouragement, guidance, and occasional solace during its composition. Many of these are persons who to the writer remain nameless—the countless librarians and desk attendants in libraries, the various audiences at conferences, the many coffee-shop owners who let us sit in their cafes for hours pondering over the latest arguments of a Ngũgĩ or a Foucault. These are the many faces that appear before me and whom I wish I could thank individually.

But in addition to these persons who continue to remain nameless are those who deeply affect one's life and who are responsible in no small measure for both the content as well as the form of one's thinking. In this regard, I owe a great debt to Simon Gikandi, who almost single-handedly steered me in the direction of a career in literary studies. As a graduate instructor at Northwestern University, he took me to my first academic conference, and it was this experience that began my academic trajectory. With the encouragement of strong mentors like Dwight Conquergood, Françoise Lionnet, Gerald Graff, and John Brenkman, I entered the graduate program in English at Duke, and it would be no exaggeration to say that the subsequent few years were some of the most exciting years I have had in the academy. It was at Duke that *Subject to Colonialism* began to take shape, and although the book has seen many reincarnations before its final version, the comments I received at this early stage from Barbara Herrnstein Smith, V. Y. Mudimbe, Stanley Fish, Kenneth Surin, and Marianna Torgovnick have made a permanent mark on my thinking. I feel fortunate, too, to have had the opportunity for frequent conversations with Kwame Anthony Appiah while he was at Duke and especially for the privilege of reading early drafts of *In My Father's House* before it was published.

Over the years of its writing, this project has also benefited from numerous conversations with friends and colleagues, in some cases extensive, in others, alas, all too infrequent. Sangeeta Luthra, Ananyo Basu, Todd Davis, David Chioni Moore, Faith Smith, and Ambreen Hai will all recognize their various traces in this work. Thanks, too, to Ken Wissoker and the entire editorial team at Duke University Press for their support of this project. The comments of the two anonymous readers of the manuscript were so helpful that to them I make a public plea—identify yourselves—dinner is on me! Although I have had the opportunity to share portions of this book with various audiences, I want in particular to thank David William Cohen for inviting me to present a paper on Akiga Sai at the Institute for Advanced Study and Research in the African Humanities at Northwestern University. The workshop was seminal to my thinking about the project, and the encouragement that I received there from Johannes Fabian and Louise White, among others, has helped me sustain my energy for the enterprise.

Beyond these debts, I thank my various students and colleagues at the University at Albany and at Tulane for providing me with support of various kinds. At Tulane, the manuscript has benefited from the scrutiny of the "first-book group" of the Program of African and African Diaspora Studies. My heartfelt appreciation to its members—Rosanne Adderley, Adeline Masquelier, and Christopher Dunn. For helping create a wonderful sense of community in the program, I wish to thank Felipe Smith. My colleagues in the English department and in the Program of African and African Diaspora Studies at Tulane consistently confirm my faith in the values of academic as well as personal integrity. Of these colleagues, Geoff Harpham, Janice Carlisle, Maaja Stewart, and Jim Kilroy have been both friends and sources of inspiration. My office neighbors Molly Travis, Teresa Toulouse, and Amy Koritz have always been a source of delight. Supriya Nair has sustained this project in its final stages in every way imaginable. Girish, Ruta, and my sister Geeta have influenced this project right from its inception, and little Sameer has offered on many an occasion to embellish the book with crayon illustrations. But my final debt, which is also my greatest, remains to my parents, who have always encouraged me to be an independent thinker and who have made great sacrifices to this end. It is to them that I dedicate this book, with love.

Dangerous Supplements

Critical (Mis)understandings

In October 1848, about forty years before the formal European partitioning of Africa, the British lieutenant governor Winniett visited the king of the Asante in the city of Kumasi. Winniett notes:

> We immediately entered into conversation, and after briefly adverting to the kindly feelings of Her Majesty's Government towards him, I embraced the favourable opportunity thus offered for speaking to him on the subject of human sacrifices; I told him of the anxious desire on the part of Her Majesty, that these sanguinary rites should be abolished, and begged his serious attention to a question so important to the cause of humanity.[1]

Upon hearing this the Asantehene, we are told, asked whether the governor had himself witnessed any such sacrifices. When Winniett responded in the negative, the governor's journal records the king's response as follows: "He then observed that although human sacrifices were the custom of his forefathers, he was reducing their number and extent in his kingdom, and that the wishes of Her Majesty should not be forgotten."[2]

The fact that this last utterance is as much a product of Winniett's official discourse as it is perhaps that of the Asantehene should be self-evident to any student of colonial discourse. The particular historical circumstances in

---

1. W. Winniett, "Journal of Lieutenant Governor Winniett's Visit to the King of Ashantee," in *British Parliamentary Papers, 1949*, 235.
2. Ibid.

which this report emerges, the circumstances of growing colonial commercial interest and the sure encroachment of political rule, mark this utterance as emblematic of the moment of early colonialism in Africa. The trope is that of a savage Africa awakening from its ugly history of "cruelty" and "doom" (two of the most common descriptive terms employed in the official letters, telegrams, memoranda, and directives) to face a more "civilized," "humane" culture personified in the very being of "Her Majesty" the English queen. The "civilizing mission," in other words, is here seen to promise positive results and vindicate Winniett's ambassadorial mission. Yet ironically, this particular image of a changing Africa has always to be put in check by the fear of the possible return of the repressed. Thus even over half a century later, with British rule well under way, the threat of an African return to "savagery" must remain to legitimate the project and the presence of colonialism.

Consider here the report of Sir Frederick Hodgson writing from the same space—Kumasi—in the year 1900. In response to the Asante demands for increased political autonomy and the return of Prempeh (the Asantehene deposed and banished by the British), Hodgson resorts to the traditional argument for colonialism. Equating African political autonomy with indigenous desire for commerce in slavery, Hodgson employs the familiar rhetoric of a British humanitarianism: "As regards the buying and selling of slaves," he informs the Asantehene, "black men might regard themselves as no better than cattle, to be bought and sold as opportunity offered or as circumstances dictated, but the white man [does] not and would not so regard them."[3] Through a convenient forgetting of the earlier non-African locus of the transatlantic slave trade, the traffic in slaves becomes in Hodgson's rhetoric yet another manifestation of an inhumane and savage custom from which the natives must be saved.

If these images of an Africa capable of change but only under British tutelage become canonical ones, they do so because they fulfill the dreams and the promises of the colonial project itself—the "dual mandate," as Frederick Lugard would later name it, of spreading "civilization" and humanitarianism while simultaneously expanding British economic interests.[4] But even at the heart of these legitimating discourses, there are undercurrents of ambivalence

3. Frederick Hodgson, "Hodgson to Chamberlain, The Fort, Kumasi, 16 April 1900," in *Great Britain and Ghana: Documents of Ghana History, 1807–1957*, ed. G. E. Metcalfe (Accra: University of Ghana, 1964), 512.
4. See Lugard, *The Dual Mandate in British Tropical Africa* (1922; rpt., London: Frank Cass, 1965).

and anxiety. If we were to return to our opening encounter between Winniett and the Asantehene, we would notice precisely such an anxiety. For we find in Winniett's records that the governor has been censured by the Asantehene not only when he is asked about his own encounters with human sacrifice, but also when the two men converse the following day:

> [The King] then observed, that the number of human sacrifices were not so numerous in Kumasi as they had been represented, and expressed a hope that mere reports relative to such a subject, flying about the country would not be listened to; and he then observed, "I remember that when I was a little boy, I heard that the English came to the coast of Africa with their ships, for cargoes of slaves, for the purpose of taking them to their own country and eating them, but I have long since known that the report was false."[5]

Here, then, all the familiar accusations are reversed, and Reason and knowledge are seen to be on the side not of the British but of the Asante: just as the English invent a "savage" Africa, so do the Asante invent a "savage" English nation; slavery and homicide (in the form of cannibalism) are read here as English features, not African; the Asantehene through a period of cultural contact has overcome his prejudices; the English, however, have failed to do so. The Asantehene's story is not just meant to be didactic—in light of the encroachments on land and liberty that are soon to come, it is also a performative event intended to demonstrate his own critical awareness of the colonial uses of such tropes as "human sacrifices" for the purpose of legitimation.

If what is at work here is a form of critical (mis)understanding between cultures, then it is "critical" in at least three senses: "critical" as necessary or essential (since without such "mis-understanding" the project of colonialism would lose some of its legitimation); "critical" as incorporating the potential of critique (as we notice in the rebuke of the Asantehene); and finally "critical" in the sense of crises-ridden. Critical (mis)understanding in all these three senses becomes the very motor of colonial growth, and the trajectory of its functioning can be discerned at various moments in the colonial archive.[6]

---

5. Winniett, "Journal," 236.
6. See, for instance, the discussion of "profound misconceptions" between the missionaries and the Tswana in Jean Comaroff and John Comaroff, *Of Revelation and Revolution: Christianity, Colonialism, and Consciousness in South Africa*, Vol. 1 (Chicago: University of Chicago Press, 1991), 170–97.

The Colonial Library

If Winniett's narrative is about the critical (mis)understandings that the colonial encounter engenders, then it is also, at another level, about the processes of invention and counterinvention that take place between two cultures in contact. Functioning so effectively as a parable of the possibilities of native agency in a colonial context, Winniett's narrative speaks directly to the central issues of this book.

Concerned with a rethinking of what V. Y. Mudimbe has called the "colonial library"—the set of representations and texts that have collectively "invented" Africa as a locus of difference and alterity—*Subject to Colonialism* attempts to reimagine the colonial library as a space of contestation. Mudimbe's claim is that along with the physical colonization of geographical spaces and human lives in Africa, there existed an epistemological "colonization" that was responsible for reorganizing "native" African minds.[7] My project is to investigate the conditions of possibility and the actual manifestations of precisely such an epistemological colonization as it emerges through the study of the colonial library. Inspired by the Asantehene's rebuke, however, my aim has been to understand the construction of the library and of the colonial process itself as a complex series of interactions between the colonizers and the colonized rather than as a unidirectional practice. African resistance, collaboration, and accommodation in all their forms are as much part of the history of colonialism, both on the social as well as epistemological plane, as are the various actions and intents of the European colonizers. I have sought to study the culture and practices of colonialism precisely as such a struggle between the colonizers and the colonized.

In proceeding with such a study, I have asked myself to be mindful of five caveats. First, that although the "colonial library" is a convenient label, it is by no means a body of texts that can be isolated in any absolute or rigid way. The constitution of this body of texts is in itself a subject of concern, as the system of inclusions and exclusions that are enacted in a given framework—disciplinary or otherwise—provide much ground for a political analysis of both epistemic and ontic relations. Much of the discussion in the second chapter is geared precisely to such a questioning. Here, in a historical interrogation of the concept of African rationality and its alleged basis in "race," I quite intentionally

---

7. Mudimbe, *The Invention of Africa: Gnosis, Philosophy, and the Order of Knowledge* (Bloomington: Indiana University Press, 1988).

read those colonial texts that have been excluded from consideration even in the most sophisticated postcolonial discussions of the concept of rationality. These texts, primarily written by psychologists and eugenicists, are integral to an understanding of the more widely read corollary discourses of anthropology or philosophy. To read these latter discourses without the backdrop of the former is to lose a great deal of their own historicity and their potentially interventionist intent. Furthermore, it is to have a very limited and skewed perspective of the constitution of the colonial library itself. Of course, any such widening of the scope of the colonial library must remind us that such pushing of its limits is endless, and any of our own readings of the colonial archives must remain at best partial and tentative.

My second caveat is that the most productive readings of the colonial library are bound to be those that read the texts not as reflections of particular colonial relations but rather as constitutive of them. This is a lesson I learn not only from the cultural materialism of Raymond Williams but also from the more recent work of speech-act theorists who insist on recognizing that even the most innocently constative utterance is at once a performative one.[8] Discourses, in other words, *do* things with and in the world, and their very entry into the social is a subject of great importance to students of culture. The question to ask of a discourse is not so much what it says but what it does. And the results of such an investigation—of a reading for "rhetoric" rather than a reading for "sense," as Andrzej Warminski puts it—will on occasion entail a paradox or *aporia*.[9] For the literal meaning of a discourse may well contradict its rhetoric or its functioning in the larger context of its utterance. Throughout this book, I have been particularly interested in the rhetorical strategies deployed by various agents in securing their interests. Whether it is the advocacy of a particular pedagogical preference on the part of a South African inspector of schools (Charles Loram), or the marketing of a disciplinary agenda (Edwin Smith and Bronislaw Malinowski), or instead the framing of a nationalist project based on the ideas of culture and history (Jomo Kenyatta and Akiga Sai), I have found that the rhetorical ingenuity of these particular individuals makes their work all the more compelling.

8. See Raymond Williams, *Marxism and Literature* (New York: Oxford University Press, 1977). For an account of the collapsing of the constative and the performative in speech acts, see Stanley Fish's reading of J. L. Austin, "With the Compliments of the Author: Reflections on Austin and Derrida," in *Doing What Comes Naturally* (Durham: Duke University Press, 1989), 37–67.
9. Andrezj Warminski, *Readings in Interpretation: Hölderlin, Hegel, Heidegger* (Minneapolis: University of Minnesota Press, 1987).

A third caveat that I have been mindful of is the importance of a revised notion of subjectivity—however decentered—that nevertheless retains a sense of human agency and practice. Here I find most compelling the work of Pierre Bourdieu, and his notion of the *habitus* as a structuring structure that limits but does not efface individual agency. The individual's habitus predisposes him or her to act in certain ways but does not limit him or her from choosing a wholly other set of options. One exciting task of interpretation is just this exposition of how a given subject functions when confronted with a set of options. The notion of the subject that underwrites this treatise is precisely such a Bourdieuian one, even though Bourdieu himself is invoked in a limited manner.[10] Indeed, the most specific instances of such workings of subjectivity are my readings of Bronislaw Malinowski and Akiga Sai, the former an intellectual in exile attempting to find himself a home in a disciplinary and professional locus, and the latter a protonationalist subject attempting to gain political legitimacy in a colonial context. Such a focus on agency is indispensable for a critical understanding of the nexus of various discursive and institutional

---

10. Here I want to register my difference with a terminological distinction made by Bourdieu between "agents" and "subjects." Bourdieu, working against the grain of a Lévi-Straussian humanism, is wary of the term *subject* because within the discourse of humanism, "subjectivity" and "subjectivism" has often implied an unlimited capacity of the "will" to rise above social constraint. As opposed to this free-willing and boundless "subject," Bourdieu proposes "agents" who "fall" into the game of living and develop strategies (sometimes even unselfconsciously) that maximize their interests while acting within the rules of the game (Bourdieu, *In Other Words: Essays Towards a Reflexive Sociology* [Stanford: Stanford University Press, 1990], 62–63). In a related move Chantal Mouffe writes, "We can . . . conceive the social agent as constituted by an ensemble of 'subject positions' that can never totally be fixed in a closed system of differences, constructed by a diversity of discourses among which there is no necessary relation, but a constant movement of overdetermination and displacement. The 'identity' of such a multiple and contradictory subject is therefore always contingent and precarious, temporarily fixed at the intersection of those subject positions and dependent on specific forms of identification. It is therefore impossible to speak of the social agent as if we were dealing with a unified, homogenous entity" (Mouffe, "Feminism, Citizenship, and Radical Democratic Politics," in *Feminists Theorize the Political,* ed. Judith Butler and Joan W. Scott [New York: Routledge, 1992], 372). I am persuaded by both Bourdieu's and Mouffe's accounts of "agents" but am not worried about calling them "subjects." So I choose instead to work with a revised and redefined understanding of subjects and subjectivity along the lines advocated by Bourdieu and Mouffe and to relieve the category of its earlier connotations. After all, who is to say that "unity" and "homogeneity" must always underwrite every conceptualization of the "subject"? Could we not—do many of us already not—think of ourselves as "subjects" and recognize that such subjectivity is split, multiply mediated, often contradictory and ambivalent?

formations in colonial Africa, and any attempt to efface such human agency is, I suggest, politically suspect.[11]

My fourth caveat, and this is perhaps the most radical, is that the colonial library must include those African subjects who took it on themselves to engage with the discourses of the colonizers and to produce their own inventions of Africa. There seems to be no conceptual, theoretical, or even political advantage in reading the works of these African subjects as somehow removed from the colonial library. Africanism, like Said's Orientalism, was a discourse that permeated the lives of both the observed as well as the observers—the colonized as well as the colonizers—and both participated, albeit unequally, in the constitution of the colonial library. To say this is not to erase the distinction between the colonizer and the colonized but to understand the colonial library as itself an important terrain of colonial tension and struggle. Seeking to represent themselves from their own perspectives and worldview was indeed an important aspect of African cultural nationalism and resistance, and to undermine these attempts by placing the writings of such important thinkers as Jomo Kenyatta or Akiga Sai in a space tangential rather than central to the colonial library does both them as well as us a great disservice.

My fifth and last caveat is that just as the inclusion of Africans in the colonial library forces us to reshape our understanding of its configurations, so it is that the attempt to hear the voices of "other others" in the archives forces us to recognize its continued limitations. The most obvious instantiation—though not by any means the only one—is the marginalization of African women in the colonial library both by European as well as by African writers. Thus, for instance, when issues of rationality and pedagogy are discussed in this library, they almost exclusively revolve around male education. It may well be the case, as some may want to argue, that no exclusion of girls was intended, but the absence of any discussion of gender, particularly in light of the fact that on many an occasion the pedagogical situation did reflect gender divisions (with girls taking courses on "home education"), renders this claim implausible. Yet as my own project shows, particularly in the context of the Af-

11. Or as Simon Gikandi eloquently puts it, "If there is any political motivation behind my book, it is the absolute rejection of the popular image of the colonial borderland as a victimized margin, one without a voice in the shaping of the larger imperial event, one without its own strengths and interests, one without agency in the shaping or representation of modern identities. The colonial archive contains many instances of what I consider to be peripheral agency" (*Maps of Englishness: Writing Identity in the Culture of Colonialism* [New York: Columbia University Press, 1996], 38).

rican texts that I read, the issue of gender and the issue of "woman" become central to the work of a nativist imagination. The central thematic of Kenyatta's text and its reception is the question of female circumcision, and as I argue extensively in my last chapter on the Tiv historian Akiga Sai, "woman" becomes a synecdoche for tradition.

These five caveats—the constitution of the colonial library as essentially open; the reading of discourses as actions rather than reflections; a revised notion of subjectivity and agency; the central rather than marginal character of African texts in the colonial library; and the importance of gender as the often unspoken category of analysis—underwrite the claims that I make herein. The book as a whole moves analytically from the outside in as well as from the panoramic to the particular. Thus, for instance, the first chapter on race and rationality almost exclusively reads the texts of non-Africans, the second chapter reads two Europeans and ends with a Kenyan, and the last chapter focuses exclusively on a Tiv historian. This intentional move is paralleled by a move from an interest in larger disciplinary or discursive issues to an interest in very particular and local articulations of colonial modernity. Both these levels of analysis are necessary for an understanding of the colonial library, and taken together, they enable us to rethink the workings of colonialism.

At the most general level, this book attempts to generate a historical understanding of some of the issues that continue to permeate our own "postcolonial" discussions of Africa. What happens when Africa, for so long the great aporia of postcolonial thought, takes center stage? How must the discourses of postcolonial studies—discourses such as those of hybridity, colonial subjectivity, subalternity—necessarily be revised, given a more elaborated understanding of their manifestations in colonial Africa?[12] It is important to rec-

---

12. Abiola Irele writes in this regard: "In very significant ways, African discourse, along with other 'minority discourses,' has urgently anticipated some of the current preoccupations in Western thought. These anticipations were not necessarily theorized, or if they were, as in the case of Fanon mentioned earlier, they were not formulated in exactly the same terms as in currents of thought now commonly grouped under poststructuralism and postmodernism. But the ideas that are coming out of the Western world today strike us with a certain familiarity, for they address issues of authority, pluralism, and especially the relation between discourse and power. These ideas are concerned crucially with the question of discursivity and its crucial function in the claims to legitimacy and normativity in the social sphere, a question that goes to the very heart of our modern experience stemming from our encounter with Europe" ("Dimensions of African Discourse," in *Order and Partialities: Theory, Pedagogy, and the "Postcolonial,"* ed. Kostas Myrsiades and Jerry McGuire [Albany: State University of New York Press, 1995], 24–25).

ognize that although guided by postcolonial agendas, the story that I tell is primarily focused on the *colonial* moment. Much of the discussion of African discourse has revolved around *post*colonial writers and philosophers. Although certainly significant in itself, a singular focus on *post*colonial African discourse runs the risk of assuming an easy binary between Empire and Nation, the former being characterized as a condition of absolute domination and subaltern voicelessness and the latter by a triumphant revolutionary consciousness. One point of my story is to show that for better or worse a careful study of the colonial archive shows that this binary cannot be retained.[13]

The valence of the binary Empire/Nation is often at work in ways that sometime escape us. Why else, if not as a result of this binarism, would a text like *Things Fall Apart* (1958), written on the eve of Nigerian independence, continue to be characterized in the popular consciousness as one of the "earliest" written literary texts of Africa?[14] Or why again does a discussion of African history before the postcolonial moment become synonymous in our minds with the tradition of the griots? Let it be clear that I am not suggesting that *Things Fall Apart* is an unimportant book or that griots were not crucial carriers and indeed propagators of historical consciousness in various African societies. Instead, I am pointing to our unacknowledged conceptual divide between the colonial and postcolonial moment that leads us to falsely equate the colonial moment with the oral and the postcolonial with the written. What happens then, to the works of those Africans who were *writing* under colonialism? What might a careful attention to writers such as Jomo Kenyatta and Akiga Sai do to our own stable periodization of the colonial-postcolonial divide?

It is here that the workings of the "dangerous supplement" that Jacques Derrida first elaborated in his reading of Rousseau become useful to my own

13. In his most recent book, Simon Gikandi makes exactly this claim. I see Gikandi's project along with the recent work by Ato Quayson and Carolyn Martin Shaw as sharing the same intellectual dispositions as my own project. Although Gikandi's project is an interrogation of the constitution of Englishness itself and in particular the gaze of the colonized, Quayson's a rigorous study of Nigerian literary tradition, and Shaw's an interrogation of race, sex, and class in Kenya, all of our projects are rooted in a desire to take the cultural production of African *colonial* subjects seriously. See Gikandi, *Maps of Englishness*; Quayson, *Strategic Transformations of Nigerian Writing* (Bloomington: Indiana University Press, 1997); and Carolyn Martin Shaw, *Colonial Inscriptions: Race, Sex, and Class in Kenya* (Minneapolis: University of Minnesota Press, 1995).
14. What happens to texts by earlier writers such as Herbert Dhlomo, Sol Plaatje, Samuel Ntara, and Paul Hazoumé?

analysis.[15] As Derrida elaborates, the dangerous supplement is that part of a given binary structure that is at first relegated to the outside, to the margin, to the position of inferiority, but works its way to the very center of the dichotomy, putting under erasure the earlier political hierarchy of the binary. Thus, for instance, in his various readings, Derrida shows how Woman, the supposedly subjugated figure of the male/female binary, begins to emerge in Nietzsche's thinking as the carrier of truth and power; or again, writing, often thought of as a debased form of speech in Western logocentric thought, often appears in the texts of Ferdinand de Saussure and Claude Lévi-Strauss as always already structurally implicit in oral societies.[16]

This simple insight of the workings of the dangerous supplement is a powerful way to think about the African colonial library. If, instead of ignoring the cultural and intellectual production of *colonial* Africans, we take them seriously, we would see them precisely as the dangerous supplements of the colonial archive. My aim in reading Jomo Kenyatta and the Tiv historian Akiga Sai is quite explicitly to read them as such and to show that no matter how pernicious the colonial library may have seemed in the hands of some colonial agents such as eugenicists and clinical psychologists, it did not go unchallenged. Although postcolonial African thinkers must certainly be credited for extending the critiques and taking them in new directions, we must not forget their colonial predecessors.

Indeed, we cannot afford to forget them, since in an important way colonial writers such as Kenyatta and Sai serve the double function of being the dangerous supplements of both the colonial archive as well as our own postcolonial consciousness. For if it is clear that by including their voices in the archive of the colonial library the library is itself rendered fractured, incomplete, subject to internal critique, then it is no less clear that these thinkers most effectively put under erasure our all too easy schematization of the colonial-postcolonial divide.

In many ways, then, this book presents a study of colonialism not as a singular, monolithic structure but rather as a practice fraught with contradictions and tensions.[17] *Subject to Colonialism* draws its inspiration from recent

15. The working of the "dangerous supplement" is illustrated by Derrida in ". . . That Dangerous Supplement . . . ," in *Of Grammatology,* trans. Gayatri Chakravorty Spivak (Baltimore: Johns Hopkins University Press, 1976), 141–64.

16. Derrida calls this structural possibility *arche-writing*.

17. See Frederick Cooper and Ann Laura Stoler, eds., *Tensions of Empire: Colonial Cultures in a Bourgeois World* (Berkeley: University of California Press, 1997).

efforts at constructing postfoundationalist accounts of colonialisms most explicitly articulated by Gyan Prakash, but also discernible in the work of scholars such as Kwame Anthony Appiah and V. Y. Mudimbe. Distinguished from *anti*-foundationalism, *post*-foundationalism is interested not so much in debunking foundations but rather in historicizing their emergence. If the antifoundationalist project seeks to critique accounts that rely on a fixed, essentializing identity that is itself indivisible, then the postfoundationalist project seeks to understand and help explain this felt need on the part of some for a foundation. Such historicizing continues the project of a constructivist epistemology already in place in the antifoundational moment, but is presented with a greater awareness of the hold of foundationalist claims over people — even when those claims have already been demonstrated as being "socially constructed."[18]

It seems to me that the appeal of a post- as opposed to anti-foundationalism thus described is precisely its ability to continue to be skeptical of monolithic

18. I often think of the move from an antifoundational project to a postfoundational one in terms parallel to the move from an *anti*-colonial critique to a *post*-colonial one. Thus, while an anticolonial critique tends to be heavily influenced by the structures of colonialism that it wishes to reject and overthrow, a postcolonial critique downplays the seeming singularity and overwhelming overdeterminations of colonialism as a structure. Arising in the nationalist struggle for independence and in the immediate aftermath of formal colonialism, anticolonial thought measures its victories and failures against what it sees as the singular, foundational cause of the people's woes — formal colonialism by an external force. Emerging later in a context often of disillusionment, postcolonial thought recognizes that responsibility must now be located not only in the colonial legacy but also in the multiply opportunistic and often selfish practices by various indigenous agents with competing claims. Likewise, the early emergence of antifoundational thought is characterized by the desire to demystify a category such as "race" or "tradition" or even the "subject" in the interests of preventing the continued misuse of the category by, in these cases, racists, authenticists, or "white-male-humanists-of-the-Enlightenment." Antifoundational demystification is of two main sorts: (1) a syntagmatic critique that demonstrates a logical flaw in the category, as Appiah does with "race" in *In My Father's House*; and (2) a diachronic critique that demonstrates the biased and often intentionally manipulated historical emergence of the category, as Ranger does with the category of "tribe" in Africa. Postfoundationalists, although in the majority sympathetic to the politics of antifoundationalism, are less anxious about discarding the problematic categories and are more interested in how categories may be manipulated for multiple political uses in varied circumstances. In some senses one might say that postfoundationalism takes anti-essentialism seriously insofar as it recognizes that categories — even flawed and historically misused categories — are not static and are subject to reappropriation. This is why, for instance, as I suggested earlier, a postfoundational politics is not afraid to reappropriate the category of the human "subject." See Kwame Anthony Appiah, *In My Father's House* (New York: Oxford University Press, 1992; Terence Ranger, *The Invention of Tribalism in Zimbabwe* (Gweru, Zimbabwe: Mambo, 1985).

foundationalisms without making the critique of foundationalism its own foundation.[19] Further, and indeed more importantly, such postfoundationalism is less dismissive of the appeal to the foundational even as it recognizes the desperation behind such an appeal. Thus although an antifoundationalist position focuses on deconstructing a foundational category such as "race," the postfoundationalist makes the further move of historicizing the emergence of such a category *as* a foundational one. The shift here is a subtle one, not so much a shift in the evaluation of the legitimacy of the category itself but rather one of paying greater attention to the historical uses to which the category has been put.[20] Or again, if the antifoundationalist focuses on the further divisibility or heterogeneity of the seemingly irreducible foundation, then the postfoundationalist emphasizes that a foundationalist account of, say, "race and ethnicity" or "gender" or the "global flow of capital" often ends up taking for granted precisely that which it seeks to explain. Thus writes Gyan Prakash about foundationalist Indian historiography:

> The difficulty with an approach that regards history as a record of such founding agents as modes of production and class structures is that it begs the next series of questions: How was class signified? By what discursive logic did the identification of class interests lead the chain of signification to economic relations? If such a logic was cultural (or historical), then how do we account for its formation and its hegemonic position? The point here is not that class and structural analyses are unimportant but

19. Judith Butler puts this well, "The point is not to do away with foundations, or even to champion a position that goes under the name of antifoundationalism. Both of those positions belong together as different versions of foundationalism and the skeptical problematic it engenders. Rather, the task is to interrogate what the theoretical move that establishes foundations *authorizes,* and what precisely it excludes or forecloses" ("Contingent Foundations: Feminism and the Question of 'Postmodernism,'" in Butler and Scott, *Feminists Theorize the Political,* 7).

20. Although early readings of Mudimbe's *Invention of Africa* and Appiah's *In My Father's House* cast them as antifoundational critiques (see, for instance, William Slaymaker, "Agents and Actors in African Antifoundationalist Aesthetics: Theory and Narrative in Appiah and Mudimbe," *Research in African Literatures* 27 [spring 1996]: 119–28), I think that these texts already begin to engage in the historicizing of "foundational" categories resulting in the kind of "postfoundational" critique that I describe here. But ultimately the difference is one of degree rather than kind. For instance, in his handling of the issue of "race," Appiah seems to work more in the antifoundational mode in *In My Father's House* and more in the postfoundational mode in his more recent book *Color Conscious* (Kwame Anthony Appiah and Amy Gutman, *Color Conscious: The Political Morality of Race* [Princeton: Princeton University Press, 1996]).

that to regard them as originating causes and subjects of history is to neglect an important question: namely, how did class, or any other subject
for that matter, come to acquire the status of an originating subject?[21]

In addition to deploying a historicist mode of analysis, postfoundational
thought emphasizes such issues as processes, performances, and the practices
of everyday life. It reevaluates the processes of inclusion and exclusion, textual
as well as conceptual, that have canonized certain texts and the ideas, themat-
ics, and concepts associated with them. It willfully reads "against the grain" of
such a canonicity and takes risks by placing unknown, unread, or intentionally marginalized texts next to those that have hitherto been hailed as exemplary. Furthermore, it unlearns the demands of a foundational criticism that
insists that the texts of a colonial situation must be read through a certain set
of foundational nodes—be they Empire, the Nation, the world-system, or
even race. Instead, it shows how these undoubtedly important problematics
are best understood only as they enter the lives of specific subjects, whether
those of the colonizers or the colonized, further mediated by such other less
epic moments as professional desires, political convictions, obligations to
friends, religious beliefs, and, indeed, the enactment of a gendered identity.[22]
Put differently, one might say that postfoundational criticism seeks to study
the cultures of colonization even as it remains interested in the colonization
of cultures. In so doing, it remains vigilant to the minoritarian voices that
emerge at odds with the dominant cultural logic of its time. Postfoundational
accounts understand that colonialism, like every other social formation, is
messy, and even though it may attempt to put on a systematic face, it remains
susceptible to a derailing.

---

21. Gyan Prakash, "Writing Post-Orientalist Histories of the Third World: Indian Historiography
Is Good to Think," in *Colonialism and Culture*, ed. Nicholas Dirks (Ann Arbor: University of
Michigan Press, 1992), 368–69).
22. The point is vividly made by the Ugandan writer R. H. Kakembo, a veteran of World War II,
who in 1944 wrote an account of his involvement in the war. At one point he writes, "I would like
to make it clear that the majority of the African soldiers came into the Army not to fight for King
George VI nor to defend the Empire. No. The King and the Empire meant and still mean nothing
to them. Men you see in the forces came to help a certain kindly lady missionary, or a good District
Commissioner whose wife plays with their children. They came to help because their friend and
lady told them that back home in Britain her or his mother was in trouble, a fierce bully was threatening to make them slaves, and if they joined the Army they might help to avert that threat and
danger to their beloved ones" (*An African Soldier Speaks* [London: Livingstone Press, 1947], 8).

Literary Studies and Colonial Discourse

One final question remains: Why should a literary critic such as myself attempt to undertake the kind of task that I have undertaken here, and what good can come of it? I shall leave the answer to the latter part of that question to the generosity of my readers, but let me attempt an answer to the first half by recourse to a brief history.

One irony surrounding the sudden growth of institutionalized literary criticism ever since the late 1960s is the fact that it gained momentum precisely at the moment at which it gave up on a rigid conception of "literature." It was, arguably, the structuralist preoccupation with the linguistic nature of myths and other cultural artifacts that allowed for innovations in the study, not only of literary "works" as they had been hitherto conceived but of various other entities, which began to be seen as "texts" functioning within the domains of multiply articulated *systems*. What many perceive today to be the hegemony of English and literature departments in the discourses of the humanities is directly related to what Arjun Appadurai has called "the hijack of culture by literary studies . . . a many-sided hijack (where a hundred Blooms flower) with many internal debates about texts and antitexts, reference and structure, theory and practice."[23] Indeed, as Appadurai continues, "social scientists look on with bewilderment as their colleagues in English and Comparative literature talk (and fight) about matters which, until as recently as fifteen years ago, would have seemed about as relevant to English departments as, say, quantum mechanics."[24]

But bewilderment is not the only response social scientists have had to the emergence of a poststructural literary criticism. In some cases the response by social scientists has been a denial of poststructuralism's usefulness, if not an outright rejection of the enterprise. Thus, for instance, in a landmark case against what she calls "postmodern" thought, Megan Vaughan seems perfectly content with the fact that "postmodern" theory in general and colonial discourse studies in particular have passed Africa by.[25] Vaughan suggests that

---

23. Arjun Appadurai, "Global Ethnoscapes: Notes and Queries for a Transnational Anthropology," in *Recapturing Anthropology: Working in the Present*, ed. Richard Fox (Santa Fe: School of American Research, 1991), 195–96.

24. Ibid., 196.

25. Vaughan uses the terms *poststructuralism* and *postmodernism* interchangeably, but the critical edge of her essay suggests that it is "poststructuralism" in particular rather than "postmodern theory" in general that is the subject of her critique. Thus I have chosen in this discussion to speak

colonial discourse theorists write under the influence of poststructuralism and produce texts whose aim "appears less one of explication, than of obfuscation and endless referral of meaning"(2). Thankfully, suggests Vaughan, for various reasons having to do with such things as the relatively shorter period of formal colonialism in Africa as opposed to South Asia, the relatively fewer written discourses on Africa as opposed to South Asia, and the relatively marginal space of Africanists as opposed to South Asianists in the international academic world, "postmodernism" has never really bothered the better and more productive work done by anthropologists and historians in Africa. Africanists, suggests Vaughan, have been more interested in "invented traditions" and have focused on issues such as "hegemony" rather than what she sees as the exclusivist "great books" approach of colonial discourse theory (8–9).

Had this essay been written by almost anyone other that Megan Vaughan it would not, for my purposes, have been worthy of commentary. But Vaughan is the author of *Curing Their Ills*, the most impressive study of colonial power and African illness written so far, a text that I have often taught to students as an exemplary model that brings the rigors of historical scholarship to test the limits and the insights of poststructural (particularly Foucauldian) theory. Indeed, if Vaughan's book is to be accounted for, the commerce between poststructuralism and African studies not only has been healthy but also has yielded considerable profit.[26] The problem, it seems, as David Bunn correctly notes in his response to Vaughan, is not so much "poststructuralism" or "postmodernism" or even "colonial discourse theory" per se but rather a

---

more narrowly of poststructural thought (Megan Vaughan, "Colonial Discourse Theory and African History, or Has Postmodernism Passed Us By?" *Social Dynamics* 20.2 [summer 1994]: 8–9).

26. And what is important to note is that contrary to the fear and anxiety of the Africanist worried about "theory-driven" analysis, it is often the field of poststructural theory that has gained from students of colonialism. So, no longer can one teach Foucault's work on "bio-power" without also teaching Megan Vaughan's *Curing Their Ills* (Stanford: Stanford University Press, 1991). No longer can one teach Foucault's histories of sexuality without also teaching Ann Laura Stoler's *Race and the Education of Desire* (Durham: Duke University Press, 1995). My point is that it is becoming increasingly difficult to characterize in a categorical manner work that is "poststructuralist" on the one hand and "Africanist" on the other. If we look at some of the most interesting recent scholarship on Africa, including work by such scholars as V. Y. Mudimbe, Anthony Appiah, Simon Gikandi, the Comaroffs, David William Cohen, Louise White, Carolyn Martin Shaw, Annie Coombes, Timothy Burke, Nancy Hunt, and Vaughan herself, we see that even when they disavow certain trends of poststructural thought, these thinkers find themselves necessarily engaged in a dialogue with it. It seems to me then that what Vaughan loosely calls "postmodern theory" is finally beginning to undergo some major discursive shifts because of the hard work of students of colonialism. To ask for a divorce today seems to me to be self-defeating.

certain specter of it that seems to raise the social scientist's anxiety.[27] This specter is the specter of language and the literary, of aesthetics and abstractions, of high canonical culture and of literary critics sitting in their libraries completely disconnected with the "real" world.

As is often the case with such scenarios, if colonial discourse studies is indeed in the sorry state that Megan Vaughan portrays it to be in—that is, it is obfuscating, it is only interested in the canonical, it essentializes the "West," it overemphasizes the "colonial," it has an impoverished theory of colonial subjectivity, it remains uninterested in issues of power and hegemony, it privileges colonial discourses and ignores local discourses[28]—if all this were true, then it would be entirely appropriate either to leave it behind or, as Vaughan does, celebrate its marginality to the field. But this picture of a poststructuralism gone awry does not do justice either to the work that has already been influenced by it or to forthcoming work that could fruitfully extend it. Rather than wish it away or pretend that it has never really been with us, I think it is more fruitful for Africanists to engage with the insights as well as the limitations of poststructural thought. Thus in the chapters that follow, a poststructuralist orientation encourages me to focus on the ambivalent and contingent politics of discursive practices, helps me be wary of progressive teleologies, and makes me question the hierarchized binarisms that emerge as foundational structures grounding identities. But at the same time, my poststructuralist disposition does not prevent me from learning from the lessons of historians and anthropologists whose work makes me look at the practice of everyday life, at modes of resistance and accommodation to institutionalized practices, and at the emergence of colonial subjectivities.

To suggest that this book borrows from the insights of anthropologists and historians is not the same as saying that this is a work of anthropology or history. For there are at least two ways of casting histories of disciplinary exchange; one is to suggest that by borrowing from each other, each discipline has increasingly shed its earlier disciplinary blindspots and has moved toward a more comprehensive and more nuanced mode of analysis. The second is to recognize the gains made by the convergence of scholarly knowledges, but also to recognize that that convergence can be mobilized most fruitfully from a particular, situated, disciplinary perspective. Thus although much of my

27. Bunn, "The Insistence of Theory: Three Questions for Megan Vaughan," *Social Dynamics* 20.2 (1994): 24–34.
28. Vaughan, "Colonial Discourse Theory and African History," 2, 8, 4, 7, 5, 10, 11.

time has been spent over the past few years engaging with anthropologists, philosophers, and historians, and although many of their interests, anxieties, and successes have affected my own work, I am convinced that the discipline to which my work finally belongs remains literary studies. This may sound like a strange claim to make, considering my engagements with the various disciplinary discourses at work in this book, but nevertheless it is a fundamental one. Disciplines, as Foucault has reminded us, are productive as much as they are repressive, and in the case of my own work it is the skills of literary and textual analysis that have primarily informed the readings that I have engaged in here. To be sure, very few of my colleagues in the field of literary studies will recognize the objects of my study as objects that we share, but few will be able to deny that my ways of reading these texts, my methods of analysis are indeed the common methods of a newer, historically, culturally, and politically conscious literary criticism. Conversely, few if any historians or anthropologists will recognize my work as "properly" historical or anthropological —and they would be justified in reading it as something different, something alien to the field. They, unlike the literary critics, will no doubt recognize the objects of my analysis but will find me doing strange things with them.[29]

This situation could also be formulated somewhat negatively. For to find one's project in such a situation is to be open to two sets of accusations—each exactly the reverse of the other. Some literary critics may well fault me for not "doing" literature and engaging instead in history, philosophy, or anthropology. Practitioners in these other fields would rightly accuse me of foregrounding the discursive and textual at the expense of the social or historical. In their own terms both groups of critics would of course be right, and, by my own calculations, if they were not right, then my own project would have little to offer.

In other words, what I am offering here as my own contribution to the study of Africanist discourse is precisely a reevaluation of the archive from the perspective of a literary critic. The questions I ask, the examples I use, and the ways in which I go about setting up my narrative are intimately connected to my training as a student of literary criticism and theory. A historian looking

29. I am of course overstating my case. The usefulness of literary readings is not always lost on social scientists. One of the most interesting feminist historians, Joan W. Scott, has this to say: "Reading for the 'literary' does not seem at all inappropriate for those whose discipline is devoted to the study of change. It is not the only kind of reading I am advocating, although more documents than those written by literary figures are susceptible to such readings" ("Experience," in *Feminists Theorize the Political*, ed. Butler and Scott, 36).

at the very same texts I assume would come up with a different narrative, an anthropologist a different one, and a philosopher yet another. None of these accounts could, without hubris, claim to be a complete one. Rather, each would retain its own disciplinary identity and simultaneously engage in a dialogue with the other. Perhaps, it may be said, that each would supplement the other. I can only hope that my own offering here will prove worthy of the nature of such supplementarity.

CHAPTER I

"Race," Rationality, and the Pedagogical Imperative

An Archaeology of Racial Knowledge

In an intentionally provocative piece, "Race, Empire, and the Historians," Christopher Fyfe writes, "In colonial Africa, authority was manifested very simply. White gave orders, black obeyed. A white skin (or more properly, a skin imputed white) conferred authority. It was an easy rule to understand and enforce, and it upheld colonial authority in Africa for about half a century. Yet some historians seem unwilling to remember it."[1] Fyfe's project in the essay is to challenge historians, both African and non-African, to rethink the role of race in the project of African colonialism. That white historians may feel ashamed and embarrassed to raise the issue may be understandable, suggests Fyfe, but the fact that African historians in the majority also sweep the issue under the carpet seems astounding to him.[2]

Fyfe's call for a serious attention to the workings of racism in the colonial economy invites a second related set of inquiries that are the topic of this chapter. If, as Fyfe and Frantz Fanon have argued, racism was in many ways the legitimizing force of colonial authority, to what extent was it underwritten by discourses on race? And if popular discourses on race have often been the subject of scholarly analysis, why have those racial discourses having scientific as-

---

1. Christopher Fyfe, "Race, Empire, and the Historians," *Race and Class* 33.4 (1992): 15.
2. Ibid., 27.

pirations been of less interest to Africanists?[3] Could the reason partially be the disciplinary divisions that separate us, rendering such a project incomprehensible? Or could it be that today we are unmoved by the "pseudoscience" of "racial" thinking, at least in its strong biological form, since it no longer seems to pose as great a threat? Or could it be, on the contrary, that we are all too afraid that returning to the question of race may allow it to rear its ugly head?

The underlying assumption of this chapter is that by selectively drawing on texts written by a wide range of disciplinary actors we may better be able to understand the *relative* role of racial thinking at different nodes of the colonial economy. To talk of the "relative" role of racial thinking is to already move away from Fyfe's foundationalist rhetoric to a less programmatic postfoundational account. Or to put it differently, it is to insist on reintroducing "race" into the mix of African(ist) colonial discourse theory while resisting any attempt to theorize it as a "sovereign hierarchical operator."[4] For despite Fanon and Fyfe's accurate portrayal of the racially structured Manichean colonial world, the actual discursive justifications for colonial social practices were often more confused, less clear-cut. In mapping out the role of "racial" thinking in such a world, we note that the battles over biology ("race") versus culture, historical process versus essential identity, and, finally, sameness versus difference could not always be reduced to a prefigured formula. For if colonialism was at its heart about the exertion of an external political power—real or imagined—over an indigenous community, it was no less also about the establishment of a rhetorical power in the same domain.[5] The ability to call the shots of "sameness" ("they are like us") or "difference" ("they are not like us") in differently motivated circumstances, and to call these shots forcefully, was the crux of the rhetorical game.

"Race," then, was a crucial component of the rhetorical interplay between "sameness" and "difference" in the colonial context. But as Ann Laura Stoler has persuasively argued, it was always mediated by other loci of differentiation such as gender, class, religion, and sexuality, which could also be mobilized by colonial ideology in various combinations either simultaneously or with pur-

3. For two exemplary texts that address popular racist discourses see Dorothy Hammond and Alta Jablow, *The Africa That Never Was* (Prospect Heights, Ill.: Waveland Press, 1970); and Jan Nederveen Pieterse, *White on Black: Images of Africa and Blacks in Western Popular Culture* (New Haven: Yale University Press, 1992).

4. Nicholas Thomas, *Colonialism's Culture: Anthropology, Travel, and Government* (Princeton: Princeton University Press, 1994), 54.

5. See in this regard David Spurr, *The Rhetoric of Empire* (Durham: Duke University Press, 1993).

poseful contradistinction.[6] What characterizes racial discourse in the colonial context, then, is not its originary nature but rather its emergence in a form embedded in social practices and institutions. This means that "the *quality* and *intensity* of racism vary enormously in different colonial contexts and at different moments in any particular colonial encounter."[7] If in this chapter I foreground the role of "race" in the discourses of African rationality and pedagogy, I do so not to establish it as a foundational category of colonial discourse theory but rather to trace its uneven trajectory and often indeed its disappearance in this terrain. Or, put differently, one might say that I am trying to relieve the foundationalist burden often put on discourses of "race" in order to see them as sites of political contestation. By focusing on a central obsession of colonial thinking in Africa—the question of the rationality of the black African—I hope to trace the awkward relationships between constructions of race and pedagogy on the part of colonial observers and the subsequent erasure of this history in postcolonial African(ist) discourse.[8]

"Is the African capable of rational thought?"[9] This seemingly simple—not to mention—condescending colonial question was related to several others:

---

6. See Ann Laura Stoler, *Race and the Education of Desire* (Durham: Duke University Press, 1995).

7. Ann Laura Stoler, "Rethinking Colonial Categories: European Communities and the Boundaries of Rule," in *Colonialism and Culture,* ed. Nicholas Dirks (Ann Arbor: University of Michigan Press, 1992), 322.

8. In other words, this chapter clearly does not pretend to provide an exhaustive account of racial thinking in colonial Africa. For a remarkable account of the theorization of race in the South African context, see Saul Dubow, *Scientific Racism in Modern South Africa* (Cambridge: Cambridge University Press, 1995). Dubow's account, although itself focusing on the South African context, is wide ranging and traces racial thinking in the context of, among other things, early diffusionist theories, theories of criminality, South African political history as well as pedagogical imperatives.

9. The concept "rationality" is one that is "essentially contested," and even full-length treatises on the subject recognize the usefulness of its contested nature. Needless to say, I do not intend to offer here *the* proper usage of the term other than to suggest that in the context of the writers I discuss, there is sufficient interest in both the content and form of the "rational." On occasion "rational" is precisely what the "emotional" is not, "rational" is precisely what the "prelogical" is not, "rational" is indeed what the "native" is not. The question, then, becomes one of conversion—can, and if so how can, the "native" be brought under the regime of the rational? For insightful discussions of "rationality" in the context of social science, educational theory, and in particular culture contact, see Robin Horton and Ruth Finnegan, eds., *Modes of Thought: Essays on Thinking in Western and Non-Western Societies* (London: Faber, 1973); Martin Tammy and K. D. Irani, eds., *Rationality in Thought and Action* (New York: Greenwood, 1986); Stanley I. Benn and G. W. Mortimore, *Rationality and the Social Sciences* (London: Routledge, 1976); Bryan Wilson, ed., *Rationality* (Oxford: Blackwell, 1970); Martin Hollis and Steven Lukes, eds., *Rationality and Relativism* (Oxford: Blackwell, 1982).

First, on the biological order, "Does the black race possess the physiological apparatus to achieve the accomplishments of whites?" Next, "Would educational opportunities enhance the prospects of Africans or would they instead only alienate them from their people?" And, "If the introduction of Western education was seen to be detrimental, how would colonialism justify itself without claims to a strong pedagogical motive?" Again, "How does one go about selecting the Africans who would benefit the most from Western teachings and education?" Lastly, "What kind of education should be provided to those who would seem not to benefit from a Westernized education?"[10]

The question, "Is the African capable of rational thought?" is, then, considerably more complex than its seemingly simple formulation suggests, but unfortunately the answers given to it in most historical reconstructions of Africanist thought have treated it as a transparent one. Since "rationality" is more easily identifiable as a philosophical issue than is "race," much of the discussion on the subject has fallen within the purview of philosophers and to some extent anthropologists with a philosophical bent. But like the historians whom Fyfe discusses, students of African philosophy have often sidestepped the issue of race per se. This reluctance is all the more surprising, since it is clear that the anxieties surrounding the question "Is there such a thing as an African philosophy?"—a question that has plagued African studies for a long time now—have arisen in the historical context of racism. In this context, the evaluations of "rationality," "mentality," "primitive thought," "indigenous ontologies," and so on, despite the euphemisms, are often about race and racial worth. How these attributes get defined and who gets to define them, how they occasionally get measured and who goes about measuring them, are all part of the story of the racialized discourse of colonial social thought.

Within the tradition of African philosophical studies the most easily available answer to the question of African rationality has been to point to such markers as Edward Tylor and Herbert Spencer, who in their social Darwinism suggested that "primitive" cultures were just lower on the evolutionary scale, that is, that they had been unable so far to fully evolve institutions characteristic of the more civilized (i.e., European) nations. The account is thickened

10. Thus J. H. Driberg writes: "If we do not believe in the logic of the savage and in the identity of his processes of thought with our own, then we should be proved illogical ourselves in attempting to develop along logical lines peoples of an alien mentality, and in attempting to transmit our civilization to peoples mentally incapable of assimilating it" (*The Savage As He Really Is* [London: Routledge, 1929], 4).

with a few quotations from Hume, Kant, and Hegel about the incapacities of the "Negro" or the lack of history in Africa. Then comes Lucien Lévy-Bruhl, who wrote a series of books, most significantly *How Natives Think* (1910/1926) and *Primitive Mentality* (1922/1923), in which he promoted the idea of "primitive thought" as "prelogical" (a term he later renounced in favor of the term "mystical"). Lévy-Bruhl is seen by some, including E. E. Evans-Pritchard, as embodying the next stage in a "progressive" history (from evolutionary models to relativistic ones) and by yet others such as Mudimbe and Appiah as occupying a space continuous with the ethnocentric colonial paradigm.[11] The next stage in this progressive drama is usually marked by Placide Tempels, the Belgian missionary whose 1945 book *Bantu Philosophy* is seen to be a revolutionary break with the previously unsympathetic and Eurocentric tradition. Indeed, Tempels's work is repeatedly cited in the literature of postcolonial African philosophy as the paradigmatic text that opened up the conditions of possibility for an Afrocentric philosophy of Africa.[12] It is in Tempels's text that Bantu ontology (particularly of the Luba and Katanga peoples) is finally seen to find a place in a global philosophical tradition. When one notes the level of energy surrounding this text in the circles of African(ist) philosophy, one gets the distinct feeling that historically it was this text, ironically written by a white missionary, that served to vindicate black African rationality. If the African has a coherent philosophical system, then he must, of necessity, be a "rational" being.[13]

11. I discuss Evans-Pritchard's treatment of Lévy-Bruhl below. For Mudimbe's and Appiah's position on Lévy-Bruhl see their coauthored essay, "The Impact of African Studies on Philosophy," in *Africa and the Disciplines: The Contributions of Research in Africa to the Social Sciences and the Humanities,* ed. Robert Bates, V. Y. Mudimbe, and Jean O'Barr (Chicago: University of Chicago Press, 1993).

12. This narrative begs the question, of course, of the necessity of *writing* for the existence, if not of a philosophical system itself, then at least of a history of philosophy. Thus, although most critics will acknowledge the existence of indigenous philosophical systems in Africa that are unconnected with the trajectory outlined here, they nevertheless concur in the opinion that Tempels's text made the discursive scrutiny of such systems possible. A parallel development has occurred in the history of literary traditions in Africa in which written literatures, and the novel in particular, have often tended to be read as the originary moment of an African literary tradition. Although some lip service is paid to orature and indigenous theater and performance, most critical histories continue to focus on the written as the marker of literary accomplishment. For a critique of this tendency and a reappraisal of "orature" see Ngugi wa Thiong'o, *Decolonising the Mind: The Politics of Language in African Literature* (London: J. Currey, 1986).

13. For an excellent account of the role of "rationality" in the context of African philosophy see D. A. Masolo, *African Philosophy in Search of an Identity* (Bloomington: Indiana University Press,

This brief review of the literature makes the answer of the estimations of African rationality within the colonial episteme seem simple—it is a narrative of a clear teleological progression. I want to suggest, however, like most thumbnail sketches, this one is too neat to be of any great value to a serious understanding of the workings of colonial knowledge—or more accurately, colonial belief—about the African native.[14] In this regard, we may be better served if we were to follow Michel Foucault's directive to the critical archaeologist and introduce into this narrative contemporaneous texts and readings that have subsequently been left out of the conventional histories.[15]

Consider, for instance, what may seem to us today as an overly sympathetic reading of Lévy-Bruhl by anthropologists of the day such as Evans-Pritchard and Franz Boas. Why did these anthropologists, despite their own at times radical skepticism of Lévy-Bruhl's thought, find it necessary to defend him against his critics?[16] Of the many possible motives that Evans-Pritchard may have had for being a sympathetic reader of Lévy-Bruhl, surely a significant one

1994). Masolo opens his book by stating, "To a large extent, the debate about African philosophy can be summarized as a significant contribution to the discussion or definition of reason or what Hegel called the spirit. Indeed, it is commonly referred to as the 'Rationality debate'" (1). In the remainder of the chapter Masolo shows why the focus on "rationality" was central to African self-assertion in the context of centuries of racial prejudice against the black race. By building his discussion on a whole range of writers—poets, philosophers, politicians—from both sides of the Atlantic, Masolo presents a compelling account of the fate of "rationality" in the struggle over racial identity and worth.

14. The relationship between the nature of "belief" and the nature of "knowledge" is itself an issue in this chapter. "Beliefs," conventionally understood, are those ideas, thoughts, and values that a person or a group may hold regardless of their empirical validity or reliability. "Knowledges," by the same token, are held to a greater accountability. But, of course, as in any case of competing claims, one person's "knowledge" is the other person's "belief." In the specific context of this chapter, what we now know to be falsifiable "beliefs" about African natives were in the context of the colonial episteme considered to be "knowledges" about Africans. I have retained the term *knowledges* in the discussion, since my aim has been to attempt an immanent critique of the constitution of such beliefs *as* knowledges. To begin the analysis with the demystification of the knowledges as "only beliefs" would preempt the analysis presented here.

15. One such person who could be introduced into the history of African philosophy is W. C. Willoughby, who in 1928 (many years before Tempels) published a book, *The Soul of the Bantu: A Sympathetic Study of the Magico-Religious Practices and Beliefs of the Bantu Tribes of Africa* (London: Student Christian Movement, 1928). Willoughby's work has been completely ignored by historians of African philosophy even though the claims he makes are very close to those made by Tempels much later. I have written on this curious forgetting elsewhere (unpublished manuscript).

16. Thus even though Evans-Pritchard may have been responsible for the most significant critique of Lévy-Bruhl's thesis (in *Witchcraft, Oracles, and Magic among the Azande* (1937; rpt., London: Oxford University Press, 1976), he nevertheless wrote a very sympathetic entry on Lévy-Bruhl in

was the recognition that Lévy-Bruhl did depart from what was increasingly threatening to be one of the orthodoxies of the day—a biologism that reduced mentality to the brain. It was important for Evans-Pritchard (as it was for perhaps the most ardent critic of "race thinking" in the early twentieth century—Franz Boas),[17] to recognize that Lévy-Bruhl was "speaking not of a biological or psychological difference between primitives and ourselves, but of a social one."[18] Let us remember that anthropology was at this time struggling to formulate models of cultural relativism that were not founded on—indeed, that attempted to debunk—any biologism. Thus for all his misconceptions, anthropologists of his day were disposed to reading Lévy-Bruhl as a fellow traveler fighting against the real enemy of biological determinism.

To understand the protectionism of an Evans-Pritchard or a Boas toward a figure like Lévy-Bruhl is to understand that intellectual paradigms are always judged diacritically. Against the biologism of the day, Lévy-Bruhl seemed to these "culturalists," even if misguided, nevertheless one of their own. If this protectionism is lost on observers today, it is because in our own poststructuralist and anti-essentialist dispositions we have lost the diacritical lens through which biological or racial essentialism seems a threat. Unlike in their own times, when the world was divided between the biological determinists and the culturalists, we seem retrospectively in our own histories to divide the world of the early twentieth century between the "primitivists" (Lévy-Bruhl) and the "rationalists" (Evans-Pritchard). But to continue to do so with no regard to the strategic similarities that these scholars themselves perceived among themselves is to engage in an act not only of bad faith but also of bad scholarship.

As critical archaeologists attentive to the absences and gaps in the conventional disciplinary histories, we need to reread the colonial library with an eye attuned to such alliances that today seem to us insignificant. Doing so leads us to listen to voices that were undoubtedly important in their day but seem to have lost their resonance in our more recent histories of colonial discourse. Such a revisionary project of a critical archaeology of African(ist) philosophy would, for instance, find renewed interest in a text such as *Primitive Philosophy*,

---

his *History of Anthropological Thought* (Boston: Faber and Faber, 1981). See also Franz Boas, *The Mind of Primitive Man* (1911; rpt., New York: Free Press, 1965).

17. Thus Boas reads Lévy-Bruhl's work as a discussion of cultural rather than racial differences. See Boas, *Mind of Primitive Man*, 43.

18. Evans-Pritchard, *History of Anthropological Thought*, 123.

which was offered by a district officer in what was then northern Rhodesia, as a specifically philosophical as opposed to anthropological contribution to the debate.[19] Virtually written out of every contemporary history of colonial discourse on Africa, *Primitive Philosophy* by Vernon Brelsford is at the most basic level an attempt to review and critique the existing literature on primitive thought and mentality. At the same time it may also be read as a text that seeks, in its own limited way, to open out a new branch of investigation—theorizing "race." In many ways, Brelsford participates in some of the common misconceptions of his day—references to Africans as "savage" or "childlike" are not at all uncommon in his text. But although he does not give up an uncritical developmentalist model, he marks an important moment in the trajectory of African(ist) thought *in so far as he most directly addresses what he sees as the errors of biologism*. Brelsford opens his chapter "Savage Mentality and Thought" by commenting on Francis Galton, who in his search for racial attributes and abilities once compared the intelligence of the Demara with a dog, only to conclude that "the comparison reflected no great honor on the man."[20] Writing in the early 1930s, Brelsford argues that although one would expect such absurd conclusions to be criticized or at least ignored, they are instead increasingly gaining the authority of a science that claims to be able to correlate mental ability with racial (physiological) attributes. Brelsford sees this project not only as dangerously racist but also as scientifically wrong. Although theories of the mind may best be left to philosophers, Brelsford claims that even good science disproves the theories of the eugenicists: "Medical science is increasingly tending to prove, by its wonderful operations in which whole pieces of the brain are removed without any observed interference with mental processes, that mind is, to a great extent, independent of the brain."[21]

Thus although Brelsford's *Primitive Mentality* has been virtually ignored by historians of African(ist) colonial discourse, it signals us to the important battles being fought against eugenics in the early half of the century and directs us to a path that can be usefully followed in the trajectory of African(ist) knowledge. My aim in the rest of this chapter is to follow Brelsford's lead and to present an alternative account of the historical discourses associated with

19. In some ways the desire to spell out this distinction is a premonition of what is to come in later debates between "ethnophilosophy" and "scientific philosophy."
20. Francis Galton, quoted in Vernon Brelsford, *Primitive Philosophy* (London: John Bale, 1935), 9.
21. Brelsford, *Primitive Philosophy*, 16. One need not affirm Brelsford's radical disjuncture between the "mind" and the "brain" in order to retain his skepticism of a scientific racism involving brain sizes or head shapes.

African rational ability. Although acknowledging the important contributions of students of African philosophy, I seek to complicate the standard account offered by the discipline by adding into the picture texts drawn from two different but related traditions: (1) the writings of the ethnopsychiatrists and their critics—the former a rather heterogenous group who at various points articulated theories of the "arrested development" of Africans, oftentimes argued for race differentials on hereditary grounds, and in some cases went about devising intelligence tests and other such calibrations that could be used to question the ultimate educability of Africans; and (2) those texts written in the psychoanalytic tradition, drawing primarily on Freud and Adler and including the works of J. F. Ritchie, Octave Mannoni, and Fanon. Although a comprehensive history of the practices of colonial education is beyond the purview of this chapter, I do provide a symptomatic reading of the anxieties around "literary" and "industrial" education in Africa, since it is clear that the discourses on black rationality and mental ability were often propagated against the backdrop of the pedagogical project.

Of Race and Reason

It would, of course, be impossible to cover within the boundaries of this chapter the genealogical development of the concept of "race" in colonial Africa.[22] What interests us here is the relationship that certain scientists, working in the first half of the twentieth century, sought to establish between physiological characteristics and mental and behavioral ones. Regardless of the specific physiological characteristics under scrutiny, the psychological effects were, in the work of these scientists, always "read off" against the quantifiable aspects of these characteristics. The strategy was one of correlating physiological measurements and calculations with mental and psychological attributes. Whether it was in establishing a correlation between brain size and temperament or between race and intelligence, the strategy was essentially, as Stephen Jay Gould has rightly suggested, one of reification—reducing a complex and abstract phenomenon such as temperament or intelligence to a set of numbers that could in turn be put in a hierarchical order.[23]

22. See in particular Ashley Montagu's *Man's Most Dangerous Myth: The Fallacy of Race* (New York: Columbia, 1942).
23. See Stephen Jay Gould, *The Mismeasure of Man* (New York: Vintage, 1981). Gould's insight that correlation is not the same as causation is lost on many of these investigators.

The psychometric projects in the high colonial period in Africa had their origins in various nineteenth-century practices and their associated theories of evolution. Philip Curtin, for instance, has documented the rise of the phrenologists who attempted to understand the nature of the African societies in order to place them in an evolutionary grid. Thus George Combe in his 1836 edition of *A System of Phrenology* attempted to demonstrate through various measurements of African skulls that "the organs of Philoprogenitiveness and Concentrativeness are largely developed; the former of which produces love of children, and the latter that concentration of mind which is favorable to settled and sedentary employments. The organs of Veneration and Hope are also considerable in size. The greatest deficiencies lie in Conscientiousness, Ideality and Reflection."[24] Although Combe's aim was to establish through phrenology a hierarchy in which the skulls of Africans were more developed than those of American Indians and Australian Aborigines but less than those of Europeans, Curtin points out that in effect Combe's project did no more than draw significantly on the prejudicial travelers' accounts of the period, which in turn looked to phrenology for "scientific" corroboration—rendering the whole enterprise circular and self-fulfilling.[25]

If the early travelers' accounts encouraged the "scientific" projects of the phrenologists, a similar exchange took place later in the 1920s and 1930s as the discourses of the "arrested development" of African natives primarily advocated by Piaget-influenced theorists were taken up in turn by educators and ethnopsychiatrists. Drawing on the methods of child psychology, these Piagetian scholars argued that the comparative development of European and African children occurred at an equal pace, but that at the onset of puberty, the African child stopped growing intellectually and emotionally.[26] According to most of these scholars, the causes of this alleged arrest were environmental and cultural, the most famous one being the relatively greater sexual activity of the African.[27] What is curious about this intellectual school is the use they

---

24. George Combe, *A System of Phrenology*, 4th ed., (1845), 433, cited in *The Image of Africa: British Ideas and Action, 1780–1850*, by Philip Curtin (Madison: University of Wisconsin Press, 1964), 366–67.

25. See Curtin, *Image of Africa*, 367.

26. Although we do not know what Piaget himself thought of such studies in the African context, he did believe in the importance of examining his claims cross-culturally. See J. Piaget, "Need and Significance of Cross-Cultural Studies in Genetic Psychology," *International Journal of Psychology* 1 (1966) 3–13.

27. These arguments were on occasion extended to account for the "arrested development" of the

made of their argument. When, in a classic essay titled "Characteristics of African Thought," James W. C. Dougall presented his theory of arrested development, his agenda was to counter the Lévy-Bruhlian claim about differences between "logical" and "mystical" thought. Dougall thought that Lévy-Bruhl had undermined the essential similarities between the civilized and the primitive that he believed could be seen in the similarities between the African adult and the European child. If there is more than a hint of racism and paternalism here, we should remember that Dougall and his fellow psychologists thought that by arguing for a difference in degree rather than in kind they were themselves countering a more dangerous racism that, by asserting insurmountable difference, conspired to keep the African in a subordinate space.[28]

The importance of foregrounding the similarity rather than the differences between races was promoted by these advocates of modernity both as a logical necessity for legitimizing the pedagogical motives of colonialism and as an ethical duty. Thus we find Raoul Allier suggesting at the close of his book *The Mind of the Savage* that despite some of the observable differences between Africans and Europeans, it is important to be optimistic along with the missionary, who wants to believe in "a humanity that is one in essence and one in destiny."[29] It is only such a belief, thinks Allier, that will discourage the racist conception that some people are born to rule and others to serve. Like Dougall, Allier read the "arrested development" of the African native as a link between Europe and Africa and not as a separation. Given the existence of this link, suggested Allier, it is the responsibility of the colonizer to help the African "grow." "If they are to rise higher, they need some intervention external to themselves."[30] Allier's work is a passionate defense of the colonial system and also of the educability of the African native. But what is important to note is that if "arrested development" was to be used by the advocates of African educability by foregrounding sameness and by asserting the primacy of environmental factors for the alleged "arrest," the same observation could and was

---

entire culture. See Joseph Daniel Unwin's *Sex and Culture* (London: Humphrey Milford, 1934), which argued that there was a demonstrable inverse correlation between the expenditure of libidinal energies sanctioned by a given culture and its intellectual and particularly architectural achievements. For a critical exposé on these correlations, see Sander Gilman, "Sexology, Psychoanalysis, and Degeneration," in *Difference and Pathology* (Ithaca: Cornell University Press, 1985), 191–216.

28. James W. C. Dougall, "Characteristics of African Thought," *Africa* 5.3 (July 1932): 249–65.

29. Raoul Allier, *The Mind of the Savage*, trans. Fred Rothwell (London: G. Bell and Sons, 1929), 274.

30. Ibid., 212.

used by others to precisely the opposite effect. In the war between asserting sameness or difference and between asserting the primacy of the environment or heredity it is not always clear whether it was science that guided policy or rather the reverse.

Measuring Brains

Although the heyday of phrenology and other cranial-measurement-oriented study was certainly the early to mid–nineteenth century, it continued to have its supporters in the African contexts of the twentieth century. In a lecture presented at the Eugenics Society of London in 1933, Dr. L. H. Gordon, one of the senior physicians working in colonial Kenya, presented his theory of African "amentia." By "amentia" Gordon was referring to the condition of being "feeble-minded," "imbecile," or just generally mentally deficient. This condition, Gordon alleged, was common in a higher proportion among the African natives than their European counterparts and was a result of the inability of their literally "lighter" brains from coping with European education in particular and cultural contact in general.[31] Gordon developed this theme in a series of papers and lectures delivered in Nairobi and insisted that the clue to the African mind and personality lay in the relatively handicapped nature of the African's physiological apparatus.[32] Thus, in a characteristic gesture, Gordon

31. See H. L. Gordon, "Amentia in the East African," *Eugenics Review* 25 (1934): 223–35.
32. The debate on the relationship between brain weight and intellectual ability deserves a study of its own. I call attention here to only one scholar who wrote a full-length book on the problems of this correlation—Cedric Dover. Published in 1937, Dover's *Half Caste* (London: Martin Secker and Warburg, 1937) is primarily a critique of the biological literature on "race" and the problems of racial hybridity. Dover's project is to show that the discourses on the potential genetic dysfunctionality of racially mixed subjects is more politically than empirically motivated. The backbone of Dover's thesis is that theories of miscegenation are problematic because the ideas of "race" and "racial purity" on which they are based are in themselves problematic ones: "The concept of race, or subspecies according to modern biological preference, is so untenable in its application to our much mongrelised species that anthropologists have never been able to agree on a racial classification of mankind, the number of proposed races ranging from the three sanctioned by the earlier naturalists to a hundred and more created by later enthusiasts" (51). Thus Dover suggests that "racethinking," although seeking to draw its authority from science, has resulted in bad science, sometimes even fraud. He cites the studies of R. B. Bean published in the *American Journal of Anatomy* at the beginning of the century, which claimed "significant mean differences in the weight of a series of one hundred and fifty white and Negro brains respectively." Bean's studies, Dover points out, were empirically disputed by F. P. Mall, who claimed in a 1909 paper that Dr. Bean had "not

wrote in a 1935 essay that "'Mind,' as you know, is just a convenient working theory to explain the mysteries of the brain"[33] and proceeded to explicate the problems of native mentality and the futility of any hope for the intellectual growth of the African in terms of the undue pressures put on the African's frontal brain by "scholastic education." Gordon's research was extended further by his colleague F. W. Vint, who worked at the Pathological Research Laboratory in Nairobi. Vint attempted to refine the earlier claims based purely on brain weight to now include features such as the effects of a marked flattening of the African brain and particularly of the differentials in the development of the cortex.[34] Vint's study of the cortical development of the African brain led him to conclude that the brain of the African adult was as developed as the brain of a European child of seven or eight years of age.[35] As such, Vint's work could be read as an extension of the "arrested development" school of thought that had manifested itself in the earlier work of writers such as James W. C. Dougall and Raoul Allier but with an important difference: as opposed to the emphasis that Dougall and Allier had placed on the role of the environment in the arrested development of the African, Vint (and Gordon) located this arrest in the structural attributes of the black African brain. Here, then, physiology was seen to be destiny, and the implicit message was that no amount of social intervention would change the lowly mental status of the black race. The fact that Gordon was an avowed supporter of a eugenicist program of social engineering and praised the Germans in their racial project should come, then, as no surprise.[36]

The emphasis on the African as child persisted well into the 1950s in the work of such colonial medical practitioners as J. C. Carothers. Carothers, per-

---

only underweighed the majority of Negro brains, but had also helped comparisons along by over-weighing those of the white series" (42).

33. H. L. Gordon, "An Inquiry into the Correlation of Civilization and Mental Disorder in the Kenya Native," *East African Medical Journal* 12 (1935–36): 327.

34. F. W. Vint, "The Brain of the Kenyan Native," *Journal of Anatomy* 68 (1934): 216–23.

35. F. W. Vint, "A Preliminary Note on the Cell Content of the Prefrontal Cortex of the East African Native," *East African Medical Journal* 9 (1932–33), 30–55.

36. See H. L. Gordon, "Is War Eugenic or Dysgenic?: That Is Does War Improve or Impair the Physical or Mental Qualities of Future Generations?" *East African Medical Journal* 19 (1942): 94. I owe this reference to an insightful book by Jock McCullogh, *Colonial Psychiatry and "the African Mind"* (Cambridge: Cambridge University Press, 1995). McCullogh's treatise, though less interested in the aspects of educability and of the ethnophilosophical tradition in Africa, would be of interest to readers of this chapter.

haps the most prolific and influential commentator on African mentality, was appointed in 1938 as senior medical officer at the Mathari Mental Hospital in Kenya.[37] During his career Carothers published several articles on mental illnesses among Africans. Although Carothers may rightly be seen to have introduced environmental factors and especially the traumas of colonial cultural contact into the account of African mentality, it is clear that he never quite challenged the physiological aspects foregrounded by Gordon and Vint.[38] Even in a book published as late as 1953, *The African Mind in Health and Disease,* Carothers could not reject the physiological argument about what had by then come to be known as the "frontal lobe deficiency" of the African, nor did he question the implications of Vint's infantilization of the African native. Echoing the earlier claims of Dougall and Allier, but without endorsing their educational program on behalf of the African native, Carothers's authoritative study did little to disrupt the claims of physiology. Published in 1953 under the auspices of the World Health Organization, well after the supposed revolution in Africanist thinking established by Tempels's *Bantu Philosophy,* Carothers's work, predisposed to reading "arrested development" as a physiological rather than sociological condition, presents a sobering note on our faith in such revolutions in particular and the march of intellectual progress in general.[39]

Eugenics and Intelligence Testing

If the earlier half of the nineteenth century saw the rise of phrenology, it was the latter half of the century that saw the rise of the eugenics movement, fueled

37. Carothers had no prior training in psychiatry, but by the time he retired in 1951 he was a well-respected commentator in the field. He was, for instance, commissioned by the World Health Organization to publish a study on mental health in Africa. Frantz Fanon, in his critique of colonial psychiatry, singled out Carothers for attack, further suggesting the influence he had.

38. Jock McCullogh suggests that Carothers was one of the first to develop a link between African culture and mentality. But despite this attention to culture, blacks and whites were, in the final analysis for Carothers, different in kind and not just degree. As McCullogh himself suggests when it came to the question of the fundamental differences between blacks and whites, Carothers appealed in his 1953 treatise (discussed below) not only to Vint and Gordon but also to American studies "showing the brain of the Negro to be inferior to that of the Caucasian" (McCullogh, *Colonial Psychiatry and "the African Mind,"* 59).

39. For a rigorous treatment of the issue of "progress" in science and social science, see Larry Laudan's *Progress and Its Problems: Towards a Theory of Scientific Growth* (Berkeley: University of California Press, 1977). Readers skeptical of this claim about the dubiousness of intellectual progress

by its own (mis)appropriations of Darwin's *Origin of Species*. In what we may call its constative moment this school was interested in tracing the hereditary nature of human characteristics; in its performative moment it was interested in a social program whereby only socially desirable traits were to be encouraged to reproduce and socially undesirable ones eliminated. Francis Galton, author of the book *Hereditary Genius* (1892) and intellectual leader of the eugenicist movement,[40] believed that such a social program was in accord with the processes of natural selection and the "survival of the fittest." Given the counternatural tendencies of protecting the weak and disabled that "civilized" society encouraged, it was all the more necessary, thought Galton, to actively engage in such a genetic program lest weak and undesirable traits were continually reproduced.[41]

Although in the context of colonial Africa Galton's strong social program thankfully never came to pass, it was indeed an important precursor to the various debates on the role of heredity in human development.[42] In particular, the entire field of intelligence testing that grew in the African context was based on this understanding of hereditary carryover and the immutability of genetically based character traits. The African, in the logical extension of this theory, could not really be educated, since he lacked the adequate "genetic make-up" for such an education. It was, then, the threat of such a reductionist model of understanding African mentality, intelligence, and potential that, I am suggesting, worried the likes of Boas, Lévy-Bruhl, and Brelsford, and it is in the context of this thinking that we finally need to evaluate their work. Yet, despite their efforts, it seems that these early anthropologists did not have the decisive censoring effects that they may have hoped for. The battle between the

---

are directed to the research of J. Philippe Rushton. In his article "Evolutionary Biology and Heritable Traits" (*Psychological Reports* 71.3 [December 1992]: 811–23), Rushton continues the project of determining intelligence and ability on physiological grounds. In Rushton's project, brains and penises are two areas of particular scrutiny.

40. Galton, *Hereditary Genius* (London: Macmillan, 1892).

41. Galton's *Hereditary Genius* presents a hierarchy of racial "comparative worth." The "Negro African," not surprisingly for Galton, appears low on the scale, even though he is deemed a higher type than the native Australian (325–37).

42. It is interesting, however, to recognize that a good amount of Galton's theorizing about hereditary characteristics grew out of his own experiences traveling in Africa—once again, some of the circular mechanisms that we noted at work in the phrenologists' projects are to be seen here. For a fascinating account of Galton in Africa see Raymond E. Fancher, "Francis Galton's African Ethnography and Its Role in the Development of His Psychology," *British Journal for the History of Science* 15 (March 1983): 67–79.

psychometrics and their critics was yet to come, and to the extent that it came, it did so not so much from anthropologists as from more sociologically bent psychologists and from philosophers of education.

At the turn of the century, Alfred Binet developed the first usable intelligence test in France, and this test was subsequently modified in 1916 by a Stanford University professor, Lewis Terman. The Stanford-Binet test, as it subsequently came to be called, was in effect an effort to come up with an objective intelligence scale on which any person could be mapped. The location of a particular individual on the scale would depend on that individual's performance on a set of standardized problem-solving tests. Although Binet's original intent was to develop a test that was exclusively to be used to measure the variation of intelligence and ability within a cultural group, the Stanford-Binet test increasingly became available to those wishing to establish cross-cultural comparisons.[43] In the case of colonial Africa, the tests were first used by Richard A. C. Oliver in the 1930s to counter precisely the kind of racial comparisons that were being made by Gordon and Vint using cranial measurements. The argument against such cross-racial comparisons was made by Oliver in 1932, when he published a guide, *General Intelligence Test for Africans: Manual for Directions*.[44] The guide outlined the use of the Stanford-Binet test and assessed the usability, in the colonial Kenyan context, of a variety of others such as the Porteus Maze test and the Goodenough test (designed to focus on diagrams rather than language).[45] And yet although Oliver's stated aim was to devise tests that could test for differences of ability among Africans, the tests nevertheless were insufficiently adapted to African cultural contexts and thus risked imposing an alien conception of intelligence itself.[46] Despite this risk, how-

---

43. It is important to note that intelligence tests need not always be misused. Used as Binet originally intended them, they can be useful tools in diagnosing learning-disabled children. Stephen Jay Gould has this to say in this context, "I feel that tests of the IQ type were helpful in the proper diagnosis of my own learning-disabled son. His average score, the IQ itself, meant nothing, for it was only an amalgam of some very high and very low scores; but the pattern of low values indicated his areas of deficit. The misuse of mental tests is not inherent in the idea of testing itself" (*Mismeasure of Man,* 155).

44. R. A. C. Oliver, *General Intelligence Tests for Africans: Manual for Directions* (Nairobi: Government Printers Kenya, 1932).

45. See also R. A. C. Oliver, "Mental Tests in the Study of the African," *Africa* (1934): 40–46; Oliver, "Mental Tests for Primitive Races," *Year Book of Education* (1935): 560–70; W. B. Mumford and C. E. Smith, "Racial Comparisons and Intelligence Testing" *Journal of the Royal African Society* 37 (1938): 46–57.

46. See Griffith Quick, Review, *Africa* (1934).

ever, Oliver's tests were increasingly utilized in Kenya for the purposes of school selection and other screening processes.[47]

Although Oliver's own work explicitly warned against the use of the tests to make cross-racial comparisons, the intelligence testing movement entered its most controversial moment at times when it attempted to make precisely such calculations. First in the United States, and then in South Africa and other parts of colonial Africa, the tests were increasingly utilized not only to ascertain the "intelligence quotient" (IQ) of a particular individual but also to measure the comparative ability and worth of races.[48] The debate on the African continent was most heated in the South African context, and we could use the work of Charles T. Loram, M. Laurence Fick, and Simon Biesheuval as significant markers of its three moments. It is in the trajectory of this debate that we see the closest and most blatant relationship between the discourses of African ability and rationality and of the various vested interests of a colonial settler economy.

We begin with the South African inspector of schools, Charles Templeman Loram. Loram, who later participated in the American-sponsored Phelps-Stokes Commission on African Education and became the Sterling Professor of Education at Yale University, wrote his 1915 doctoral dissertation on South African native education policy at Teachers College, Columbia University. He began his study, *The Education of the South African Native,* with the assumption that was to resonate throughout the literature of intelligence testing to come: that to have an effective educational policy, one needed to have a proper understanding of native ability. "There is a good deal of *opinion* on the subject, but nothing which can altogether be relied on as a basis for the structure of an educational practice," he argued.[49] Loram's project was to replicate, in the South African context, some of the psychological tests that were being conducted in the United States at the time.[50] These tests, Loram believed, would

47. Charles Lyons, *To Wash an Aethiop White: British Ideas about Black African Educability, 1530–1960* (New York: Teachers College Press, 1975), 145.
48. This is not to suggest that such tests were uncontested in the African context. As I discuss below in my reading of Simon Biesheuval, the very idea of a measurable intelligence was the subject of much critique. In addition to the refutation by Biesheuval, see also J. W. Winterbottom, "Can We Measure the African's Intelligence?" *Rhodes-Livingston Journal* 6.6 (1948): 53–59; and Mumford and Smith, "Racial Comparisons and Intelligence Testing," 46–57.
49. Charles Templeman Loram, *The Education of the South African Native* (London: Longmans Green, 1917), viii.
50. At the time Loram was working on his dissertation, the Binet test was still being modified by

provide the foundation for a better understanding of the mental capacities and educability of the African native.

The question that Loram sought to answer was that of the validity of the theory of the arrest of mental development of the native. He attempted to verify this arrest "scientifically," that is, through the mechanism of intelligence testing. The most interesting aspect of Loram's book, however, is not so much what he did with the results of the tests as what he wouldn't do with them. After using the tests devised by the American psychologist W. H. Pyle in the South African context, Loram discovered that although there was evidence of "undoubted mental slowness and sluggishness of many of the older pupils in Native schools,"[51] this was not a peculiar racial characteristic of the natives. His test results had shown that a decrease in efficiency at the onset of puberty was a characteristic that was common to all the three races studied (Europeans, Indians, and Native Africans). If there were indeed observable differences between older native students and European students of the same age, these were to be accounted for not by innate capacities but rather by environmental factors. Loram suggested that native students, as opposed to European ones, found the educational experience unsatisfactory and were more likely to be frustrated by the uncertain and tenuous rewards that such education offered. It was this sense of dissatisfaction with the larger societal structure that resulted in a greater sense of apathy among the older native students. To change this situation, Loram made the following suggestion: "For many years to come, separate courses of study, as well as separate schools, for the Natives will be necessary. The courses of study should take account of the peculiar experiences of the Natives, and the teaching, in the earlier stages at least, should be in the vernacular. From the beginning the education given should be meaningful to the Natives, and to this end should lead up to the future occupations open to them."[52]

Thus Loram, rather than rejecting wholesale the cross-cultural validity of intelligence testing, sought the "scientific" authority rendered by these tests to side with the environmentalists rather than the hereditarians. It is important to remember that Loram was speaking not just as a scholar but as an important participant in the field of South African educational policy. He had his own

---

Lewis Terman. Loram relied instead on tests developed by the American psychologist W. H. Pyle, who had devised them to measure logic, memory, and substitution.

51. Loram, *Education of the South African Native,* 218.

52. Ibid., 225.

agendas and beliefs, which clearly entered his reading of the issues. The chapter titled "Why Educate the Native," in which Loram presents extensive arguments for increased state support for Bantu education, was arguably written to "scare" the white South Africans into agreeing to support Bantu education—the horrors of an uneducated native population portrayed by Loram here attest to an astute awareness on the writer's part that the only way to get the Europeans to pay any attention to the issue would be to present them with a specter of a savage world encroaching on their own.[53]

If Loram's agendas included greater support for a "relevant" native education, it is important to recognize that the debates that were to later take place in the larger African context over "literary" versus "industrial" education were already making an appearance in Loram's work. Loram's own position in this debate is somewhat uncertain and ambiguous, and he may indeed have changed his views on the matter during his career.[54] Thus, for instance, we

53. Loram engaged in a similar calculated rhetorical move when he chose to write the foreword to Ray E. Phillips's *The Bantu Are Coming*, a book that was extremely critical of white South African attitudes toward the native Africans. Phillips's book deplored the working conditions in mines; discussed the contradictions of capital; demythologized the colonial Christianity, which wanted to save souls but leave the people empty-stomached; and argued vehemently for enlarging the scope of the native economy. Loram wrote in his foreword: "While Mr. Phillips excoriates our cant beliefs about natives, criticizes the attitude of the government whites toward the native people with real indignation, his object is perfectly plain. He sees the absolute necessity for a basis of adjustment between the two races who have to live side by side: he realizes clearly that the interests of both whites and blacks are inextricably bound up together so that the prosperity of one depends on the prosperity of the other. . . . while dissociating myself entirely from the political opinions expressed herein, I, as a South African, commend to my fellow-countrymen this burning appeal for a change of heart in the consideration of our grave and difficult problem" (foreword to *The Bantu Are Coming*, by Ray E. Phillips [New York: Richard R. Smith, 1930], 8–9). I will leave it to the reader to work through the wonderfully convoluted message here—recommending a change of heart in public policy and race relations without endorsing the "political opinions expressed herein" is only one such move. My point is that Loram was aware of the limitations of what he could and could not say as a government employee, and he did his best to help advocate change without seeming to do as much. Here it should suffice to say that Loram's influence was felt by actors who fashioned themselves as relatively progressive in the South African scene. For instance, in a book titled *Sons of Africa* intended to foreground the heroic biographies of black Africans of the past and present, Georgina A. Gollock acknowledges Loram as an important friend and influence (Gollock, *Sons of Africa* [New York: Friendship Press, 1928], ix).

54. R. Hunt Davis Jr. suggests in his study of Loram that he was a firm believer of the industrial education model advocated by Booker T. Washington at Tuskegee. Although it is true that Loram continued to work closely with advocates of industrial education for Africans, including Thomas Hesse Jones, it is unclear, as I suggest in my reading, whether this collaboration was based more on funding opportunities for the study of African education or on deep ideological convictions. See

find Thomas Jesse Jones, the leader of the Phelps-Stokes Commission, citing Loram in the introductory section of the 1921 report as a fellow skeptic of the literary education prevalent in Africa.[55] But a reading of *The Education of the South African Native* suggests that Loram was aware of the importance of balancing the two kinds of education and perhaps even of encouraging "literary" education. When in the late 1920s the Phelps-Stokes Commission encouraged "industrial" education for Africans based on Booker T. Washington's Tuskegee model, the idea was received with much enthusiasm by most colonial officers but not by the missionaries and many Africans who opted for a more "literary" education. The missionaries opposed the "industrial" model because it threatened to take time away from the study of the Scriptures and from spiritual and moral growth; the Africans questioned the model as being just another way to put natives in their place by encouraging them to engage in manual labor and not in the more lucrative possibilities offered by the intellectual labor of colonial capitalism. Thus the "industrial" education model was seen by the Africans as a way of "learning to labor." The colonial officers, on the other hand, spouted the rhetoric of "relevance" to emphasize the need for such manual training.

Loram's own book, as we have suggested, made a plea for increased educational facilities for Africans and in doing so emphasized the importance of "literary education." In the chapter "The Present System of Industrial Education," Loram agreed with the consensus that industrial education was indeed important for South African natives. Yet Loram's aim in the chapter is not so much to applaud "industrial education" but to caution against its uncritical use. In a curious twist to the prevalent orthodoxy that held that educating natives (in the "literary" fashion) was dangerous because they would demand clerical jobs and more upward mobility, Loram suggested instead that the increased "industrial training" of natives was a threat to the white industrial

---

R. Hunt Davis Jr., "Charles T. Loram and an American Model for African Education in South Africa," *African Studies Review* 19.2 (September 1976): 87–99.

55. Loram is quoted as writing: "It is estimated that thousands of pounds are wasted yearly through the undiscriminating charity of philanthropists, and this is especially the case with Negro education, for many good people think it sufficient if the black folk have churches and schools without inquiring what kinds of schools and what kinds of churches they have and ought to have" (*Education in Africa: Report by Thomas Jesse Jones* [New York: Phelps-Stokes, 1921], xvii). Although this statement was made by Loram specifically as a review of the work of the commission, it does not, it seems, commit him to the emphasis of the industrial education preferences of the commission itself.

classes who would be displaced by the natives. Thus, according to Loram, given the fact that there was no evidence of a greater need of skilled labor in the South African workplace, the exclusive focus on the creation of native "skilled labor" would only lead to further racial tensions among the working class.[56] Added to the higher costs of industrial as opposed to literary education, and the resistance of the natives themselves to purely industrial education, the wholesale adoption of such education would be problematic in the South African context. Thus in contradistinction to the hegemonic view that literary education of natives leads to social tensions and demands, Loram argued that in the particular context of South Africa, with a substantial white working class, industrial education would lead to similar tensions. Unlike the rest of Africa, where "industrial education" may indeed serve colonial interest, in South Africa, suggested Loram, a balance between the two must be maintained.

If Loram's project was to argue for a separate educational system for South African blacks balancing literary with industrial training, such a goal was considered to be futile by his intellectual rival M. Laurence Fick. As staunchly hereditarian as Loram was environmentalist, Fick, a psychologist who worked for the National Bureau of Educational and Social Research, had less faith in the educability of black Africans. In 1939 Fick published *The Educability of the South African Native*, which essentially refuted Loram's claim that the arrested development of Africans had to do with environmental factors. Fick attempted to show through a series of tests that he claimed were adequately adapted to suit African cultural factors that no matter how culturally relevant the testing could be made, Africans would still not measure up to their European counterparts.[57] As proof of the accuracy of his results, Fick correlated the lower scores of African native students taking the tests with their already observed lower performance in school examinations.[58] Given his strategic em-

---

56. See Loram, *Education of the South African Native*, 156–59.

57. See Laurence Fick, *The Educability of the South African Native* (Pretoria: South African Council for Educational and Social Research, 1939), 56.

58. The problematic logic here is well outlined by J. M. Winterbottom in his "Can We Measure the African's Intelligence?" 53–59. He writes: "Fick's claim that his tests are valid because they agree with the results of school attainment tests is therefore in itself conclusive proof of their invalidity. It proves that these tests, in so far as they measure anything at all, are merely measuring school attainments and can have no claim whatever to measure (innate) intelligence" (55). Along with the Biesheuval text discussed below, this essay is an excellent critique of the practice of intelligence testing in South Africa.

ployment position, Fick became an important adviser to South African policy makers who were content with deriving from his theories an educational policy that undermined the importance of native education. If black South Africans were limited by hereditary factors from accomplishing higher forms of education, then, so the argument went, what was the point in wasting financial resources on such educational efforts?[59]

Perhaps recognizing the dangers of having a hereditarian program advising the educational board, Simon Biesheuval, a psychologist on the staff of the South African Institute of Race Relations, offered a book-length critique and refutation of Fick's work. Indeed, Biesheuval's critique, titled *African Intelligence,* is a significant moment in the rethinking not only of Fick's methods and results but of the dangerous ideological uses to which intelligence testing can be put in a cross-cultural setting.[60] According to Beisheuval, Fick's greatest error lay in his belief that intelligence tests determine innate ability rather than "a hereditary potentiality as it happens to have been realized by specific environmental circumstances."[61] As such, the role of factors such as prenatal intrauterine syphilitic infections or postnatal malnutrition, to name only two, are absent in Fick's account. So are the multiple social variables of urban versus rural environments, economic differentials, age differentials, and sex differentials. The effects of "detribalization" and the relative effects of culture contact, including the familiarity of students with the test situation, the effects of the presence of a European tester, the indigenous attitudes toward such tests, all add up, argued Biesheuval, to undermine the confidence with which Fick establishes absolute innate difference. "If there should prove to be real and fundamental differences between the minds of Africans and those of Europeans," wrote Biesheuval, "it would be strange indeed if a mere index was able to summarize these differences adequately, however useful this index might

59. See Lyons, *To Wash an Aethiop White,* 142–43, for a further development of this underwriting of South African educational policy and in particular of the appropriation of Fick's work by the then South African chief inspector of native education, Dr. W. W. M. Eiselen.

60. And in many ways, Biesheuval's fundamental critique has not been surpassed even today. Many of the counterarguments against the social programming resulting from cross-racial intelligence correlations made today are in fact already to be seen in Biesheuval's work. A parallel reading of Biesheuval's book written in 1943 and the recent volume of essays, Russell Jacoby and Naomi Glauberman, eds., *The Bell Curve Debate: History, Documents, Opinions* (New York: Random House, 1995), shows that surprisingly little has changed over time in the nature of the debate.

61. Simon Biesheuval, *African Intelligence* (Johannesburg: South African Institute of Race Relations, 1943), 18.

be in predicting successful adaptation to European culture in the case of Europeans themselves. A detailed statement of the assets and liabilities, the potentialities and drawbacks, of the intellectual processes of Africans might serve as a far more useful basis for the formulation of an educational policy and for the objective assessment of the future of Africans in Western civilization than an estimate of the range of African intelligence quotients."[62] The fact that Biesheuval's claims found some currency among liberal intellectuals but not among the South African policy makers at that time speaks more to the nature of the political appropriation of academic thought than to the values and rigor of scholarship itself.[63] As I have suggested earlier, the relationships between the development of an academic discourse and the use of that discourse to underwrite policy issues is always an ambivalent one. Although social institutions always attempt to present their own limits on the trajectory of intellectual thought and debate, there is, as Foucault has shown, a certain discursive logic and order internal to discourse that ensures that it retains its own relative autonomy. To these issues, and in particular to the relationship between the theories of African mentality and educational policy, we shall return, but meanwhile let us move to the psychoanalytic treatment of the study of African mentality.

The Psychoanalytic Call

In contrast to the primarily anthropological readings of "primitive mentality" (which were characterized by an early cultural relativism with an ambivalent relationship to the discourses of evolution), and the ethnopsychiatrists' emphasis on the physiological or hereditary differences between races, other scholars foregrounded the differences between "African natives" and "civilized Europeans" on a psychoanalytic model. These scholars insisted that any understanding of the mentality of the African, and any determination of the native's rational capabilities, would have to draw on a consideration of the social growth of the African from childhood to maturity. The history of psychoanalysis in Africa in the first half of the twentieth century is as yet extremely

---

62. Ibid., 11.
63. See in particular the work of R. F. Alfred Hoernle, whose *Race and Reason* (Johannesburg: Witwatersrand University Press, 1945) is an important collection of essays calling for liberalism in the South African context.

sketchy, and the exact affiliations of the critics to various psychoanalytic schools is at best problematic. Yet, for our purposes, a consideration of some of these early efforts at psychoanalyzing the native condition is important to gain a perspective on the multiplicity of discourses on African mentality.

The first thing to note about this group of texts is their focus on the "temperament" and "personality" of the African. The idea is that if there are lessons to be drawn about the African and his rational potential, they may be better learned from an understanding of his behavior and character traits than from a set of numerical results either of a cranial or of an intelligence test kind.[64] The psychoanalysts did not, of course, have to work hard at providing empirical "evidence" for any particular character traits, since the negative stereotypes were commonplace both in the academic as well as in popular discourses of the time. A convenient summary may be found in Adolphe Louis Cureau's *Savage Man in Central Africa: A Study of Primitive Races in the French Congo.* In the second book of this work, titled "Psychology of the Individual," Cureau juxtaposes the African native with the European. Thus the African, suggests Cureau, "is rather inferior to the European in the acuteness of the senses, . . . has no courage when attacked by internal diseases, but moans and complains over the mildest indispositions, . . . has a fickle instability of impressions and sensations, which merely graze his consciousness, leaving nothing but a transient mark on it, . . . [has] feelings of affection [which] are superficial, . . . [has] a conception of truth far more imperfect [than that of] the superior races, . . .

64. It should be noted that some of the developers of the various intelligence tests were aware of the limitations of the tests in evaluating "temperament." Thus Porteus and Babcock write, "There is no doubt whatsoever that the present methods of measuring intelligence are distinctly inadequate and that the next steps in research must be in the direction of the examination of the volitional, emotional or temperamental traits which are usually included under the heading of character." The definition of "temperament" offered by Porteus and Babcock is worthy of quotation here, since it matches that of the psychoanalysts: "It is the focusing of the lens of mental capacity upon the field of life's experience, and without this focusing, no matter how excellent the lens, the picture will be blurred and indistinct. Temperament is the energizing of the intellect, that which determines the strength of one's interest, the angle and latent force of one's bent, and thus has a profound influence on a man's achievement by determining his attitude to life's situations. It does not influence a man's capacity for thinking so much as his capacity for action, so that temperamental deficiencies often underlie that wide gulf which frequently yawns between capability and performance. Its relation to character is therefore intimate. It vivifies motivation, so that temperamental traits and qualities together make up the force for those 'drives' or 'sets' which so largely influence our effectiveness in adjustment to the situations that lie in the path of experience" (Stanley Porteus and Marjorie Babcock, *Temperament and Race* [Boston: R. G. Badger, 1926], 268–70).

does not understand abstract ideas [such as honesty], . . . is inert, indifferent and fatalistic, . . . is melancholy."[65]

It was precisely such characterizations of the native that interested the psychoanalysts not so much as a subject of refutation as much as attributes to be explained.[66] The most notorious of such attempts was a pamphlet written by the principal of the Barotse National School in northern Rhodesia. Published in 1943 under the auspices of the Rhodes-Livingstone Institute, "The African as Suckling and Adult: A Psychological Study" is an attempt to understand the ambivalences prevalent in the life of an adult African native. Drawing on depth psychology and Freud in particular, J. F. Ritchie argues that the most decisive influence on the African's adult life is the long duration of his nursing period as a child. Unlike European children, who are nursed for a shorter period of time and whose breast-feeding is more regulated, the African child, argues Ritchie, is overindulged to the point where he ceases to learn restraint. Furthermore, since nursing continues past an age where the child is conscious of himself as a separate person, the child develops a sense of omnipotence, since his mother is in effect his slave, always available to feed him at his beck and call. Thus when the child is weaned, he suffers a powerful moment of recognition in which his power is lost and, indeed, is replaced by his father (who reinitiates sexual relations with the mother at the end of the nursing period). The child begins to be resentful of the mother, and his hate, though temporarily overcome by the immediate "will to hold on to life and enjoy it," reasserts itself; "later in life," says Ritchie, "it colors the whole African attitude to women."[67] Similarly, "the repressed conception of the father as a thief and bully is . . . one of the deepest reasons for the typical African distrust of authority, authority being a father-surrogate" (13).

Needless to say, in Ritchie's account, everything that supposedly characterizes the African native is rooted in the particular dynamics of African nursing and weaning. Thus if the African, as Cureau tells us, "has a fickle instability of impressions and sensations, which merely graze his consciousness, leaving nothing but a transient mark on it," it is because, Ritchie would inform us, of

65. Adolphe Louis Cureau, *Savage Man in Central Africa: A Study of the Primitive Races of the French Congo* (London: T. F. Unwin, 1915), 43–68.
66. However, some alleged characteristics, such as sensory differences between Europeans and Africans for instance, were either rejected or downplayed by the psychoanalysts.
67. J. F. Ritchie, "The African as Suckling and Adult: A Psychological Study," Rhodes-Livingstone Papers, no. 9 (1943): 13.

his past trauma as an infant: "Constantly indulged for so long, the nursling is not obliged to look back to the past nor forward to the future for satisfaction. Then when the shock of weaning does come, he dare not think of time at all. . . . In later life an unconscious activation of the memory of that intolerable period may express itself in a fit of absent-mindedness, a sort of mild hysterical unconsciousness" (15). Or again, the African lacks creative imagination because as a child, "hardly ever separated from his mother during his first year or more, [he] is not obliged to use his latent powers of imagination, and so does not learn to think for himself or rely on himself" (16). This leads, then, not only to a lack of imagination but also to the dependency complex for which he is infamous.

Ritchie's explanation of the problems of rational thinking on the part of the African are somewhat complicated. For the African child, after weaning, nursing is established as the absolute standard of "good" and weaning as the absolute standard of "bad." But in addition, the child feels that he is bad, since he has himself lost his control over his mother. This feeling of badness causes him pain, and so the child must do anything to convince himself that he is good. "He cannot look critically at himself and the world and see that neither the goodness nor the badness is absolute, and accept himself and the world for the mixture of potential good and potential bad that everyone and everything really is" (28). As a result, the African child grows up to be a biased thinker incapable of critical evaluation. Indeed, for Ritchie this early experience is so formative that it is not affected even by the possibility of a Western education. The sphere of education only furthers the African's condition—education becomes no more than an obsession in which "unconsciously he believes that (it) is a pathway back to his mother's breast, and the examination is the doorway at the end of it" (35). And yet although the African is eager to receive such an education, Ritchie believes that he is bound to fail since (1) the African can assimilate very little of the abstract order of Western education; (2) he lacks initiative and independence of mind and "expects his teacher to think for him and somehow to insert the finished thought into his mind"; and (3) Western education takes on a "mysterious" air for the African and is always identified with his own ambivalent emotions and parental intercourse after his weaning (37).

If Ritchie's treatise was published by the Rhodes-Livingstone Institute, it may well be that it was published more for its lessons on other potential uses of psychoanalysis in the African context than for Ritchie's own interpretive claims.[68] Although generally supportive of Ritchie's project, Max Gluckman, the director of the institute, wrote in his introductory note that Ritchie had exaggerated the psychological factors that inhibit the African's potential intelligence. Furthermore, Gluckman ended his note by asking for the patience of readers trained in psychoanalysis when dealing with the long sections in the essay that explain basic concepts in the field. "It is I who requested him to explain these concepts for many of the readers of this paper will be unacquainted with them," writes Gluckman, suggesting that for him the paper's most valuable assets were not Ritchie's conclusions but rather the premises and methods of psychoanalysis itself. Indeed, this reading is further confirmed by Meyer Fortes's review of the work in the journal *Africa*. Fortes, like Gluckman, welcomed the work's psychoanalytic emphasis as a necessary intervention in the discourses of African mentality and personality but found Ritchie's conclusions unpersuasive. Alluding to the various clichés about African personality that pervade Ritchie's work, Fortes notes that they "make one wonder if Mr. Ritchie knows anything about Africans outside of the schoolroom or the Europeans compound."[69]

Fortes ends his review of Ritchie's work with a comment that serves as an important moment of transition to a later development in psychologically oriented studies of African personality. He writes, "What significance is to be attached to Mr. Ritchie's interpretation of his data? For their authenticity is beyond question. Internal evidence suggests that his subjects were mainly African teachers, schoolboys, and servants, individuals whose personality would be under the constant strain of seeking a satisfactory adjustment within the fringe of quasi-European culture and economy. They would be persons who might stand in a relationship of acute ambivalence towards Mr. Ritchie. It is possible, therefore, that Mr. Ritchie's data represent only an analysis of a difficult transference-relationship existing between himself and his subjects."[70] In other words, Ritchie's blindspot is the larger social situation in

---

68. Although we should note that Ritchie's work did influence other scholars. Carothers addressed it at some length in his World Health Organization study, and it was also favorably cited and to some extent followed by Wulf Sachs, a South African psychoanalyst who did a major psychoanalytic case study of a Manyika healer-diviner, "John Chavafambira," during 1933–36. See Wulf Sachs, *Black Hamlet*, new intro. by Saul Dubow and Jacqueline Rose (Baltimore: Johns Hopkins University Press, 1996).

69. Fortes, Review of "The African as Suckling and Adult," *Africa* (1945): 166.

70. Ibid., 167.

which his subjects function and, in particular, their relationship to him as a colonial other. Fortes's point is one that has been extensively emphasized in contemporary ethnographic critique—that there is no such thing as a purely objective, noninterventionist ethnographic position and that the observer is not fully isolatable from the observed.[71] In Ritchie's case, the ambivalence that he keeps finding in natives may be something that he doesn't just discover, but indeed helps generate.

It is this concern with the social context of colonialism that motivated Octave Mannoni's *Prospero and Caliban: The Psychology of Colonization*. Emphasis on the "colonial situation" promised the possibility of a sociopolitical critique of the discourses on African personality and perhaps also of colonialism itself. *Prospero and Caliban* was originally written in 1948 (published 1950), in the aftermath of the Madagascar rebellion. Mannoni's note to the second edition of the text insists that the writing of the study was for him as much a lesson about himself as it was about the Malagasies. Writing a study in a society fraught with cultural and racial tensions, Mannoni found it unable to present the "other" in the conventional manner in which the observer would retain pure objective distance. In his own estimation, the dissemination of his book took effect in breaking down the facade of the "scientific objectivity" of his colleagues: "Their attitude of scientific objectivity, which forced them to keep their own personality outside the field of observation, disconcertingly began to appear as a White Privilege and seemed to be a source of difficulties—almost a symptom of their refusal to understand certain aspects of the situation."[72] Fortes could not have put it better.

Yet, despite his own disbelief in anything as decontextualized as a "primitive" mentality (22), Mannoni's account presupposes the conventional accounts of the psychology of the natives. The only difference here is that the colonizer too has a psychological condition that leads him to the colonial encounter. Thus the Malagasy is fraught with a dependency complex that if threatened leads to an inferiority complex. The native, then, needs a paternal figure to look after and provide for him, and resists any attempt at withdrawal

71. For such contemporary critique, see James Clifford and George Marcus, eds., *Writing Culture: The Poetics and Politics of Ethnography* (Berkeley: University of California Press, 1986); George Marcus and Michael M. J. Fischer, *Anthropology as Cultural Critique: An Experimental Moment in the Human Sciences* (Chicago: University of Chicago Press, 1986).
72. Octave Mannoni, *Prospero and Caliban: The Psychology of Colonization*, 2d ed. (New York: Praeger, 1964), 7.

on this figure's part. He begins to see the provider's protection as a right and feels no need to respond with any excessive show of gratitude.

Although the "native" is thus left relatively homogenized in Mannoni's account, the European is not. Not all Europeans are attracted to and participate in the colonial project. The "predestined colonial" (98) is one who has certain latent complexes that are made manifest in the colonial situation. The most important of these is a desire to escape from the company of other men, a desire for solitude. The colonial rejects his own society, and "rejection of that world is combined with an urge to dominate, an urge which is infantile in origin and which social adaptation has failed to discipline" (108). This, dubbed by Mannoni as the "Prospero complex," predisposes some Europeans into becoming colonials.

It should come as no surprise that such readings of the colonial situation were bound to annoy the nationalists and the Marxists, for they tend to downplay the economic and political and foreground the psychological.[73] Yet in Mannoni's defense it should be said that he was in support of the freedom struggles, and rather than explaining away the colonial situation through social psychology, he attempted to comment on them as a pathology. Thus in no uncertain terms Mannoni commits a certain kind of "class-suicide" as a colonial when he urges for an end to colonialism:

> It seems, then, that there is no alternative to the painful apprenticeship to freedom; that alone will solve all the problems amid which both Malagasies and Europeans are floundering—it is a medicine which will cure them both. If it appears sweet to the one and bitter to the other, it is an illusion in both cases. The way will be much harder for the Malagasies than they imagine, while the Europeans have no idea of the extent to which a genuine and successful liberation of their subject peoples—if it could be brought about without conflict, which unfortunately they make unlikely—would liberate them too, without harming their "interests" to anything like the extent they fear.[74]

73. Mannoni explicitly addresses this critique by saying that he doesn't wish to discount materialist theories, but rather to enhance them with his psychoanalytic reflections. It is interesting in this light that a similar work, albeit originating more in the existentialist tradition than in a psychoanalytic one, Albert Memmi's *The Colonizer and the Colonized*, also devotes considerable attention to the critique of the leftist European. See Memmi, *The Colonizer and the Colonized*, trans. Howard Greenfield, intro. by Jean-Paul Sartre (Boston: Beacon Press, 1969).

74. Mannoni, *Prospero and Caliban*, 66–67.

If Mannoni's work attempted, in its own limited way, to account for African mentality and personality by reading it within the context of colonialism, it was Frantz Fanon who most explicitly made the move from such study to nationalist politics. On his way there, however, Fanon found occasion to launch a scathing critique of *Prospero and Caliban.* In *Black Skins, White Masks,* Fanon claims that Mannoni erred in his reading of colonial racism as a limited phenomenon that can be located in the unconscious feelings of the colonizer's inferiority complex rather than in the originary culture of the colonizer. For Fanon, Mannoni's defense of French culture evident in his attempt to demarcate divisions between benevolent Frenchmen and the racist kind was intolerable. Racism to Fanon was not a question of individual attitudes and behaviors but rather structural mechanisms of societal control. French society and its colonial policies, Fanon argued, partook of a global racism that pervaded not only the colonial world but also the metropolitan one.[75]

For Fanon, Mannoni's greatest error lay in his undermining of the violence done to the native psyche by colonialism itself. He argued that it is wrong to suggest, as Mannoni did, that the native inferiority complex predated colonialism and rendered for it an important condition of possibility. Rather, the violence of colonialism, suggested Fanon, is itself responsible for encouraging such a complex where it does arise. As a practicing psychiatrist in Algeria, Fanon had several occasions to study and analyze native schizophrenia and other mental traumas. In his essay "Colonial War and Mental Disorders," published as the last chapter of *The Wretched of the Earth,* he discusses various case studies of European and native Algerian patients. Fanon's attentions are centered on the condition of the Algerian native of whom he writes: "The Algerian's criminality, his impulsivity, and the violence of his murders are therefore not the consequence of the organization of his nervous system or of characterial originality, but the direct product of the colonial situation."[76] What is significant here is that at no point did Fanon himself refute any of the *specifics* of the conventional discourse on the native personality—it is only the *explanations* of the causes of that personality that he refuted. Thus even in this late work, Fanon's aim was not to counter the stereotypical claims about native violence or for that matter, native impulsiveness. His project, rather, was to ac-

75. Frantz Fanon, *Black Skin, White Masks* (1952; rpt., New York: Grove Press, 1966), 91–93.
76. Frantz Fanon, *The Wretched of the Earth,* trans. Constance Farrington, preface by Jean-Paul Sartre (New York: Grove Press, 1965), 309. Fanon was originally from Martinique but worked in Algeria.

count for them, not as physiological characteristics as in the theories of the biological determinists, nor as cultural differences as in the theories of the anthropologists, nor even as moral shortcomings as in the allegations of the missionaries, but rather as political and psychological consequences of a colonial system that alienated the native and made him hate himself.

Educating the African

In considering the development of the racialized (and often racist) colonial discourses on African mentality, it is important to recognize that many of these discourses were articulated within institutional sites of pedagogy and conversion.[77] One way to understand these institutional contexts is to recognize, for instance, that whereas the missionaries tended to focus more on such matters as native moral and religious systems revealing signs of a systemic alterity, the more secular educators focused on such issues as logical processes of thought and the ability of Africans to follow "scientific" reasoning and methods. Yet whether the motivations were primarily the more secular ones of creating normative colonial subjects who could adapt to the rapidly changing colonial economies, or the more religious ones of saving souls, the concerns over the mental dispositions, personality traits, and temperament of the African natives were equally salient.

In terms of the relationship between the discourses of rationality and their institutional contexts, if we remember for instance, that James W. C. Dougall, one of the scholars who insisted on emphasizing the essential similarities as opposed to differences between Europeans and Africans, was also early on in

---

77. This section, as much of this chapter, should more appropriately be titled "Educating the African Male." Most of the discussions of African educability privilege boys and men as the normative African subjects. Very little reference is made to women's education in general, and even studies that otherwise focus on women's issues leave the question of women's formal education undeveloped. An exception to this is Adelaide Casely-Hayford's early essay "A Girl's School in West Africa" (*Southern Workman* [October 1926]), but the primary focus here is on training the "African girl of today for the highest vocation of all—the vocation of motherhood tomorrow" (454), and consequently the educational efforts are directed toward learning needlework, making baskets, and cooking. Later anthropological studies of the colonial and early postcolonial period did not necessarily advance the issue: in *African Women* (New York: Praeger, 1965), a study of the Ibo, Sylvia Leith-Ross is relatively silent on the issue of women's education. Although there is some discussion of young girls' socialization into the traditional work roles for women in the community, Leith-Ross's only note vis-à-vis girls' formal schooling is that coeducation is detrimental to their well being.

his career a missionary, and later to be the first principal of the Jeanes School (teacher training) in Kenya, then we could read pedagogical zeal in his theorizations of native mentality.[78] If again, we see a Charles Templeman Loram play a fine rhetorical game with his white South African readers, "scaring" them, as I have suggested, into accepting the importance of Bantu education, then we see this only in the light of his being an inspector of schools preoccupied with pedagogical policies. If, finally, we give weight to Meyer Fortes's reading of J. F. Ritchie in which the latter's misreading of African dependency is really no more than a reflection of Ritchie's own fostering of dependence in his students, then once again the relationship between the theorization of African rationality and its emergence in the context of the pedagogical situation becomes urgent. Nevertheless, it is important to keep in mind that the precise nature of this relationship between institutional locus and discursive formation is not always easily calculable.

The classic materialist account of the relationship between institutional structures and emergent discourses attempts to read the "superstructural" discourses off of the educational practices forming the "base."[79] Further, if the institutional locus of the discourses of rationality is the pedagogical situation, then it is no less true, argue the classic materialists, that in a colonial context, both the educational practices as well as the discourses theorizing them are compromised by colonial interests. Such is the argument advocated most famously by Martin Carnoy, who in his *Education as Cultural Imperialism* claims that in the colonial situation, "knowledge itself is colonized" and is only concerned with retaining the colonial hierarchies in place.[80] Carnoy sug-

---

78. For a careful assessment of the Jeanes School in Kenya and of James Dougall's integral role in it, see Richard Heyman, "The Initial Years of the Jeanes School in Kenya, 1924–1931," in *Essays in the History of African Education,* ed. Vincent M. Battle and Charles H. Lyons (New York: Teachers College Press, 1970), 105–23.

79. It is true that some thinkers such as Raymond Williams successfully complicate the base-superstructure model without giving up a materialist perspective. Such a revised notion of cultural materialism is quite compatible with my own account. My critique here, however, is aimed at thinkers who have too reductionist a model of understanding the pedagogical situation. I am afraid that this model is not unique to Carnoy (discussed below), but rather saturates the Marxist tradition on pedagogy. Even the now canonical essay by Althusser on ideological state apparatuses does not escape such thinking. See Raymond Williams, *Marxism and Literature* (New York: Oxford University Press, 1977); Louis Althusser, "Ideology and Ideological State Apparatuses," in *Lenin and Philosophy and Other Essays* (New York: Monthly Review Press, 1971), 127–86.

80. Martin Carnoy, *Education as Cultural Imperialism* (New York: David McKay Co., 1974), 3.

gests that rather than "freeing" the native from tradition, the colonial education system, coterminus with the transition from feudalism to capitalism, makes the native dependent and enslaves him to a "clock system." Originally, claims Carnoy, the native was free to stay at home and not go to the farm.[81] Now, he has lost that choice. Furthermore, not only is the colonial educational system really a handmaiden to capitalist structures, Carnoy suggests that even the one potential use commonly cited for it, that is, its potential to propagate "Western" ideas of liberty, is unfounded, since ideas of liberty and resistance to oppression were already present in Africa before the arrival of the colonial educational system.

Carnoy's thesis of the colonization of the native mind by the colonial educational system is one that has had great currency in the legacy of anticolonial thinking. Frantz Fanon and Ngũgĩ wa Thiong'o, to name only two such critics, advocate the thesis with different emphases.[82] Although some recent revisionist work in the history of colonial education questions this early thesis,[83] our interest here is not so much to take sides in this debate as to touch on just one aspect of it. This aspect has to do not so much with the actual effects of the system of colonial education on Africans but with what Carnoy and others associated with his project conceive of as its perfect theorization. In other words, although Carnoy may be correct in evaluating the consequences of the system, he pays little attention to the complicated and at times contradictory relationships between ideologies and interests prevalent in the colonial moment. In other words, there is too quick a move made from the claim that the colonial educational system was inherently oppressive to the rather more debatable claim that such oppression was backed up by a purposively masterminded and internally coherent theoretical system immune to any slippage. A closer look at some of the contradictions shows that to suggest that all these were perfectly visualized in a Machiavellian theoretical system would be to grant too much ingenuity and forethought to the British colonizers.

81. We can hear echoes here of Lévi-Strauss's dismay at the "arrival of writing" among the Nambikwara. The subtext of the desire for the "pure" untouched other, the "noble" savage uncorrupted by "Western" capitalism, is ever present. Derrida's response to Lévi-Strauss in *Of Grammatology* is equally appropriable here. See Jacques Derrida, *Of Grammatology,* trans. Gayatri Chakravorty Spivak (Baltimore: Johns Hopkins University Press, 1976), 101–40.
82. See, for instance, Fanon's *Wretched of the Earth;* and Ngũgĩ wa Thiong'o's *Decolonising the Mind.*
83. See Clive Whitehead, "British Colonial Policy: A Synonym for Cultural Imperialism?" in *Benefits Bestowed?* ed. J. A. Mangam (Manchester: Manchester University Press, 1988), 211–30.

The point, essentially, is one of the relationship of theories to practices. Rather than seeing a linear, unidirectional linkage between a colonial interest (here, economic), to a theory (here, a pedagogical one), to a practice (here, a particular form of schooling), as outlined by Carnoy, I suggest that it would be more appropriate to recognize that institutional practices and discursive formations are in a continuous "feedback loop" or in processes in which each is affecting the other in no predetermined manner. For even a cursory look at Carnoy's classic micronarrative shows that no step in it can remain uncontested. First, to reduce "colonial interest" purely to the economic is to lose sight of the tremendous efforts and discursive justifications that had to be mounted against the "idealist" goals by colonial administrators and is, indeed, to write out of significance the rhetorical importance of a book like Lugard's *Dual Mandate in British Tropical Africa*. One of the most important aims of that book was to establish the importance of the economic interest of Britain and not to allow the idealist desires of missionaries and other philanthropists to interfere with this goal.[84] In other words, if the "idealist" motives had to be curtailed, then we must realize that they must have existed as a serious contender in the first place. The "colonial interest," then, seems to have been split between the desires for the economic advancement of the colonizers and their desire to help "advance" the conditions of the Africans. This "dual mandate," as Lugard calls it, caused considerable confusion in educational policy, resulting in what F. Clarke, in 1932, dubbed the "double mind in African education."[85] Referring to Clarke's article of the same name, Bronislaw Malinowski later summarized the situation as follows:

> The onslaught of white civilization on native cultures is carried out by two columns, the column of goodwill towards the African and the column of "good-sense"—or the column of "good-gain" for the European, as some like to call it, if perhaps not quite fairly. The first are prepared to

84. Thus Lugard writes, "Let it be admitted at the outset that European brains, capital, and energy have not been, and never will be, expended in developing the resources of Africa from motives of pure philanthropy; that Europe is in Africa for the mutual benefit of her own industrial classes and of the native races in their progress to a higher plane; that the benefit can be made reciprocal, and that it is the aim and desire of civilised administration to fulfill this dual mandate" (Frederick Lugard, *The Dual Mandate in British Tropical Africa* [1922; rpt., Edinburgh: Blackwood and Sons, 1926], 617).
85. See F. Clarke, "The Double Mind in African Education," in *Africa* (1932): 158–68.

give the Native unstintingly our knowledge and our Christianity, our love of sport and our predilection for cotton and linen. The others, while realizing that the educated African may be useful as a laborer, clerk or assistant, soon become aware that he also grows into a dangerous competitor.[86]

Thus colonial "interest" is itself divided, and although it may well be the case that the economic motivations may ultimately triumph, they remain susceptible to the "idealist" inclinations that may indeed function as a "dangerous supplement."[87] If this is the case, then the second and third junctures of Carnoy's micronarrative also become open to critique. There can be no absolute pedagogical theory in a situation in which there is no absolute interest, and furthermore the relationship between pedagogical theories and practices is in itself never absolutely linear. Thus we have a plurality of educational ideas, some emphasizing "literary" education, others "industrial" education, yet others worrying about "deracination" and "assimilation"; some attempting to base themselves on biological evaluations of native abilities, others on psychoanalytic versions, and yet others on anticolonial nationalisms.

As an illustration of these claims, we may turn briefly to two texts, one a novel and the other a real-life account of the workings of a colonial school in Nigeria. Both texts illustrate the contradictions of the "double mind" in African education, as it manifested itself in the debate over industrial versus literary education. In this debate, too, various arguments were mustered up, at times unpredictably by people on either side, some citing the African's "arrested development" as evidence that he should not be burdened with the demands of a "literary" education, others citing "relevance" as a factor for choosing industrial education.[88] In Mark Freshfield's 1946 novel *The Stormy Dawn*

86. Bronislaw Malinowski, "Native Education and Culture Contact," *International Review of Missions* 25 (1936): 484.

87. It is important to emphasize that to argue thus is not to undermine the real material conditions in which theoretical discourses operate. It is only to recognize that it is unhelpful to reduce the material merely to the economic. Indeed, it is precisely material conditions in all their forms that a careful analysis must respect, since it must recognize that a major role of theoretical discourses, especially in the colonial context, is precisely to engage in a doublespeak in which the material—and indeed the economic—is conveniently undermined or even effaced. The task of the cultural critic then, is to take these discourses seriously and to examine how they attempt to accomplish this project.

88. Incidentally, a fascinating account could be provided of the concept of "relevance" in African

for instance, two brothers, Dinkura and Folu, exemplify the two different paths to an African education. Folu, the brother who opts for the "literary" educational system, is offended by the inclusion of personal hygiene and agriculture as required subjects:

> The other subject offensive to Folu, and indeed to most of the boys and to the innermost convictions of the teachers, was agriculture. The colony's Education Department, which prescribed the curriculum of all schools receiving Government grants, had decreed that education must have "an agricultural bias." All school-children were, therefore, condemned, on certain hot afternoons in the week, to grub up the school grounds and plant vegetables in small rectangular plots. The mission further insisted that boys' boarding school should grow a part of their own food. As the boys had come to school with the idea of emancipating themselves from menial labor, they regarded this as a deep-laid plot to keep the African down. Therefore, they hoed and planted with rebellion in their heads and scowls upon their faces.[89]

Suspicious of an educational system that he is sure is designed to keep him in an inferior place, Folu does his best to succeed, and when he does not get a fellowship to go to England, he manages to steal some money to cover the expenses. Heading the Socrates society and presenting talks and lectures at various gatherings in England, Folu begins to organize his fellow compatriots to seek independence. In this, however, he fails, as he consistently gets into arguments of strategy, and finally his political frustrations and his growing sense of guilt along with his fear of being exposed as a thief lead to a nervous breakdown and ultimately to his suicide. Meanwhile, Dinkura, his brother, who has always kept in touch with the traditional skills such as woodworking and masonry, finally ends up getting an award to study architecture and by all accounts lives happily ever after. Freshfield's novel, then, is a didactic novel with a pointed message about "relevance" of education

---

education through colonial and postcolonial times. For instance, when the postcolonial Ngũgĩ wa Thiong'o argues that colonial education was not "relevant" to the needs of the natives, he hardly means it in the way in which some colonial educators argued for "relevance" in colonial education—for the latter "relevance" meant teaching Africans agricultural and industrial skills. Indeed, as we will see below, many colonial Africans objected to this particular form of "relevance," since it seemed to them no more than a ploy to keep them in their place as colonial laborers.

89. Mark Freshfield, *The Stormy Dawn* (London: Faber and Faber, 1946), 71.

and the risks for Westernized Africans. Borrowing from a strand of popular colonial discourse of the time, the book offers a sense that Western-style education is not only irrelevant but also leads to a psychological as well as physiological breakdown. The best education for Africa, suggests this novel, is one that does not alienate the African from his "organic" environment and its needs.[90] But such a confident support of "agricultural" education along with a disavowal of "literary" education is not the only picture to be found.

Consider the case of the Omu school, which opened in Omu, Nigeria, on September 15, 1931. This boarding school, catering primarily to elementary and lower-middle-school boys (ages eight to sixteen), modeled itself on the "adaptationist" principles of cross-cultural education. The idea was that educational methods and practices should be made "relevant" to the lived environments of the African students and not just uncritically imported from Europe. As the first principal of the school, J. D. Clarke put it, "Let us make it clear to him [the African] that by avoiding a slavish imitation of Western civilization he yet may be able to enjoy its benefits and learn from its mistakes."[91] But Clarke, knowing that the kind of education he had in mind was not necessarily the one demanded by the Africans, feels compelled to continue, "To admit that we must necessarily provide what any and every African wants in the way of education would be a denial of any justification for our presence in Africa" (135).

Perhaps a brief look at some of the incoherences of Clarke's positions may explain why some Africans may have been skeptical of the "adaptationist" model. The first moment is when Clarke defends the inclusion of manual labor, in particular gardening and farm labor, as an important part of the daily schedule and the curriculum. Clarke writes,

> I consider that manual work, real hard dirty work, is an essential element of any system of education worthy of the name. The tragedy of education, both in Europe and Africa, is that it tends to set up a barrier between the brain and the hand-worker, to encourage the idea that there is something dishonorable in honest sweat. That is all wrong, for there will always be

90. Again, notice how "relevant" education and "organic" needs draw on the rhetoric of "nonintervention." Yet to many colonial Africans such as Folu, this was in itself a form of colonial racism meant to withhold the privilege of "literary" education from African subjects.

91. J. D. Clarke, *Omu: An African Experiment in Education* (London: Longman, 1936), 135.

many who do unpleasant tasks for the community, and it should be one of the aims of education to cultivate sympathy between those who will be manual workers in later life. (25)

Although Clarke thus opts to redefine education by moving away from the model of book learning or "literary" education, he nevertheless uses rigorous intelligence as criteria for admissions to his school. He argues, "In a country in which only a very small proportion of the children go to school at all such weeding out of the unintelligent at the start is very necessary, for it is essential that our efforts be concentrated upon the best brains" (16). In other words, the smart children should be taught the virtues of manual labor so that they can evolve into "sympathetic" subjects; the less able are best left alone. An educational philosophy that begins by wanting to take the totality of a different cultural order into account in its own workings ends up instead by selecting its subjects according to its own criteria (of "intelligence") and then making them answer to what is supposedly their own cultural good ("manual labor").

If this in itself is not sufficient, as in Freshfield's novel, to arouse the skepticism of the students, making them wonder whether this kind of education is not indeed meant to "keep them in their own place," then surely a more visible slippage does—a slippage involving the management of gardening. In his write-up, Clarke describes the manner in which the schoolboys are divided in four groups, each of which cultivates a vegetable garden and sells the produce to the school kitchen or to Clarke himself. In case one wonders who determines the price of the goods—in this scenario in which students labor under the supervision of a teacher only to sell the produce to him—Clarke provides a ready answer: "The chance of making a bit of pocket-money has been a great inducement to the boys to grow new vegetables. In fact the competition has become so keen that the young market gardeners arrive at my house at 6 am with their produce for sale. The records which they keep of their dealings also form a useful bit of practical arithmetic" (43). The price, we are told then, is set not by the arbitrariness of the school principal but rather by the laws of competitive market relations. Further, if a close reading of Clarke's text suggests that this gardening practice in fact makes up for Clarke's own failures in the garden,[92] ensuring that no compromises are made on the European school

---

92. Clarke: "The boys are very successful in their gardening, for although insects invariably eat my carefully reared plants, theirs always seem to escape" (*Omu,* 43–44).

principal's palate, we are called on to focus instead on the pedagogical opportunities provided by the math lesson.

The contradictions of the gardening practice are not lost on the students. Clarke writes,

> One evening when we were discussing the season's seed requirements one of the boys asked why it was necessary to buy new seed from England every year, and asked whether we could not save our own seed. It was a sensible question; the answer of course being that most English vegetables are as susceptible to the climate as the white men who bring them to Africa; and I told him that just as European children do not thrive in Nigeria, so also European vegetables reproduce themselves best in their own country. (44)

Even if the answer misreads the gist of the question,[93] the question, itself, is more than "sensible"—indeed it is no less than a critique of dependency. Why, in the midst of all this talk about making education "relevant" to the lives and needs of the students, are seeds being imported at higher cost from England? If the sole purpose of this exercise is to make students "sympathetic" to hard manual labor, why can't the local seed be used to teach this same lesson? If English seed needs English soil, why not use African seed for African soil? The answer given by the principal, in the form of an observation of his students, betrays the hypocrisy:

> They did not readily eat the exotic vegetables which they learnt to grow, for the Yoruba, like many other Africans, is very conservative in his diet. He is a yam connoisseur, and little more. Eventually they acquired a taste for tomatoes, and although they do not like the "bitterness" of fresh lettuce it is eaten, as they eat spinach, as one of the ingredients in their palm-oil soups. (44)

And so it is that the implementation of the "adaptationist" philosophy is fraught with contradictions—manual labor is to be an important part of the curriculum in order to espouse sympathy for manual workers, and yet students are to be selected purely on their intellectual attributes; gardening and other such manual activities are meant to be lessons in arithmetic and per-

---

93. Clarke reads the question as "Why do we need *new* seeds every year?" when the question really is "Why do we need to get seeds from Europe every year when we can use our own Nigerian seeds?"

haps economics, yet they most obviously serve the function of providing the school principal with daily fresh vegetables of his liking; and although so-called literary education is to be questioned for encouraging natives to slavishly imitate European mannerisms, in matters of the palate, European tastes are imposed and complete indifference paid to native desires, customs, and interests.

"Race" and Its Contingencies

Students of African philosophy have often focused on the discourses of rationality as they emerged in the philosophical and anthropological traditions of the twentieth century. But, as I have suggested in this chapter, the colonial question of "rationality" and the "mental ability" of Africans was an attempt to put a scientific mask on popular racist (mis)conceptions of Africans in colonial times. Histories of African(ist) rationality that ignore these allegedly scientific discourses of mentality do so at their own peril. The work of the colonial ethnopsychiatrists must be squarely put into these histories, since scientific racism was never far removed from social policy even if it did not always successfully drive it. And conversely, although remaining skeptical of the overdetermined nature of the anthropological project, we should remember that the cultural relativism and critique of biological essentialism offered by anthropologists was an important discursive alternative to the dangerous social engineering that was the lingering legacy of eugenicist thought.

In the next chapter I pay closer attention to anthropology as a discipline, focusing on three anthropologists—Edwin Smith, Bronislaw Malinowski, and Jomo Kenyatta—in particular. My aim there will be to assert that anthropological activity in colonial Africa was by its very nature politically ambivalent. But before I move on, it would be useful to rearticulate some of the more general claims that I have made in this chapter.

PROGRESS AND ITS PROBLEMS   The idea of intellectual progress as a cumulative enterprise is a particularly problematic one. As markers in this chapter, one can look at the 1953 publication by J. C. Carothers of the "childlike" mentality of the African, or one can even look at the more recent work of scholars such as J. Philippe Rushton. Furthermore, it is important to remember that just because there is a consensus of opinion in a specific locus (such as the scholarly community), there is no guarantee that such a consensus will necessarily be translated to other institutional locations. Simon Biesheuval's predominance in the liberal scholarly community in South Africa and the general acceptance of his critique of cross-cultural intelligence testing by the academic community made little difference to the choice of educational policy makers who "fell back" on an earlier understanding of the intellectual potential of black Africans. Thus even if there may be intellectual progress, it need not be reflected in the larger social world.

THE POLITICS OF DISCOURSE   A stronger way to articulate this disjuncture would be to suggest that contrary to widespread conviction, there is no direct correlation between a theoretical observation and a political goal or practice. In other words, although a particular theoretical observation may be appropriated in a specific context to serve a particular political function, such a function is not an intrinsic property of the observation itself but a contingent use of that observation. This is also to say that the same or similar theoretical observation may be used, in a different context, by different political agents with different agendas, for entirely different and even opposite political goals. The classic example of this, of course, is the negritude movement in Africa—the same "observation" of the African's "emotional" as opposed to "rational" tendencies made by the racist Hegel are here appropriated for a liberatory politics by black Africans. One could extend this observation to Lucien Lévy-Bruhl as well—he too is caught in between these two political moments; downplaying the African's rationality, although racist in the context of an earlier ultraconfident rational era, is not so in the context of a more questioning, skeptical moment of the critique of rationality itself.

In a similar vein, we could also note that theoretical arguments and claims rarely travel outside their original locus in a holistic manner. In other words, arguments developed in a particular context may only be selectively drawn on in the service of other contexts. Thus, for instance, the observation about the "arrested development" of Africans, in the context of the advocates of African education such as Raoul Allier, becomes one that foregrounds the essential similarity between Europeans and Africans and proposes greater educational funding and support. In the hands of the hereditarians and their supporters, the "arrested development" observation turns into a statement of essential and indeed irreparable difference, thereby making any additional educational resources, funding, and efforts futile. Related here are the basic formulations of "sameness" or "difference" in a comparative analysis of two cultures. But there is no clear political valence to foregrounding either of these as informing moments of cultural analysis. In the context of the majority of the thinkers I have discussed in this chapter, "sameness" translated into more attention to colonial education, whereas "difference" meant the futility of the pedagogical project. But if the modernist imaginary might favor the tendencies of the advocates of "sameness," by the same token the anticolonial and noninterventionist (and indeed the neotraditionalist) imaginery would perhaps be happier with the "difference"-based account. Or again, establishing the relative "sameness" of a particular African culture with the colonial one would lead to, say, an emphasis on a "literary" education—this in turn would be read as "progressive" by many colonial African subjects and later as "reactionary" by many nationalist and postcolonial subjects. Or conversely, the emphasis on "difference" would lead to the call for "relevance" in education on the part of some colonial educators for whom "relevance" is reduced to industrial and agricultural education—but "relevance," which in theory is precisely what the nationalist and postcolonial intellectuals argue was lacking in the colonial education system, is clearly not what these earlier educators meant by it. In short, the observation, "Educational practices must be based on the lives and needs of the people and should be made relevant to their concerns," the kind of statement quite prevalent both in colonial as well as postcolonial times, is completely and I argue necessarily devoid of any specific plan of action.

SOCIAL PRACTICES EXCEED SOCIAL THEORIES   Finally, from this we are led to observe that social practices are driven by more than social theory. This claim is at once banal and significant. It is intended as a corrective to the assumption, ironically made as much by materialists as by nonmaterialists, that social practices are the result of coherent ideologies or theories. It is this assumption that leads someone like Carnoy into suggesting that there is a holistic ideological system at work that must necessarily lead to particular forms of social practices (here pedagogical) that in turn must necessarily create particular subject positions. This scenario not only ignores the nuanced differences between the subjects of these practices, it also assumes a very hermetic situation with absolutely no leakages, no "noise," no interruptions or digressions. It fails to recognize that ideologies themselves are never solitary but always embattling competing ideologies (which is why they are necessary in the first place), and that this competition is always in tension with the pragmatic concerns and other material factors affecting the practices (pedagogical or otherwise) that they supposedly dictate. The practices,[94] in turn, are certainly in-

94. Here I mean practices other than the practices of theorizing itself.

formed by these ideological competitions, but are not entirely determined by them. Rather, practitioners, in as eclectic a fashion as necessary, draw on whatever theoretical, intellectual observations they can to underwrite their practices, and that too only when they feel such an underwriting useful or necessary. Thus the sobering lesson here is that, much to the dismay of intellectuals, the world does not depend entirely on the work of philosophers or other theorists to function, and, much to the satisfaction of those attempting liberation, ideologies (including "colonial ideology") are never absolute and always contain within them the possibilities of emancipation.

Dangerous Liaisons? Frustrated Radicals, Master Professionals

Guilt by Association—The History of a Debate

One of the most memorable characters in Yambo Ouologuem's 1968 novel *Bound to Violence* is the anthropologist Fritz Shrobenius. Intent on research-ing the "night of the Nakem civilization and of African history," Shrobenius and his family arrive in Nakem in July 1910. It is clear, however, that the resi-dents of Nakem are only interested in Shrobenius for the gold bullion, fabrics, and other commodities he brings them and in exchange are willing to put up with the "harassing" and "interminable questions" that are put to them by him and his wife. Indeed, Ouologuem takes a certain pleasure in the perver-sity of this exchange:

> Saif made up stories and the interpreter translated, Madoubo repeated in French, refining on the subtleties to the delight of Shrobenius, that hu-man crayfish afflicted with a groping mania for resuscitating an African universe—cultural autonomy, he called it—which had lost all living real-ity; dressed with the flashy elegance of a colonial on holiday, a great laugh-ter, he was determined to find metaphysical meaning in everything, even in the shape of the palaver tree under which the notables met to chat. Ges-ticulating at every word, he displayed his love of Africa and his tempestu-ous knowledge with the assurance of a high school student who had slipped through his final examinations by the skin of his teeth. African

life, he held, was pure art, intense religious symbolism, and a civilization once grandiose—but alas a victim of the white man's vicissitudes.[1]

If Ouologuem's Shrobenius is arguably an allusion to the real-life anthropologist Leo Frobenius and to his legacy as it evolved in the work of the negritude thinkers on the one hand and francophone anthropologists such as Marcel Griaule on the other, it may nevertheless serve more generally to indict Africanist anthropology as a whole. Written in the late 1960s, Ouologuem's passage, despite its unique recourse to fiction, irony, and satire, must be read as part of the larger postcolonial critique of anthropology that emerged both in the newly independent nations and the metropoles. No discussion of twentieth-century anthropology can afford to sidestep this debate. Since it has largely receded in academic memory, and since the "epistemological upheaval" in anthropology often referred to today is not this earlier debate but rather the later "postmodern" textualist revolution of the 1980s, it may be prudent to take a quick look at some of its contours. Without engaging in an exhaustive review of the various positions articulated then, we may note as markers the following five important moments in the debate.

1. James R. Hooker's 1963 essay, "The Anthropologist's Frontier: The Last Phase of African Exploitation," was one of the first to argue that anthropologists came to Africa after World War I as "the handmaidens of colonial governments."[2] Hooker suggested that if African "informants" may seem to have cultivated relationships with such anthropologists, it was only because they were seen as potential mediators between the local peoples and the colonial administrators. To read this relationship as one that afforded the possibility of true understanding of alterity was, suggested Hooker, to misconstrue it. Hooker also claimed that if there was any anti-European sentiment on the part of the anthropologist, it was only emergent late in the day—after World War II. Thus for the greater part of the first half of the century, the anthropologist could only be read as a colonial collaborator. Looking to the future of anthropology, Hooker suggested that if anthropologists were to sustain themselves

1. Yambo Ouologuem, *Bound to Violence,* trans. Ralph Manheim (London: Heinemann, 1971), 87.
2. Hooker, "The Anthropologist's Frontier: The Last Phase of African Exploitation," *Journal of Modern African Studies* 1.4 (1963): 455.

in the postcolonial era, they would have to "become historians or sociologists" (455).

2. Soon to follow Hooker's piece was an essay by a Belgian anthropologist Jacques Maquet. Published in the American journal *Current Anthropology* as part of a series of essays dedicated in honor of the doyen of cultural relativism, Melville J. Herskovits, this essay was to be the anchor of the debate as it evolved in the American academy. Maquet's "Objectivity in Anthropology" was the first explicitly political treatment of the existential situation of the anthropologist in a colonial world. About these anthropologists Maquet wrote, "They were scholars whose material and professional interests lay in their home countries but who participated in the privileges of the dominant caste during their stay in Africa."[3] Despite their occasional liberal beliefs, claims Maquet, the professional and career interests of anthropologists were far too vested in retaining the colonial situation. It is by referring to such vested interests, suggests Maquet, that one can appreciate the "perspectival" aspect of anthropological observation. In a statement that seems everyday to our own postmodern sensibilities but that seems to have taken the anthropological world by surprise in 1964, Maquet wrote, "There is no picture without a perspective, that is to say, not taken from a definite point of view."[4] Yet to say this, Maquet realized, was not to find immediate access to any *particular* "interest" as *singularly* operative for *all* anthropologists in the colonial situation, since any such singling out would always be put into question by other potential candidates. Thus "socioeconomic" interest could not be the sole kind of interest at work, nor could "professionalism" or "scientificity." The individual subject (i.e., anthropologist) would have to be understood as driven by a whole set of interests—conscious or not—that would derive from and in turn constitute (to borrow a term from Barbara Herrnstein Smith) their own "personal economy."[5] Thus sophisticating his account of the contingency of cross-

3. Jaques Maquet, "Objectivity in Anthropology," *Current Anthropology* 5 (February 1964): 48.
4. Ibid., 51.
5. Maquet refers to this as "individuality" and suggests that it is an important aspect of the anthropologist's activities and judgments. "By 'individuality,' we understand what Kluckhorn and Murray describe as the product of countless and successive interactions between the maturing constitution and different environing situations from birth onward, that is to say, the innate equipment developed by different educational processes and moulded by the personal history" (Maquet, "Objectivity in Anthropology," 52). For a more contemporary account of the notion of "personal economy" and its relationship to judgment (here to include cognitive judgment) see Barbara Herrnstein Smith, *Contingencies of Value* (Cambridge: Harvard University Press, 1988), 30–32, 42–43.

cultural cognition, Maquet goes on to argue that the recognition of such a situation need not be a sign of defeat. The argument that anthropology needed to retain its "objectivity" in order to retain the status of a "science," suggested Maquet, was itself problematic because it granted too much cognitive objectivity to science itself—far more than science could achieve. Anticipating the line of argument later to be popularized in the discipline by Clifford Geertz,[6] Maquet was arguing here for a "local knowledge": "A perspectivistic knowl edge is not as such nonobjective; it is partial."[7] If it was "relativism" that Maquet was foregrounding, it was one very different from the "cultural relativism" of Herskovits—rather than focusing on differences between cultures, Maquet's project was one more concerned with confronting the partiality of truth claims, the limitations of theories, and the interestedness of science. His goal was not to debunk anthropology but rather first to show how the emergence of postcolonial voices was beginning to question the epistemological foundations of the discipline, and second to offer a way for anthropologists to live with and through "partial" knowledges.

The publication of Maquet's article in *Current Anthropology* was to set in motion a whole range of rethinkings of the discipline by postcolonial, Continental and American anthropologists,[8] and the most elaborate of these was the publication by the journal of a forum, "Social Responsibilities." The three lead articles, by Gerald Berreman, Gutorm Gjessing, and Kathleen Gough, and the responses they generated by anthropologists from around the world are particularly worthy of mention.[9] Berreman, Gjessing, and Gough were controversial not so much because they elaborated on Maquet's thesis of the value-laden nature of anthropological research but rather because they were read by some as going too far in outlining the particularities of a radical an-

6. See Clifford Geertz, *Local Knowledge: Further Essays in Interpretive Anthropology* (New York: Basic Books, 1983).

7. "Objectivity in Anthropology," 54.

8. The British critiques were somewhat different insofar as they focused on the theoretical losses to anthropology in its alliance with colonialism. American and Continental European critics, along with several African ones, focused, however, on the more ethical and moral aspects of the alliance.

9. This forum remains the single most substantial critique that emerged from the space of the American anthropological community. See Gerald D. Berreman, "Is Anthropology Alive? Social Responsibility in Social Anthropology"; Gutorm Gjessing, "The Social Responsibility of the Social Scientist"; Kathleen Gough, "New Proposals for Anthropologists"; "Comments" by various anthropologists from Prague, Berlin, Bergen, Hamilton, Calcutta, Cagayan de Oro, Leningrad, etc. (407–25); "Replies" by Berreman, Gjessing, and Gough (425–35); all in *Current Anthropology* 9.5 (December 1968).

thropology. Yet although all three essays did exhibit leftist tendencies, they were by no means equally revolutionary. Gjessing, for instance, simply suggested that anthropologists would do well to recognize their unconscious motives and to see how, notwithstanding their liberal beliefs, they often align themselves with the ruling classes.[10] Berreman went a little further by suggesting that anthropologists ought to control how their research was appropriated by the ruling classes. Such vigilance, suggested Berreman, was where the social responsibility of the researcher lay, but exactly how the control over research was to be established Berreman could not say.[11] The position that seems to have upset other anthropologists most was that of Gough, who after pronouncing that anthropology was "a child of Western imperialism" stated that the only corrective measure open to a "relevant" anthropology of the future was to join hands with revolutionary, anticapitalist forces in the developing world.[12] There is perhaps no better demonstration of the anger generated when a liberal academy is confronted with a "lefter than thou" position than the debate that ensued, and I leave it to individual readers to make their own way through the numerous angry responses that Gough's piece in particular provoked.[13] My own interest in calling attention to the publication of the fo-

10. "Social Responsibility of the Social Scientist," 399–400.

11. "Is Anthropology Alive?" 393.

12. "New Proposals for Anthropologists," 403, 407. See also John Moore, "Perspective for a Partisan Anthropology," *Liberation* (1971): 34–43, for a further development along the same general lines. Diane Lewis's "Anthropology and Colonialism" (*Current Anthropology* 14.5 [1973]: 581–99) has a less polemical thrust and is more in keeping with the attempt to present a symmetrical account also evident in the contemporaneous publication of *Anthropology and the Colonial Encounter*, ed. Talal Asad (Atlantic Heights, N.J.: Humanities Press, 1973).

13. But just as teasers, I include here a few snippets of the responses: "The social anthropologist is in a better position than most members of his society to reach an understanding of other cultures, and the increasing intercultural contact of a shrinking world creates an increasing need for such understanding" (P. M. Butler, Surrey, U. K., 408); "I am baffled by the black-white approach of these papers. . . . I fail to see any connection between anthropology and, indeed, science as such and any type of moral commitment. Morally, the scientists are not better off than any other kind of people, and their mastery of facts does *not* necessarily lead them to deeper moral insight" (Erik Cohen, Jerusalem, Israel, 410); "There is nothing 'anthropological' about the American Anthropological Association's resolution against genocide; and Chomsky's eloquent condemnation of American actions in Vietnam is an expression of his feelings of outrage, not the result of any application of linguistics to the problem" (John Gulick, Chapel Hill, N.C., 414); "The world is not simply divided into 'good' revolutionary and 'bad' counter-revolutionary regimes; there are revolutions and revolutions, who is to decide, and by what means, the 'real,' 'true,' 'good' revolution has at last occurred? What is posed here is a moral question, which anthropologists are not necessarily

rum is only to indicate that at the heart of this call for social responsibility was an appeal to some notion of "relevance." The form of this appeal—if not its content—as will later become clear in my reading of Bronislaw Malinowski, was the same as that employed by some colonial anthropologists, and it was precisely such advocacy of "relevance" that made them the public enemy of a postcolonial consciousness. Indeed, one contributor to the forum picks up on precisely this issue: "I am worried however, about the implication that we should reduce the aims of social anthropology to such narrowly pragmatic ones. Does this not turn out to be the same as Malinowski's functionalism, but inside out—the same pragmatism, merely diverted from the British colonial administration to the local national interests?"[14]

3. A third significant articulation in the critique was that of Claude Lévi-Strauss, who was arguably already at this point in history the single most important anthropologist responsible for taking anthropology in a whole new direction. Although Lévi-Straussian structuralism is not the subject of this chapter, we may briefly say that this new direction was the formulation of an abstract theory based on mathematical correlations and complex linguistic analysis, a theory that may be seen to emerge not only as a dialogue with contemporaneous innovations in linguistics but more importantly as a reaction to the crisis felt by anthropology. Structuralism, which offered neither the pleasures of historical analysis (much encouraged in two different versions by the American descendants of Boas, on the one hand, and of a later school of historical anthropologists that emerged in southern Africa, on the other)[15] nor the sense of "relevance" offered by the school of "practical" or "applied" anthropology favored by Malinowski, offered instead its own kind of motor for the growth of the discipline. This motor was based on what we may in general call the pleasure of theory or, more specifically, the pleasures of aestheticized theory, which took as its driving force "elegance" rather than "relevance."[16] But as I have already indicated, if Lévi-Straussian structuralism took,

---

better placed to judge than others, and which different anthropologists will in any case answer differently according not only to the facts of the situation but also to their own ideological convictions" (I. M. Lewis, London, U. K., 418); all in *Current Anthropology* 9.5 (December 1968).

14. Leo S. Klejn (Leningrad), *Current Anthropology* 9.5 (December 1968): 416.

15. A school in the legacy of Isaac Schapera and whose most prominent contemporary descendants are John Comaroff and Jean Comaroff.

16. Although the reading of structuralism as an aestheticized theory is my own, critiques of structuralism by Jan Vansina and Anthony Appiah have been useful in my own thinking. See Jan Van-

it did so precisely as a response to the discipline's felt awareness of crisis. It is in this sense that Lévi-Strauss's "Anthropology: Its Achievements and Future," published in 1966, becomes not only a moment of self-critical reflection but also a manifesto for disciplinary change. In a remarkably clear paragraph, Lévi-Strauss presents the basic crises, both theoretical and moral, of the anthropology of his moment:

> Contemporary anthropology thus finds itself in a paradoxical situation. For it is out of a deep respect for cultures other than our own that the doctrine of cultural relativism evolved; and it now appears that this doctrine is deemed unacceptable by the very people on whose behalf it was upheld, while those ethnologists who favour unilinear evolutionism find unexpected support from peoples who desire nothing more than to share in the benefits of industrialization, and who prefer to look at themselves as temporarily backward rather than permanently different.[17]

It is perhaps because structuralism had already proved itself successful in providing Lévi-Strauss and others an escape route both from relativism and from evolutionism, that he does not feel it necessary to indulge here in a direct advocacy of his own methodological offerings. Instead, Lévi-Strauss focuses on the urgency of disciplinary change itself. Similar in tone to Jean Paul Sartre's 1948 introduction to negritude in the essay "Black Orpheus,"[18] Lévi-Strauss recognizes the need for Western thinkers (here anthropologists) to take into account the increasingly emergent claims of hitherto unheard speakers from the ex-colonies. Yet such attention, Lévi-Strauss warns, should not mean mere reversals of disciplinary agents, where for instance African anthropologists would study Western societies. Anthropology would best cope with this "new threat to our studies," as he puts it, by "allowing itself to perish in order to be born again under a new guise."[19] Such a new guise would discard the emphasis on *outsideness* as a privileged position of observation and would

---

sina, "Is Elegance Proof? Structuralism and African History," *History in Africa* 10 (1983): 307–48; Kwame Anthony Appiah, "Strictures on Structures: The Prospects for a Structuralist Poetics of African Fiction," in *Black Literature and Literary Theory,* ed. Henry Louis Gates Jr. (New York: Methuen, 1984), 127–50.

17. Claude Lévi-Strauss, "Anthropology: Its Achievement and Future," *Current Anthropology* 7.2 (1966): 125.

18. Jean-Paul Sartre, *Black Orpheus* (Paris: Presence Africaine, 1976).

19. Lévi-Strauss, "Anthropology," 125, 126.

encourage instead the possibilities of what were later to be called "native anthropologies."[20]

4. The fourth moment in our roughly chronological schema is the critique offered by what Philip Marfleet calls the "British New Left."[21] The New Left critique, consisting primarily of Perry Anderson's "Components of the National Culture," David Goddard's "Limits of British Anthropology," Jarius Banaji's "The Crisis of British Anthropology," and Peter Worsley's "The End of Anthropology," focused primarily on the theoretical developments (or rather the lack thereof) in the trajectory of twentieth-century British anthropology.[22] According to these critics, the failure of British anthropology was a failure "to articulate a total conception of the colonial situation."[23] Thus, argued Anderson, anthropology served the ideological function of the British ruling classes by displacing the idea of "totality" onto the colonial world of "primitive" cultures, thereby blinding them to the contradictions in the domestic political scene. Such working was particularly true of British functionalism, argued Goddard, since it was satisfied in merely observing cultural differences without any substantial efforts made toward achieving a structural understanding of the relationship between cultural phenomena. If, in suggesting that a structural focus may well reinvigorate anthropology, Goddard was in keeping with the growing interest in a scientific Marxist methodology on the part of the majority of his *New Left Review* colleagues, such enthusiasm was not shared by all. Banaji, for instance, whose essay was soon to follow Goddard's, not only denounced functionalism as a retrograde form of naive empiricism but also suggested that any potential radicalism of a structural anthropology had already been "naturalized" by the likes of Leach and "sterilized" by the likes of Needham.[24] Like Worsley, who in his own contribution

20. Francophone readers will note that in this brief survey, which does not claim to be exhaustive, I have not given consideration to the school of French Marxists such as Emmanuel Terray and Jean Copans. Although this school is important in its own right, it had few engagements with the more Anglocentric functionalism that is the primary subject of this chapter.
21. See Philip Marfleet, "Bibliographical Notes," in Asad, *Anthropology and the Colonial Encounter,* for a parallel bibliographical account of the debate.
22. See Perry Anderson, "Components of the National Culture," *New Left Review* 50 (1968): 3–57; David Goddard, "Limits of British Anthropology," *New Left Review* 58 (1969): 79–89; Jairus Banaji, "The Crisis of British Anthropology," *New Left Review* 64 (1970): 70–85; Peter Worsley, "The End of Anthropology," *Transactions of the Sixth World Congress of Sociology* (1970): 121–29.
23. Goddard, "Limits of British Anthropology," 80.
24. Banaji, "Crises of British Anthropology," 84.

announced the "end" of anthropology, Banaji too saw its sure death, but unlike Worsley or Lévi-Strauss or even the radical anthropologists speaking from the United States, Banaji saw little use in resuscitating this dying subject. The New Left critique, although important in its moment, seems in retrospect to have been stillborn, and even some of the critics who at first glance were sympathetic to it gradually parted ways.[25] One can only speculate whether the lack of an explicit ethical and moral appeal had something to do with this abandonment.[26] The critiques of anthropology that resonated the most in this period of disciplinary upheaval were those that appealed to the ethical rather than purely theoretical aspects of the discipline.

5. At the very center of the critique of anthropology were the positions taken up by various postcolonial critics in the debate. Situated in the interstices of the practical-ethical-moral aspects of the debate as it emerged in the American scene and its theoretical-methodological-historical aspects as developed in the British academy, the two most significant essays were Bernard Magubane's "A Critical Look at Indices Used in the Study of Social Change in Colonial Africa," which appeared in 1971, and an important revisionist rethinking of the entire debate in 1976 by the South African anthropologist Archie Mafeje.[27] Magubane's strategy was to critique the ethnocentrism of anthropology, as it had hitherto been practiced in Africa, through a close reading of two anthropologists who had done research in Zambia. Focusing on the work of A. L. Epstein and J. Clyde Mitchell, Magubane argued that

25. Thus, for instance, the essays in the 1973 collection edited by Talal Asad (*Anthropology and the Colonial Encounter*), although emerging in the context of the New Left critique, parted ways not only by focusing on individual anthropological careers but also by foregrounding practical rather than largely theoretical concerns.

26. The role of ethics and morality has always been a contentious issue in Marxist thinking. Although the precise configurations of the divisions are beyond the scope of this chapter, one could conveniently follow Alvin Gouldner's categorization of the "Two Marxisms"—one "scientific" the other "cultural"—and say that although ethical claims often took center stage in the work of "cultural" Marxists, they were quite consciously suppressed by the "scientific" Marxists. The New Left critique appears to emerge within this "scientific" strain. See Alvin Gouldner, *The Two Marxisms: Contradictions and Anomalies in the Development of Theory* (New York: Seabury Press, 1980).

27. See Bernard Magubane, "A Critical Look at Indices Used in the Study of Social Change in Colonial Africa," *Current Anthropology* 12.4–5 (1971): 419–31 (see also "Comments" to the piece by various international anthropologists, 431–39; and Magubane's "Reply," 439–45); and Archie Mafeje, "The Problem of Anthropology in Historical Perspective: An Inquiry into the Growth of the Social Sciences," *Canadian Journal of African Studies* 10.2 (1976): 307–33.

their choice of focusing on the adaptability of the Zambian, and in particular their emphasis on the "Westernization" of the native as reflected in the choice of wearing "Western clothes," was misguided. When Epstein and Mitchell measure the supposed Westernization of the natives through the indice of clothing, they make it seem, says Magubane, "as though (the Africans) exerted free choice."[28] Furthermore, such a focus on the "acculturation" of the native becomes an implicit validation of the colonial "civilizing mission" itself, and in the process the entire history of violence, not only physical but also psychological, is erased. The donning of Western clothes, argues Magubane, is more appropriately read as the mark of the psychological colonization of the native and of the "politics of survival" (420) of the African in a colonial world. To simply state, as do Mitchell and Epstein, that Africans endow prestige to "Western" forms, commodities, jobs, and so on, suggests Magubane, is to be smugly complacent with the mission of colonialism. To ask, instead, how "urbanization as a way of life" (422) had historically pressed itself on Africans and how they had been normatized into being urban subjects[29] is to engage in a politically responsible critique. Moreover, Magubane asserts it is necessary to recognize that such urbanization and "Westernization" was not devoid of a politics of resistance. Mimicry was not a sign of the colonized's absolute love of the colonizer, but rather, to put it in a more contemporary vocabulary, a form of "sly civility."[30]

Magubane's piece generated a good deal of controversy among his readers, some suggesting that he had misread the intentions of Mitchell and Epstein, others suggesting that Magubane's critique was more the result of the current postcolonial thrashing of anthropology than of any major sins of the anthro-

---

28. "Critical Look at Indices," 419.

29. Magubane writes, "The Africans they describe as seeking Europeanization are men who, though politically enslaved and economically exploited, were nevertheless successfully creating a new cultural synthesis to correspond to the new situation and to express more accurately their ego ideals." Further, "The acquisition of 'European' goods was not, therefore, in any sense 'imitative' or indicative of status, but a necessary consequence of being absorbed in a milieu dominated by factory-made goods" ("Critical Look at Indices," 423, 425).

30. The term *sly civility* is of course most associated with Homi Bhabha, who has made it available for the contemporary academy along with terms such as *hybridity* and *mimicry*. Although being grateful to Bhabha for his sustained theorizing of such terms, we may also turn to earlier instances of their treatment. Magubane's essay is one such significant moment in the theorization of "mimicry" in the colonial world, and one hopes that it will be subject to a fuller reading than I can engage in here. See Homi Bhabha, *The Location of Culture* (New York: Routledge, 1994).

pologists themselves, yet others accusing him of being polemical and emotional.[31] But regardless of the clearly defensive rhetoric, sometimes even coming from anthropologists in the ex-colonies, Magubane's provocative argument had made a permanent mark on the discipline. Five years later, Magubane's piece and the controversy surrounding it was to take center stage in Archie Mafeje's critical rethinking of the entire history of the debate.

Although clearly sympathetic to the gist of Magubane's claims, Mafeje's offering was at once more devastating to the colonial formation of social science and less harshly judgmental toward colonial anthropology. Mafeje's strongly historical analysis provoked him to claim first that it was "ahistorical" to suggest that colonial "British anthropologists should have been something other than what they were,"[32] and second that it was equally misguided to isolate anthropology as the "black sheep" (326) of colonial social science. The subject of critique, thought Mafeje, should neither be individual anthropologists nor the discipline itself, but rather the whole constitution of "functionalism" across disciplines. "In its paradigmatic form functionalism is a product of nineteenth-century Western European bourgeois society, and was never limited to a single discipline called anthropology" (311). Mafeje saw in functionalism "a vindication of nineteenth-century utilitarianism and a consolidation of positivist intellectual gains" (315). As such, Majefe suggested, if we must point our fingers at all, then the entire episteme of late-nineteenth-century and early-twentieth-century society should be our target. If, despite this recognition, the focus were to remain anthropological, then it should at least proceed with the caveat that "the intellectual effort (of anthropology) was a service to colonialism not because of crude suppositions about direct conspiracy or collusion but mainly because of the ontology of its thought categories" (318).[33]

---

31. See "Comments" to the piece by various international anthropologists, 431–39; and Magubane's "Reply," 439–45. It should be noted that as we saw earlier with *Current Anthropology*'s publication of the "Social Responsibilities Forum," the journal's editorial policy of inviting responses to the essays published and having the author "reply" to them was crucial in fostering the debate.

32. Mafeje, "Problem of Anthropology," 309.

33. Although I find Mafeje's critique refreshing, I part company with him when he tends to put absolute weight on the role of "thought categories." In direct contrast to the more nominalist position I advocate in this chapter (and throughout this book), Mafele explicitly rejects any efforts to sort out between the different goals, politics, and projects of individual anthropologists. If Mafeje is a "lumper" rather than a "splitter" vis-à-vis disciplines, he is so vis-à-vis disciplinary agents as well. My own reservation about this position is that if all disciplinary agents are seen to be so completely consumed by the "ontology of (the discipline's) thought categories" then this leaves no

It is important to distinguish Mafeje's response to the debate in anthropology from the critiques of the British New Left, because although he shares the general leftist disposition and indeed a certain focus on the theoretical configurations of the discipline, Mafeje differs from them in one crucial way. Unlike the purely negative orientation of the British New Left, Mafeje's position is more self-aware and indeed more careful of its own limitations. "Retrodictive interpretation is always easier and safer than predictive analysis and self-criticism" (319), writes Mafeje. He claims that neither he nor Magubane would have been anthropologists had it not been for the likes of "Leo Kuper, Monica Wilson, Mitchell, Gluckman or Epstein," and as such, Mafeje continues, one could even say that these earlier anthropologists were "progressive insofar as they created grounds for their own negation" (319). Much of my own argument in this chapter hinges around this moment of negativity within the space of affirmation, and thus it seems appropriate to end this brief review of the history of the debate with Mafeje having the last word:

> Historically, we had to be a partial affirmation of bourgeois functionalism in order to be its negation, in exactly the same way as African nationalists had to be part of the colonial system in order to experience its frustrations. It is therefore, error to imagine, as Magubane does, that there could be a negation without an affirmation or a falsity without a truth. Mitchell and Epstein are the glorious truth of their time and the ignominious falsity of Magubane's time. . . . Capitalism and imperialism had to exist before a Mitchell or an Epstein could "anthropologize" in the middle of Africa. Likewise nationalism and independence had to exist before Magubane could polemicize against them and transcend his earlier petty-bourgeois intellectual preoccupations. That is the only way we can describe ourselves without falling prey to an undialectical presumptuousness. *We did not know it all long before; we are only beginning now because circumstances dictate it.* (319; my emphasis)

Finger Pointing, or, the Politics of Blame

The "undialectical presumptuousness" to which Mafeje refers in the above quotation speaks of course to the anxiety around every transhistorical or

---

room for innovation and change. Indeed, by my account such a position leaves a discipline with no motor for expansion and growth.

transcontextual critique. Through what compelling transhistorical appeal can one accuse one's predecessors of such acts of crime as collaboration with political movements of which we now disapprove? Should such guilt be attributed collectively or on an individual case-by-case basis? Students of cultural and literary theory are not novices to these debates, and perhaps the most powerful example of these concerns was the recent controversy surrounding the wartime journalism of the literary critic Paul de Man, who, it was alleged, wrote anti-Semitic articles in the Belgian newspaper *Le Soir* in the face of a rising fascism. The responses to this discovery were many, some suggesting that de Man was not in fact anti-Semitic—that his critique of "vulgar anti-Semitism" was a sign of his own disavowal of prejudice—others suggesting that although he may have been "a product of his time," he had never exhibited any anti-Semitic tendencies or prejudices later on in life (in other words, he was, if anything, a recovering anti-Semite), yet others arguing that he was in fact resisting fascism even as he was apparently supporting it (thus calling for a closer reading of the "hidden meanings" of his texts), and yet more proclaiming that de Man's personal history had finally shed light on the nihilism, ahistoricity, and bad politics of the critical movement he had come to represent: American deconstruction.[34]

The various positions that surfaced around the unveiling of de Man's articles exhibited not so much the consensus of a post-Holocaust academy but precisely its difficulty in coming to a definitive judgment. This lack of consensus had very little—I think (and hope)—to do with any disagreement over the evils of anti-Semitism or the Holocaust itself; indeed, it seems that all parties in the debate agreed that the Holocaust had been one of the greatest historical tragedies of the century. And yet this shared belief, in and of itself, could not decisively dictate a unanimous position on the attribution of guilt to Paul de Man.[35] Although one might be tempted to read the debate in terms of the dis-

34. A great majority of the debate surrounding the discovery of these articles is collected in Werner Hamacher, Neil Hertz, and Thomas Keenan, eds., *Responses: On Paul de Man's Wartime Journalism* (Lincoln: University of Nebraska Press, 1989).

35. This difficulty was in no small measure dependent on our own varied conceptions of the role, efficacy, relative centrality, and so on of the figure of the "cultural worker" itself. It need hardly be pointed out that such a difficulty would not arise around a more centrally political figure such as Hitler himself, or indeed around the many other participants more directly involved in the Nazi project. The question that arises then is how one attributes guilt relative to the degree of participation—real or perceived—in any given political project. In retrospect it seems that the "crime" of collaboration is often attributed holistically even while the question of relative involvement continues to rear its ugly head. Whether it is the case of a cultural worker writing under a totalitarian

agreement over how exactly one reads the *Le Soir* articles (or to put it in traditional literary critical terms—over "authorial intention"), the debate was really the surfacing of the anxiety of the placement of "guilt" itself; this anxiety was one rooted in the question, how does one ascribe "guilt" transhistorically, or as Mafeje might put it, without an "undialectical presumptuousness?" And one could even push this further and say, that conscious or not, the unease in such a situation is finally locatable in a self doubt; for whether the issue is the mass genocide of Native Americans in colonial America, or the mass genocide of Jews and homosexuals in Nazi Germany, or the genocide and victimization associated with the transatlantic slave trade, or even the systemic oppression of an oftentimes violent colonialism,[36] the troubling question is the same: to paraphrase Mafeje, "Had I lived then, (lived, that is, on that particular side of the racial, cultural, sexual divide) would I have known what I *now* know?— and if not—would I have exempted myself from committing such sins?"

If the question as I put it is an uncomfortable one, then at the risk of sounding moralizing, I suggest that it is better to live with such discomfort than to be smug about our own "know it all" sensibility. This, I think, is the lesson that Mafeje wants to teach those of us who all too easily absolve ourselves of our own contemporaneity by focusing on the sins of our predecessors, and it is a lesson that many of our most sophisticated thinkers preach. Jacques Derrida, to name one such visionary thinker, reminds us in his essay "The Principle of Reason: The University in the Eyes of Its Pupils" that the opposition between "applied" or "oriented" research and "pure" research is increasingly rendered problematic in our own technoscientific societies and that all knowledge production is susceptible to appropriation by the military-industrial complex.[37] No more, suggests Derrida, can any player in the university point accusingly at another without also recognizing his or her own culpability.[38] No one is exempt today from complicity or collaboration with the State, since

---

regime or that of an anthropologist writing under colonialism, the question of their relationship (relative involvement/detachment) to the dominant political practices remains the same and ultimately forces one toward a rethought account of the position of the "cultural worker" in society.

36. For a powerful critique of Totalitarianism and its connection with Imperialism and Racism, see Hannah Arendt's three-volume study, *The Origins of Totalitarianism* (New York: Harcourt Brace, 1951). The second volume, *Imperialism,* may be of particular interest to readers of this study.

37. Jacques Derrida, "The Principle of Reason: The University in the Eyes of Its Pupils," *Diacritics* (fall 1983): 3–20.

38. And no more, we may add, can we honestly pretend that colonial research was compromised politically in a way in which ours is not.

even if a particular knowledge "should remain useless in its results, in its productions, it can always serve to keep the masters of discourse busy: the experts,
professionals of rhetoric, logic or philosophy who might otherwise be
applying their energy elsewhere."[39] If the essay begins with the typically Der-
ridian negative formulation, "Today, how can we *not* speak of the University?"
(13; my emphasis) (i.e., both: "How can we afford not to speak of the University?" and "What kinds of things should we not say about the University?"),
then, the implicit question with which the essay ends is, "Today, how can we
not speak of *complicity?*" (i.e., "How can we afford not to speak of complicity
[in light of Heidegger's collaborative politics]? and "How should we avoid
speaking of complicity—i.e., in the singular—in an always already pro-
nounced way?"). To put it thus, however, is not to fall into a nihilism (the anti-
deconstructionist's favorite bogey), but simply to be ever vigilant of our locations even as we continue to judge others.[40] Returning to the context of the
postcolonial evaluation of anthropology, we might pay heed to the wisdom of
Edward Said. In the context of an important reading of the later revolution in
anthropology, Said remarks of contemporary American academics:

> And do we not by conviction and power tend to regard ourselves as some-
> how exempt from the more sordid imperial adventures that preceded
> ours precisely by pointing to our immense cultural achievements, our
> prosperity, our theoretical and epistemological awareness? And, besides,
> is there not an assumption on our part that our destiny is that we should
> rule and lead the world, a role that we have assigned to ourselves as part of
> our errand into the wilderness?[41]

39. Derrida, "Principle of Reason," 13.
40. Thus to recognize that we ourselves may also be compromised is not to suspend judgment but,
perhaps, ironically to sharpen it. Despite the anxieties of those who worry that in the absence of
universalist (transhistorical) grounding of value-judgment only anarchy is to be found (where, for
instance, no one can judge because "every claim is deemed to be as good as another"), acts of evaluation in fact continue to take place. For an account of such a postaxiological understanding of evaluation, see Herrnstein Smith, *Contingencies of Value*, 150–84.
41. Edward Said, "Representing the Colonized: Anthropology's Interlocutors," *Critical Inquiry* 15
(1989): 216. Said makes a parallel argument in his reading of Joseph Conrad: "Yet lest we think pa-
tronizingly of Conrad as the creature of his own time, we had better note that recent attitudes in
Washington and among most Western policymakers and intellectuals show little advance over his
views" (*Culture and Imperialism* [New York: Vintage, 1994], xvii). The parallel between readings
of anthropology and readings of Conrad will become clearer later, but here it suffices to pay attention to Said's warning that locating a wrong in another historical moment or another cultural context often serves to mask one's own complicity with not too different projects.

To understand, with Said, that the "real problem remains to haunt us: the relationship between anthropology as an ongoing enterprise and, on the other hand, empire as an ongoing concern" is to begin to see the complicated problematics of simultaneously affirming a Western-derived ideology of development (even though it may be under the rubric of "public policy" or "sociology") while debunking the heritage of a colonial anthropology.[42] For although it is not directly the subject of this chapter, the case could indeed be made that despite some cosmetic changes, little has changed in the deep structures of applied anthropology as it was practiced in colonial times and as it is practiced—by local and expatriate workers alike—in many African postcolonial nations today.[43]

It should be clear that my aim in bringing the de Man case into this discussion (one could just as easily have brought in the Heidegger controversy) is not by any means to reduce the Holocaust and British colonialism into the same. Rather, my point is to show that the anxieties surrounding the attribution of the "guilt" of collaboration transhistorically emerge even in situations in which the actual politics of the parties collaborated with is deemed unanimously to be reprehensible. Or to put it differently, if there is an unease about attributing guilt even in the context of a potential collaboration with something like the Holocaust, then it should be of no surprise that the guilt associated with colonial collaboration must seem harder to attribute indeed.[44] What is interesting about the treatment of these two historical experiences within the academy, however, is the somewhat different way in which they were developed. Despite the suspicions of deconstructionists that the attack on Paul de Man was really an attack on deconstruction itself, it nevertheless remains the case that deconstruction was not dethroned by the discovery. Nor was, one could add, philosophy dethroned by the discovery of Heidegger's pro-Nazi leanings. In the case of anthropology, on the other hand, the critique seems

42. Said, "Representing the Colonized," 217.
43. There is a significant literature on development anthropology. Very few scholars today argue against the actual development of infrastructure and industry in African nations even while they recognize some of its pitfalls. The project of modernity is still incomplete in many developing nations, and there are no signs that it will be renounced anytime in the near future. See, for instance, David Brokensha and Marian Pearsall, eds., *The Anthropology of Development in Sub-Saharan Africa* (Lexington: University Press of Kentucky, 1969); David Brokensha and Peter Little, eds., *Anthropology of Development and Change in East Africa* (Boulder: Westview, 1988); John Mason and Mari Clark, eds., *New Directions in U.S. Foreign Assistance and New Roles for Anthropologists* (Williamsburg, Va.: Dept. of Anthropology, College of William and Mary, 1991).
44. Since there are arguably more apologists for colonialism than there are for the Holocaust.

to have affected the discipline as a whole, with no particular anthropologist singled out for scrutiny. Here a collective guilt was attributed, and the sense was that if you were an anthropologist during colonial times, then you were, knowingly or unknowingly, willingly or unwillingly, a colonial collaborator.

Yet, as I have hinted already, regardless of this wholesale rejection, anthropology, albeit in different guises, has continued to speak to, of, and from Africa. Whether in the form of public policy or "development" specialists, or in its new alliances with the disciplines of political science, sociology, or history, anthropological knowledge—broadly construing itself as any knowledge about another culture—has continued to sell. In some quarters, particularly those of the American academy, it has even turned to literary theory. "Some time ago," write Jean Comaroff and John Comaroff, "Thompson expressed the fear that the social scientist was condemned to wait forever outside the philosophy department. Our current nightmare has us waiting still. But now we sit, the philosopher at our side, begging an audience with the literary critic."[45]

There is, it seems to me, a great amount of give-and-take possible between anthropology and literary theory. Each discipline in the exchange provides a visage of the limits of the other—anthropology showing literary theory the implicit ethnocentrisms of its own presuppositions, literary theory showing anthropology the equally problematic ideologies exhibited in its archives. Despite the implications of the Comaroffs' observation, this exchange need not be unidirectional, and if either discipline arrogantly assumes it to be such, it will only do so at its own peril. In the remainder of this chapter I offer my own work as an instantiation of such an exchange between disciplines, not so much as a way to escape the debates generated in the 1960s but rather as a way to ground them through a set of close readings. Neither accepting the wholesale rejection of the discipline of anthropology, nor its defensive validation mostly by those scholars of the older generation who feel themselves to be unduly reprimanded,[46] I propose that a close rereading of the archives with the training of a literary critic would allow one to see the wisdom of Mafeje's claims. For if every moment of affirmation has within it a potential moment of a negation, then the narrative of twentieth-century anthropology would seem very

45. Jean Comaroff and John Comaroff, *Of Revelation and Revolution: Christianity, Colonialism, and Consciousness in South Africa,* vol. 1 (Chicago: University of Chicago Press, 1991), 14.
46. See, for instance, Raymond Firth's essay, "The Sceptical Anthropologist: Social Anthropology and Marxist Views on Society," *Proceedings of the British Academy* 58 (1972): 177–213; and also the special issue of *Anthropological Forum* 4.2 (1977) devoted to personal narratives by anthropologists who had engaged in fieldwork during the colonial period.

different indeed. And although this different story may often seem alien to anthropologists, to literary critics it will seem strangely familiar—for the revisionist thinking that such an enterprise entails is not too different from the revisionist readings of the literary canon that have increasingly taken center stage in the discipline of literary studies itself.[47]

I propose, then, to engage in readings of three moments in the history of twentieth-century Africanist anthropology.[48] The first is of a liberal humanism represented here through a reading of a text by the Reverend Edwin Smith; the second, a modernist-pragmatic professionalism as represented by the father of British functional anthropology, Bronislaw Malinowski; the third, a cultural nationalism as articulated by the Kenyan leader Jomo Kenyatta. The readings are not exhaustive but "symptomatic," and my aim is to mark some of the problematics that emerge in the context of these three standpoints rather than to provide a complete evaluation of any particular stance. Indeed, on occasion, as in the case of my discussion of Malinowskian functionalism, the general reservations that I have about functionalism as a theory are backgrounded in the interest of presenting it as a pragmatic rhetoric. For it is only when we think of it as a pragmatic rhetoric rather than as a rigorous theory that we can make sense of functionalism's attractiveness not only to a whole generation of anthropologists from the metropole but also, and perhaps more interestingly, to a nationalist such as Jomo Kenyatta. Furthermore, it is such a focus on the practices of functionalism (rather than a focus on its purely theoretical premises) that allows us to mark its relatively different tra-

47. I am thinking in particular of the arguments posed for and against canon revision based on the political implications of the texts. This debate has taken place at several levels, one of them being the level of ideological representation. To put it crudely, the questions that follow are—do literary texts represent, embody, codify the subject position of the writers writing them? If they do, do they do so in a complete, holistic way or are there instead gaps in the texts for ideological positions alien to the author to make their way? Should the task of a changing academy, sensitive to the needs of a pluralistic curriculum and student body, be to decenter the canon of traditionally male and traditionally Western texts, or should it be instead to teach them with a newer emphasis on their ideological content? Does the continued teaching of these texts, despite the occasional emphasis on their ideological-political particularities, result in fostering a genuinely pluralistic and tolerant society, or does it instead reinscribe the values and prejudices of a cultural system that are today increasingly seen to be problematic?

48. Again, I insist that what follows not be read as an exhaustive history of anthropology in Africa. A fine book that takes on that task and that would be of interest to readers of this chapter is Sally Falk Moore, *Anthropology and Africa: Changing Perspectives on a Changing Scene* (Charlottesville: University Press of Virginia, 1994).

jectories in related but also differently politicized contexts such as Malinowski's British academy and Kenyatta's colonial State. But to say all this is to jump ahead of the story, which more appropriately begins with a consideration of Edwin Smith.

Edwin Smith's Liberal Humanism

There is, in the anthropological literature on Africa, an event associated with the Asante and the powers of Kumasi that is seminal to our understanding of the colonial anthropological project. Coincidentally, it involves as its central character the same Sir Frederick Hodgson whom we encountered in the introduction. The event, which was dubbed the "Golden Stool episode," is important insofar as it became the "mythological charter" of anthropological practice in Africa in the twentieth century—a "mythological charter," that is, in the Malinowskian sense of the term: a culture's account of the past produced to explain the condition of the present.[49] As such, the telling of the story is as important as the tale itself, and so I turn to one of its most prominent tellings by the missionary advocate of anthropology, the Reverend Edwin W. Smith.

Born in South Africa into a missionary family, Smith found his own calling in his family's vocation. During his career Smith wrote several important books such as *The Blessed Missionaries, African Beliefs and Christian Faith,* and the treatise of our immediate concern here, the popular 1927 book *The Golden Stool: Some Aspects of the Conflict of Cultures in Africa,* based on a set of lectures delivered at the Primitive Methodist Conference in 1926.[50] As a Fellow of the Royal Anthropological Society of Great Britain and one of the founding members of the International Institute of African Languages and Cultures, Smith gained the respect not only of fellow missionaries and educators in Africa but also of the growing numbers of Africanist anthropologists with whom he sought to form alliances. Indeed, it was Edwin Smith who was the most eloquent spokesperson for the importance of anthropology in the colonial context. Although Bronislaw Malinowski relied heavily on the political and economic aspirations of colonial agents for his own rigorous advocacy of

49. See Bronislaw Malinowski, *Magic, Science, and Religion and Other Essays* (Boston: Beacon Press, 1948), 92.
50. Edwin Smith, *The Blessed Missionaries* (London: Oxford University Press, 1950; Smith, *African Beliefs and Christian Faith* (London: Society for Christian Literature, 1936); Smith, *The Golden Stool: Some Aspects of the Conflict of Cultures in Africa,* 2d ed. (London: Holborn Publishing House, 1927).

the "science" of anthropology, Edwin Smith continued to hold the place for being the most humanistic voice of appeal for the subject. If Malinowski was the pragmatist and Smith the romanticist, I would argue that the former's continual efforts to raise funds and gain general support, well documented by several historians of anthropology,[51] could only be successful because of the simultaneous dissemination of a romantic humanism by the likes of Smith.

Smith begins his book by recounting the story of the Golden Stool. Early in the eighteenth century, we are told, "there came to the court of Osai Tutu, the fourth King of the Ashanti, a celebrated magician named Anotchi, who announced that he was specially commissioned by Onyame, the God of the Sky, to make Ashanti a great and powerful nation."[52] Anotchi proceeded to present to the king a stool covered with gold, which descended in a black cloud from Heaven. He then proclaimed that the stool was no ordinary one, since it contained the *sunsum* (the soul) of the Ashanti. The Golden Stool was thus cherished as the most sacred possession of the people. No one sat on it, and on the rare occasions on which it was publicly displayed, it was placed on an elephant skin and covered with a ceremonial cloth. "Whenever on great occasions its power was evoked, the King would pretend three times to sit upon it and would then seat himself upon his own stool and rest his arm upon the Golden Stool" (2). Gradually, empowered by the possession of the Golden Stool, the Asante became more defiant of their overlord from Denkyira, and when a neighboring chief attempted to make a replica of the stool for himself, the king of Ashanti "led an army against him, cut off his head, and melted the gold that adorned the rival stool. The gold was cast into two masks representing the face of the impious chief and these were hung as trophies upon the Golden Stool" (3).

So far, Smith's narrative is setting up the stage. The background to the story is mythical, but it is treated with the reserved respect properly accorded to any religious story of divine revelation. By emphasizing the religious elements of the Asante, Smith is working very much within the colonial missionary order of things: the African, although not necessarily (yet) Christian, nevertheless possesses the conditions of possibility for conversion. In other words, rather than being in a hopelessly fallen state with no ability to distinguish between

51. See, for instance, Henrika Kuklick, *The Savage Within: The Social History of British Anthropology, 1895–1945* (New York: Cambridge University Press, 1991); Jack Goody, *The Expansive Moment in Africa: Anthropology in Britain and Africa, 1918–1970* (New York: Cambridge University Press, 1995).
52. Smith, *Golden Stool*, 2.

such phenomenon as body and soul, the African here already exhibits these aspects in his or her own religious schema. Indeed, the agent of the critical (mis)understanding here is the colonial officer, who errs precisely in confusing these essentially different categories of "body" and "soul."[53]

This officer, Sir Frederick Hodgson, governor of the Gold Coast, enters the picture in 1899, when he decides to send his private secretary Captain Armitage on a secret expedition in pursuit of the Golden Stool. When the expedition fails and arouses the suspicion and resentment of the Asante, Hodgson decides to take matters in his own hands and visits Kumasi. "He summoned the chiefs and the people to a meeting to be held on the 28th, and they came — outwardly submissive, but inwardly boiling over with indignation. Captain Armitage's expedition, artfully conducted as it was, had aroused the nation's suspicions. It needed but a spark to set the land ablaze."[54] Hodgson proceeds in the meeting with the chiefs to demand the Golden Stool. Edwin Smith quotes from Hodgson's speech:

> "What must I do to the man, whoever he is, who has failed to give to the Queen, who is the paramount power in this country, the stool to which she is entitled? Where is the Golden Stool? Why am I not sitting on the Golden Stool at this moment? I am the representative of the paramount power in this country; why have you relegated me to this chair? Why did you not take the opportunity of my coming to Kumasi to bring the Golden Stool and give it to me to sit upon?" (6)

Smith's commentary on Hodgson's speech follows: "A singularly foolish speech! An excellent example of the blunders that are made through ignorance of the African mind!" (7). The misunderstanding, of course, as Smith makes abundantly clear, is the misconception of the stool as a mere physical object as opposed to a metaphysical one. Rather than recognizing the religious meaning of the stool as a carrier of the "soul" of the people, the governor reduces it to the equivalent of a physical (even if symbolically rich) throne. If the misunderstanding arises from the governor's desire to critique or rebuke the Asante for not paying him due homage, it is at the same time "critical" in the sense of crises-ridden. "The speech was received by the assembly in silence," writes Smith. "But the chiefs returned home to prepare for war. Within a week fighting had commenced" (7).

---

53. See the introduction for a discussion of the triple sense of "Critical (Mis)understanding."
54. Smith, *Golden Stool*, 5.

There is a lot more to be said about the turn of events here and of Smith's account of them, but for now, let us continue with the final scene in this tripartite narrative. Twenty years after the war in 1900, Smith writes, the Golden stool, which had been secretly hidden underground, was accidentally unearthed during the construction of a roadway. At this time, Danso, the native headman of the area near the construction site, collaborated with some of his friends and moved the stool to the house of an elder named Yankyira. A later turn of events resulted in Yankyira and Danso stealing the gold off the stool, and news of this desecration spread to the leaders in Kumasi. The leaders of Kumasi held a public hearing and found Danso and his collaborators guilty of stealing property and "betraying the Ashanti nation and laying it open to disgrace and ridicule" (11). The death sentence was passed on the traitors, but, Smith tells us, the British government substituted fines and banishment for the ultimate penalty.

Smith continues: "Why, it may be asked, did not the Government, which in times past had tried to secure the Golden Stool, take this opportunity of seizing it?" (13). The answer of course is predictable, and it provides the moral of Smith's story:

> In earlier days the authorities had blundered through sheer ignorance. But recently *they had appointed an anthropologist* whose business it was to study Ashanti customs and beliefs, and this officer, Captain Rattray, a man of conspicuous ability and long experience, endowed with much tact and wholly sympathetic in his attitude towards the people, had investigated and reported upon the history of the Stool. What he said enlightened the Government as to the true nature of reverence in which the Ashantis held this ancient shrine. . . . They would have gone to war again in 1920 had the Government taken advantage of the opportunity to seize the Stool. *From such a conflict the timely researches of Captain Rattray saved Britain and Ashanti.* (13–14)[55]

It is the anthropologist, then, who is the hero of the day. Sympathetic toward the indigenous Africans, knowledgeable about their ways, and equally competent in the worldview of the colonizer, the anthropologist becomes the perfect mediator between the two. As one of the earliest and most often cited stories of the triumph of anthropology and its project of humanistic intercultural understanding, Edwin Smith's story becomes the mythological charter

55. The italics here are mine, but could just as well have been Edwin Smith's.

of the entire discipline in the colonial context. The Golden Stool is no more just the sunsum of the Asante, nor is it just Hodgson's throne, it is now a symbol in the legacy of Frazer's Golden Bough, a legacy that Smith by all accounts much admired.[56]

If the story of the Golden Stool thus becomes a legitimation device for colonial anthropology, then how does it do so? We should note that in order for Smith's narrative to so compellingly function as a plea for intercultural understanding, it must conveniently cordon off a vast area of historical experience and struggle between the two cultures before the occasion of Hodgson's speech. In other words, if the transition between the first stage of religious and social harmony and the next stage of the governor's "misunderstanding" is to allow for the necessary moral to be drawn, then this transition must be immediate and absolute. Thus it is that the political struggle between the British and the Asante—with its various episodes such as the overthrow and banishment by the British of the Asante king Prempeh, or the increasing taxation imposed on the Asante by the British, or yet again, the conflicts over land and territorial rights—is downplayed in Smith's account.[57]

If the history of British-Asante relations before Hodgson's folly is, as Smith himself puts it, "passed over" in his account,[58] the events after the speech are, of course, emphasized. We are told of the 1,007 casualties on the British side in this ensuing war with the Asante, and the "terrible sufferings endured by the tiny garrison" (8) of three European officers and a hundred Hausas left behind to defend the British interest. In the entire encounter, we are told, 9 British officers were killed, 6 died of disease, and 43 were wounded. "How many of the Ashantis were killed and wounded is not known" (8). "Certainly," writes Edwin Smith, "it was a heavy price to pay for a blunder" (8).

But a heavy price for whom?[59] The ambiguity surrounding that question

56. Smith writes: "The title of this lecture will have reminded my readers of the famous Golden Bough. . . . Now the Golden Stool might lead on to as far-reaching an inquiry as the Golden Bough led Sir James Frazer. But this lecture is limited to one volume" (*Golden Stool*, 15–16).

57. For a more comprehensive account of precisely such a history, see Alan Lloyd, *The Drums of Kumasi: The Story of the Ashanti Wars* (London: Longman, 1964); David Kimble, *A Political History of Ghana: The Rise of Gold Coast Nationalism, 1850–1928* (London: Oxford University Press, 1963); W. E. F. Ward, *A History of Ghana* (London: Allen and Unwin, 1958).

58. Smith, *Golden Stool*, 3.

59. I am arguing here that the backgrounding of prior history and the subsequent focus on the dire consequences of the Hodgson blunder is a rhetorically astute narrative device employed by Smith to structure his didactic tale. Yet there does exist an alternative reading of this narrative choice— students of colonial discourse will also recognize here the familiar pattern of colonially inspired

must resonate even more in light of the next two sentences in Smith's account: "Ashanti was formally annexed as a British possession. *In the settlement nothing was said about the Golden Stool.*"[60] Despite the casualties, given the strategic importance of Kumasi and the control of its leadership for the British,[61] it is clear that the colonizers made an important gain in the process of their empire building. So what remains to be commented on is Smith's recognition of the fact that "nothing was said about the Golden Stool." For in this sentence lies the textual aporia, the moment wherein a certain blindness leads to an insight, although not for the author himself. Could it be, this sentence suggests, that despite Smith's reading of it, it was not just innocent folly on the part of a British officer that led to this catastrophe? Could it be that "nothing was said about the Golden Stool" because in fact the stool itself hardly mattered at all? Could it be, in other words, that the Ashanti War of 1900 was not really about the "misconception" of the significance of the stool but rather about something else?

Such questions are troubling to Smith's account not because they point to gaps in his narrative but rather because they undermine its most central tenet. Smith's appeal is an appeal to Reason, to understanding—it is, in other words, a belief that intercultural communication and understanding *in and of itself* is the harbinger of peace. But even the most cursory historical survey of British-Asante relations of the period shows that the ultimate issue is not one of understanding at all. Indeed, the two sides understand each other only too well. The conflict, in short, is not over two mutually incompatible worldviews— rather, it is over two mutually incompatible demands and claims for territorial, political, and economic control. As a good liberal humanist, Smith keeps calling for more tolerance, sympathy, and understanding—but these are not the ideals that either the British colonials or the Asante seek. The investments for these latter parties are more concrete—land, labor, and political autonomy.

---

histories to dwell on those events that seem most crucial from the colonizer's point of view. In Smith's narrative, for instance, the real horror seems not to be what happened to the Asante, but rather what happened to the British. Hence the offering of figures and statistics of British casualties and a vague reference to those of the Asante.

60. Smith, *Golden Stool*, 8–9; my emphasis.

61. Such a control of Kumasi leadership was a continual concern for British officers toward the end of the nineteenth century. See, for instance, Governor W. E. Maxwell's letter (9 May 1895) to the Marquis of Ripon regarding the Ashanti invasion of British protectorates in 1873–74 (in *Great Britain and Ghana: Documents of Ghana History, 1807–1957*, ed. G. E. Metcalfe [Accra: University of Ghana, 1964], 475–77).

If to make such a claim is to suggest that Smith's project (and by extension the project of the anthropology he advocates) is out-of-sync with the interests of both the colonial officers and the African subjects, then it is also to suggest that here too we encounter a version of the triple-sensed critical (mis)understanding we discussed earlier. The particular (mis)understanding exhibited by Smith here is one that is not only "critical" in the sense of "necessary" (since it legitimates the entire project of anthropology), but it also gains valence through critique (of the supposed ignorance of the "practical man"[62]) while at the same time carrying the germ of a disciplinary crises that is concurrently being asked to be "relevant" to its own contemporaneity. In so doing, it must be noted, Smith's discourse already begins to participate in the rhetoric of a professionalism to which we now turn.

A Rhetoric of Professionalism

One of the most significant episodes in the professionalization of British anthropology early in this century is a debate sparked by the 1929 publication of an essay by Bronislaw Malinowski titled "Practical Anthropology."[63] Malinowski's aim in this essay is to propose a new way of thinking about the task of the anthropologist, who has hitherto, so Malinowski claims, been interested in antiquarian activities of little contemporary relevance. Rather than continuing in this vein, Malinowski urges his fellow anthropologists to "become more interested in the changing African, and in the anthropology of the contact of white and colored, of European culture and primitive tribal life" (22). By concentrating on aspects of "primitive economics, primitive jurisprudence, questions of land tenure, a correct understanding of African indigenous education, as well as wider problems of population, hygiene and changing outlook" (23), such studies will benefit the work of the colonial administrators in the colonies. The adoption of the principle of "indirect rule" makes such studies all the more necessary, argues Malinowski, since the very principle of such rule is to respect and develop indigenous modes of governance.

Such propositions, fears Malinowski, will be "pooh-poohed" by the "practical man" in the colonial field as no more than an encroachment on his own

---

62. The term *practical man* is consistently used in the colonial anthropological literature to distinguish between anthropologists and men who are directly occupied in the tasks of governing.
63. Malinowski, "Practical Anthropology," *Africa* (1929): 22–38.

territory. But it should be pointed out that the expertise of the anthropologist, deriving from his specialized training, is indispensable for such study, which no layperson could efficiently pursue. Furthermore, Malinowski suggests, his own readings of the literature have convinced him that the layperson, because of an inadequate understanding of social theory and terminology, errs too frequently in his observations. Such mishandling of terminology and of conceptual schemes of the native African can be potentially disastrous, and to make his point Malinowski provides the ready example of the "Golden Stool."

In addition to the resistance of the "practical man," Malinowski also attempts to address the cognitive conservatism of his own colleagues. It is here perhaps that Malinowski is at his rhetorical best, for what he aims single-handedly to do is cause a radical shift in the discipline without letting it lose its identity. For if the shift were so radical as to make the disciplinary transition incoherent, then of course no reason would remain for the particular task at hand to be performed by anthropologists—it could just as easily be taken up by others—as one critic of Malinowski, P. E. Mitchell, was soon to suggest. Perhaps anticipating precisely such a position, Malinowski is careful to point out that although anthropologists have been conducting what to him seem irrelevant studies ("of dead men and origins" as he puts it), the skills necessary for this new twist in the profession are ones that are "already in existence" in a "well defined branch of our learning" (27). To further emphasize the point he writes, "I want to make it quite clear that I am not indiscriminately criticizing old anthropology or trying to revolutionize it. From the very beginning the comparative methods of old anthropology have produced work with and special studies of the greatest importance for the practical man" (28).

To understand that there is no contradiction between claiming that anthropology has had it all wrong and claiming that in fact it also had it all right, or again, to understand how the performative "I am *not* trying to . . . revolutionize (anthropology)" works precisely to revolutionize the discipline—to understand this—is to understand the workings of a rhetoric of professionalism. It is precisely by calling for change while suggesting that such change is "business as usual" that the identity of the discipline can be retained.[64] And

64. For a related point in legal theory see Stanley Fish's essay "The Law Wishes to Have a Formal Existence," in *The Fate of Law,* ed. Austin Sarat and Thomas Kearns (Ann Arbor: University of Michigan Press, 1991), 159–208. Fish claims in this essay that the most effective kind of change is one that doesn't announce itself as change but rather as "business as usual." The issues of disciplinarity and especially disciplinary identity are most forcefully made by Michel Foucault in his essay,

disciplinary identity is no small part of Malinowski's project. For Malinowski knew as any good grant writer does that to win the support of an exterior funding agency—such support being crucial for fieldwork activities—is to present oneself not as a maverick in one's own profession but rather as a representative of the best that the field has to offer.[65] Thus to assert the centrality of the functional approach and its pragmatic offerings to the colonial situation was at once to call for a change and to suggest that the change had already taken place.

Although Malinowski does not here discuss at length the change that had already taken place, the formation of a committee of missionaries and scholars dedicated to the study of the African and the establishment by this committee of the journal *Africa* is precisely the kind of change that he has in mind, and indeed that he embraces. It is significant that on Malinowski's part, there is no acknowledgment of the fact that the constituency of the committee was multidisciplinary and indeed multiprofessional.[66] This willful neglect, too, is part of the effort to get the machinery of a professional anthropology going. In a rhetoric once again familiar to the professional conscience, the suggestion here is that if anthropologists already had the skills to be the most qualified to

"The Discourse on Language," in *The Archaeology of Knowledge* (New York: Pantheon, 1972), 215–37.

65. There is a good deal of discussion in the literature on Philanthropy and Anthropology in the early twentieth century and in particular on Malinowski's efforts to get American funding to sustain his own efforts and those of his students. For some such historically illuminating accounts see Donald Fisher, "American Philanthrophy and the Social Sciences: The Reproduction of a Conservative Ideology," in *Philanthrophy and Cultural Imperialism,* ed. Robert F. Arnove (Boston: G. K. Hall, 1980), 233–68. See also Raymond Firth, "Malinowski in the History of Social Anthropology," in *Malinowski between Two Worlds: The Polish Roots of an Anthropological Tradition,* ed. Roy Ellen et al. (New York: Cambridge University Press, 1988), 12–42. In this essay Firth remembers a particular encounter with Malinowski in the capacity of being his student. "He was also very tolerant of the 'social lie' as a matter of expediency. I well remember how in 1925, when I had just become his research assistant, he asked me to add a footnote to an article of mine about to be published, acknowledging help from the Laura Spelman Rockefeller Foundation (which had financed the research assistantship) in its preparation. I objected because the article had in fact been written before this. To him this was irrelevant; it *could* have been written a bit later, and a signal of thanks to the Rockefeller authorities was to him more important than a technicality of dating, about which I seemed to have what he described as Methodist scruples. Finally, after some heated argument, I gave way on more general grounds of loyalty, to which he attached great importance" (33).

66. The founding committee members included among others, missionaries (J. H. Oldham, Father Dubois, Edwin Smith), a philosophical anthropologist (Lucien Lévy-Bruhl), colonial "practical" men (Frederick Lugard [chair], G. Van der Kerken), a scholar associated with a museum (Dr. Schachtzabel), and professional anthropologists (Seligman, Meinhof).

do the task at hand, they still needed a lot more in terms of training, research time, a place to meet, a forum to disseminate their research, and so on to do the job really well. The article "Practical Anthropology" ends with precisely such a call to further enhance the appropriate institutional structures.[67]

If Malinowski expected some resistance both from his colleagues as well as from the so-called practical men, he was certainly to receive both. Most immediately, the criticism came from the "practical men." Although one administrator, F. H. Ruxton, presented an overall welcoming attitude to the anthropological offer of helpful advice with minor quibbles about issues such as Malinowski's advocacy of indirect as opposed to direct rule,[68] another, P. E. Mitchell, a provincial commissioner in Tanganyika, was more severe. Mitchell suggested that as a quintessential scientist, the anthropologist was best adapted to the laboratory and could not, with his scientifically rigorous habits, be of much help to the practical man.[69] The "practical man," argued Mitchell, was his own best guide and needed little assistance from the specialist. Mitchell's suggestion that what disqualified, or at least severely limited, the scientist was a determination to get to the bottom of all things before reaching a judgment is an intriguing one. What was needed at certain critical moments in colonial governance, suggested Mitchell, was a decision now, not tomorrow or even later when the scientist had had the opportunity to study patiently the various contingencies of the situation. In such matters of governance, suggested Mitchell, it was the practical man who was the best judge, not the scientist.

What is intriguing about Mitchell's observation is that in some senses it was a critique not so much of anthropology per se but of any activity that re-

67. As a master professional, Malinowski took every opportunity to promote this vision of the discipline. Thus, for instance, the genre of the book review offered him a perfect space to further disseminate his views, and in a 1930 review of the *Report of the Commission on Closer Union of the Dependencies in Eastern and Central Africa* (London: H. M. Stationery Office), published in *Africa*, Malinowski suggested that the anthropologist may well read the report as "a charter of the official status of his science, because every postulate which the Commissioners lay down can only correctly be determined by anthropological inquiry" (318). For those who might have missed the message, Malinowski provides a reference to his "Practical Anthropology" essay published the previous year in the same journal and goes on to underline that his position had also become the official position of the institute by citing the "decision of the Council recorded on p. 193, vol ii, no. 2" supporting the research agendas he was advocating.

68. F. H. Ruxton, "An Anthropological No-Man's Land," *Africa* 3.1 (1930): 1–11.

69. See P. E. Mitchell, "The Anthropologist and the Practical Man—A Reply and a Question." *Africa* 3 (1930): 217–23.

fused to come to closure. And if closure was the issue, here in the form of the need to come to a judgment, then once again the heart of the matter was really professionalism itself. For although Malinowski would rebut Mitchell's point in his essay "The Rationalization of Anthropology and Administration," by arguing that closure was indeed possible in the form of circumstantial judgments, such closure could never be misunderstood as the closure or culmination of the contribution of the discipline.[70] Indeed, by pointing to the relative slowness of anthropological activity, Mitchell, perhaps unwittingly, was recognizing the workings of yet another professional credo—don't quite finish the business of what you set out to do today, for if you do, you will have nothing to do tomorrow.[71] This principle, it is sobering to note, was also the unspoken principle behind the notion of indirect rule itself. For the argument can be made that the emphasis on gradual change by the colonial advocates of indirect rule, no matter how they cloaked the policy in the garb of the "interests of the native," was nevertheless a way to ensure for themselves the longest possible stay in the African contexts.[72]

In an essay full of rich historical detail, George Stocking has suggested that Malinowski was a master rhetorician whose "instrumental rhetoric" meant that he "spoke in different voices to different audiences" in his efforts to sell

70. Thus in the colonial context the fear was that you couldn't just bring in an anthropological expert in the face of a crisis, expect him to make a quick evaluation, and then just leave immediately. The chances were greater that the anthropologist would have to be sustained for longer periods of time, through "normal" periods as well as through periods of "crisis." Such long-term existence of the anthropologist was not to be favored by many administrators who felt that the anthropologist with his "pro-native" stance would soon become a "trouble-maker."

71. Thus, for instance, Edwin Smith writes about the relative slowness of the progress of the discipline: "We cannot wonder that progress has been slow; we may perhaps say, salutarily slow." Although Smith's reference is to the past development of the field rather than its future, the argument would also hold for future developments ("Anthropology and the Practical Man," *Journal of the Royal Anthropological Institute of Great Britain and Ireland* 64, [1934]: xvii). On a parallel argument made in literary studies see Stanley Fish's essay, "No Bias, No Merit: The Case against Blind Submission," in *Doing What Comes Naturally* (Durham: Duke University Press, 1989), 171.

72. Growing up as a high school student in Tanzania and Kenya, and situated there as a son of an "expatriate" family (foreigners who were, in principle, on temporary assignments in the countries), I often heard in social gatherings debates on how far the training of indigenous Africans for specialized skills could or should go. Thus although the expatriate professionals knew fully well that their job was, in effect, to train Africans who could replace them, it was precisely the knowledge that they would be replaced that would induce some of them to conduct the training at a relatively slow pace. Very few expatriates, given the comfortable positions they had secured for themselves in these new lands, were inclined to give them up. I am making a similar argument here regarding the colonial officers in the earlier period.

anthropology.[73] Nowhere is Stocking's remark more apposite than in Malinowski's response to Mitchell. The essay "The Rationalization of Anthropology and Administration," which appeared in *Africa* in 1930, was markedly different in tone from the original piece advocating practical anthropology. Opening with a sober reflection on the inevitability of science and technology and their "relentless persistence"[74] in effecting great changes in the world, Malinowski proceeds to acknowledge the "refuge" from such change traditionally offered by anthropology, the discipline that has allowed a "romantic escape from our overstandardized culture" (406). But although such romantic escapism may still draw the occasional enthusiast to the discipline of anthropology, Malinowski suggests that its only respectable (i.e., professional) future lies in its "rationalization." "I am attempting to make anthropology into a real science," writes Malinowski, and the characteristics of this science will be "uniformity and rationalization" (406). Such "rationalization" would entail the "dispassionate study of the ordinary, the drab, the commonplace, without any preference for the sensational, the singular and the remote" (407), and would focus on the "changing native" and of populations of hybrids and in-betweens. It is such attention to the workings of modernity that would move anthropology away from its "leisurely existence in its antiquarian fool's paradise" (406) into a more rigorous and hardworking professional ethos. In the bargain, suggests Malinowski, the anthropologist would lose the sense of romance associated with the discipline but trade it in for the "other attraction which science presents, the feeling of power given by the sense of control of human reality through the establishment of general laws" (408).

If the essay "Practical Anthropology" has a prophetic element not too concerned with the actual messiness of the practicability of its own agendas, this second piece is at once more passionate about the inevitability of its insights and more attentive to the potentially disingenuous ways in which it could be appropriated. For if the essay opens with a Malinowski who passionately urges his colleagues to recognize the potential relevance of their efforts in the colonial project, then such urging is not entirely blind to the ills of colonial-

73. See George Stocking, "Maclay, Kubary, Malinowski: Archetypes from the Dreamtime of Anthropology," in *Colonial Situations: Essays on the Contextualization of Ethnographic Knowledge,* ed. George Stocking (Madison: University of Wisconsin Press, 1991), 54.

74. Bronislaw Malinowski, "The Rationalization of Anthropology and Administration," *Africa* 3.4 (1930): 405.

ism. The most direct instance of this is the point at which Malinowski takes Mitchell's "practical men" to task for their hypocritical labeling of the natives as "murderers" (because of their alleged adherence to traditions such as ritual sacrifice) while themselves engaging in horrific punitive expeditions against the colonized. Malinowski writes, "Africa is not my special field, but I have a vague idea that 'punitive expeditions,' wholesale massacre of natives by whites, strange retaliations in the name of 'justice,' 'prestige,' and the 'white man's honor' did also occur in the Dark Continent, and that it is not only the colored African there who deserves the title of 'murderer,' nor is it the white European who should use such terms of abuse as marks of his own racial superiority" (411). Indeed, continues Malinowski, the task of the functional anthropologist at the current moment is to be a sort of watchdog who "studies the white savage side by side with the colored" and is "prepared to face, as part of his problem, the turmoil of everyday life and even the chaos of maladministration and predatory politics" (419).

Historians of anthropology have suggested that there was an evolution in Malinowski's own position vis-à-vis colonialism and more particularly vis-à-vis the native's point of view, insofar as he became increasingly aware of the importance of the native viewpoint as a corrective to colonialism's own story. There is much truth to this claim, and it can be substantiated quite easily by even a cursory reading of a late work such as *The Dynamics of Culture Change: An Inquiry into Race Relations in Africa,* which was published posthumously in the 1961 but based on lectures Malinowski gave at Yale in 1941.[75] It can also be noted in his support of anthropologists from the colonies such as Jomo Kenyatta. Scholars sympathetic to Malinowski tend to focus on these later writings, implying that the man did indeed undergo a change and was not always a passionate advocate of an uncritical colonialism, as the earlier writings may sometimes tempt us to read him. The argument I make here however, is that the germ of Malinowski's critique of colonialism was already present even in his earlier writings, and as is the case in the particular article under consideration, even in his most explicit calls for collaborative work.

Thus, for instance, to continue with our reading of his essay, although much of the remainder of the text is dedicated to a point-by-point rebuttal of Mitchell's claims about the inadequacies of the anthropologist, Malinowski makes it clear that leaving the task of anthropology to the "practical man" is

75. Bronislaw Malinowski, *The Dynamics of Culture Change in Africa: An Inquiry into Race Relations,* ed. Phyllis M. Kabery (New Haven: Yale University Press, 1961).

not only bad science but also bad judgment. For the points of view that are inevitably left out of the picture in this scenario are those of the colonized subjects themselves, and no amount of "goodwill" on the part of colonial actors can adequately come to terms with those other points of view. Relying for political judgment on the "community of interests" of the practical men themselves, as Mitchell wants to do, is flawed, suggests Malinowski, because

> we know that these groups, far from having any "community of interests," are divided by profound, indeed irreconcilable differences. And why, again, is this the case? Because they have deeply-rooted, personal interests at stake, which cannot possibly be brought into harmony with each other. *And this is not because of any lack of goodwill or of knowledge. The dissensions involved far transcend any intellectual effort or emotional adjustment; they cannot be bridged over by mere goodwill.*[76]

This last point is clearly critical, and its double-edged nature should be at the heart of our reevaluations of Malinowski. Although at one level directed against Mitchell's advocacy of the "practical man" as his own guide, Malinowski here comes to recognize a truth that in many ways serves to limit his own project. For to understand, as does Malinowski, that the practical man of business in the colonies, "however much he may sympathize with the natives, is bound to have more sympathy with his wife and children, with his dream of success and constructive enterprise" (422), is also to understand that the anthropological view, too, will not triumph over its "vested interest." We have returned at this moment in Malinowski's text to the critique that I made against Edwin Smith's own liberal humanism. I suggested at that point that the problem with Smith's account of the Golden Stool was its somewhat naive belief that if only all the parties involved had "understood" each other, then a clash could have been avoided. Malinowski, a man not unaccustomed to the workings of "vested interests," is here confronting a similar situation. To be sure, he positions the anthropologist and the administrator at a remove from other colonial agents whose interests seem more transparent to him. But it seems that regardless of this somewhat problematic gesture, the logical extension of Malinowski's observation is that anthropological knowledge alone — that is, without any accompanying shifts in "vested interests" real or perceived — would not be sufficient to change, for better or for worse, the actions of the "practical man."

76. Malinowski, "Rationalization of Anthropology and Administration," 422; my emphasis.

What Malinowski here approaches is precisely the kind of understanding that Max Gluckman, in an essay that was to be later read as a definitive critique of Malinowskian functionalism, was to accuse him of lacking. Gluckman, in his 1947 essay "Malinowski's 'Functional' Analysis of Social Change," finds Malinowski guilty of ignoring the historical contingencies of colonial practices and their essentially conflictual nature.[77] "A Government unmoved by the sufferings of thousands of people," writes Gluckman, "is not likely to be moved by the pretty chart of an anthropologist. Knowledge alone cannot make a moral policy; it can as easily serve an immoral one."[78]

To recognize that anthropologists such as Malinowski and Gluckman were aware of the limits of anthropology is to recognize that contrary to a certain conception of the discipline as a willing handmaiden to the colonial project, and indeed contrary even to Malinowski's own passionate pleas for relevance, it seems that anthropologists working in colonial times already knew that the limits of the discipline had been set in places not too far from where Mitchell thought them to be.[79] But if the project of the discipline was to continue, then the recognition of such disjuncture between scientific knowledge and "moral policy," as Gluckman was to call it, had to be suppressed. What Gluckman failed to note was that Malinowski was all too aware of this disjuncture and that he knew that ultimately what would win the day would be not the sheer truth of science but rather the exhaustive process of persuasion. Yet, in order to be successful, persuasion, or rhetoric, itself had to don the mask of scientificity, and it is here that Malinowski learnt the art of claiming for himself the label of "objectivity."[80]

77. Max Gluckman, "Malinowski's 'Functional' Analysis of Social Change," *Africa* (1947): 103–21. On a somewhat tangential note it should be of interest to recognize that Gluckman, despite his critique of functionalism, presents here a rather surprising functionalist account of conflict. Blaming Malinowski for failing to focus sufficiently on colonial conflict, he writes, "This unawareness flows from Malinowski's refusal to see conflict as a mode of integrating groups and to recognize that hostility between groups is a form of social balance" (111). Thus an essay that attempts to outline the faults of functionalism becomes more functionalist than its object of critique and indeed becomes so at the greatest point of tension in the account—the point of conflict.
78. Gluckman, "Malinowski's 'Functional' Analysis of Social Change," 105.
79. To say this is not to suggest that the production of anthropological knowledge was of no use to the colonial administration. It is only to mark the limits of such knowledge production and to recognize that even anthropologists like Malinowski who preached "relevance" were conscious of these limits.
80. Understand again that "objectivity" is being rhetorically used here to advocate very specific, contingently held positions.

Consider, for instance, the example that we discussed earlier: about the label "murder" for certain ritual killings, Malinowski writes, "Whether you call it aviophagy or murder matters little, but the real anthropologist of the functional school, without calling it any names, would study its cultural context, its implications and its meanings to the natives."[81] To say that anthropologists will study the practice "without calling it any names" is to say that they will attempt to study it without any prejudice, recognizing (ironically) that the choice between the terms *murder* or *aviophagy* matters not little but rather a lot. Although we could argue along with Maquet that such a value-free study would in fact be impossible to practice, Malinowski's refusal to choose between the value-laden terms *murder* and *aviogaphy* belies his interest in actually presenting the practice from the "native's point of view," even while claiming the standpoint of objectivity.[82]

Despite the pretense of such unbiased description, then—a *necessary pretense* on the part of a discipline accused by the "practical man" of excessive "pro-native ranting"[83]—there is, in Malinowski's essay, a recognition and indeed a call for the anthropologist's interpretive bias to favor the native. But this "real anthropologist," we must recognize, in providing a sympathetic contextualization of native practices and its "meaning to the natives," would still not be guaranteed success in convincing the colonizer into overcoming his own horror of the practice. Furthermore, such an anthropological lesson may have no effect on the administrator's own vested interests—political, economic, ideological, aesthetic, or otherwise—which may provoke him to put a

---

81. "Rationalization of Anthropology and Administration," 410.

82. A remark made by Claude Lévi-Strauss about anthropological activity is apt here. "While often inclined to subversion among his own people and in revolt against traditional behaviour, the anthropologist appears respectful to the point of conservatism as soon as he is dealing with a society different from his own" (*Tristes Tropiques* [New York: Atheneum, 1981], 383).

83. The term is often used by Malinowski in moments of self-defense; e.g., at one point in his discussions of the colonial encounter Malinowski writes: "The European takes as much, in fact a great deal more, than he gives. But what he takes away are not cultural traits but land, wealth and labour. This is not an indictment nor a piece of pro-Native ranting. It is simply a strong *caveat* that an approach which eliminates from the study of change the real driving forces is insufficient" (*Dynamics of Culture Change in Africa*, 26). Incidentally, this statement should also shed light on critiques that argue that functionalism and studies of "culture change" were ineffective because they did not focus on conflict. Although it is true that the actual studies did not, in fact, sufficiently foreground the conflictual aspects of the encounter, this seems to have been less the consequence of a blindness than of a rhetorical strategy on the part of the ethnographers (see also discussion of Herskovits in footnote 87).

ban on it. Thus we reach the second limit of the discipline, a limit that is latent in Malinowski's own sense of the discipline. It was at this limit that science had to give way to a moral discourse.

If Malinowski was increasingly aware of these limits, how did they affect his sense of commitment to his profession and to the larger society? If the critics of the British New Left were right in their assessment of the theoretically impoverished state of the discipline under Malinowski's functionalist regime, then such impoverishment must be tied to Malinowski's self-consciously empiricist expansion of the discipline. In the face of critiques such as Mitchell's, which accused the anthropologist of an unpragmatic scientism, Malinowski's "professional unconscious"[84] led him to recognize that the moment of colonialism was an opportune one not for the growth of theory but for the growth of data. Theory, had it been rigorously pursued in Malinowski's moment, was not likely to have led to the degree of growth of the anthropological profession as did the emphasis on practicality, and a good example of this is the relatively stunted growth during this time (late 1920s, early 1930s) of the discipline's more abstract French mode. The later triumph of structuralism was due not only to yet another strong figure—Lévi-Strauss—but also to the changing nature of world politics and the crisis of European society in the aftermath of two world wars. Whatever problems we may have with so-called naive empiricism today, then, such historicizing of functionalism leads us to question the uncritical narrative of progress (with its own representation of the move from anthropologists as "hunters and gatherers" to complex theoreticians) that often implicitly accompanies such critiques as those of the 1960s theoreticians. This narrative of progress has a tendency to privilege theory over practice and absolute consistency over messy appropriations and partial observations. Such privileging is misguided in so far as it misconstrues the values of our own era as natural and transhistorical.

To say all this is *not* to argue that "functionalism" was, or is, a compelling *theoretical* paradigm. Rather, it is to attempt an understanding of how and why it did seem a workable analytic for anthropologists who were critical of the ex-

---

84. I use the term *professional unconscious* here in the very specific sense in which it is proposed by Bruce Robbins. Robbins adapts the psychoanalytic model to understand the "professional unconscious" as the manner in which professionals internalize versions of their various "publics" and take them into account in their own self-conceptualization of their roles and responsibilities. Such a psychic mechanism, suggests Robbins, is "not a simple rationalization or self-deception" but rather integral to the nature of a professional practice. See Bruce Robbins, *Secular Vocations: Intellectuals, Professionalism, Culture* London: Verso, 1993), 88–89.

cesses of colonialism while professionally profiting from them. Consider here just one moment in the postfunctionalist critique of Malinowski. In an essay suggestively titled "The Dismal Science of Functionalism," Dorothy Gregg and Elgin Williams suggest that functionalists are "theoretically committed to a strong and uncritical assumption that whatever is is right," and yet they seem to have a "benevolent sympathy for the 'rights' of individuals (attacked by certain institutions) and a dogged insistence on cultural autonomy." These conflicting demands lead to often confused accounts, suggest the writers, and as an example they offer Malinowski: "In a recent posthumous publication, Malinowski constantly reiterates his dictum that all institutions satisfy basic needs. And on every page he bitterly condemns imperialist exploitation and the color bar. No two positions could be more contradictory; hence the confusion."[85] Such contradiction and confusion would strike most contemporary readers as reason enough to recognize the "science" of functionalism as "dismal" without recognizing that it was precisely such "contradiction" or more accurately "selective application" of principles that allowed Malinowski and his students to at once argue on behalf of native practices (functional accounts) *and* to retain a skeptical tone about colonial intervention. In a world in which theoretical consistency were the ultimate virtue functionalism would surely be judged a failure; in a world instead in which theory and science were no more than tools for the humanitarian goals associated with defending the interests of the dominated,[86] it is not clear whether the same judgment would hold.

If Malinowski's pragmatism was subject to such critiques of theoretical inadequacy, then a similar critique was mounted against it in the name of "history." Referring to the work of Malinowski and his students, the American anthropologist Melville Herskovits wrote in 1938: "When practical results are the end of such studies, a sense of historical perspective is ordinarily lacking."[87]

---

85. Dorothy Gregg and Elgin Williams, "The Dismal Science of Functionalism," *American Anthropologist* 50.4, pt. 1 (October–December, 1948): 606.

86. Or, in other words, a world where the practice of theory is a rhetoric in its own right.

87. Herskovits, *Acculturation: The Study of Culture Contacts* (New York: J. J. Augustin Publishers, 1938), 30. It should be of some interest that despite such a call for historicizing, Herskovits's own speculations on the nature of colonial culture contact seem rather ahistorical. Suggesting that cultures have always been in contact with each other throughout history, and citing the expansion of "the Empires of the Far East as well as of Europe in ancient and medieval times" (31), Herskovits proposes that there is no essential difference between such earlier culture contacts and those of more contemporary colonialism. The only reason these contemporary contacts have become privileged sites of study, suggests Herskovits, is because of the demands of "practicality" and not be-

Herskovits suggested that ethnocentric bias could never be avoided in the analysis of a culture contact in which the anthropologist's own culture was involved, and that therefore "the utmost scientific gain" was to be found in studies of "those situations where nations of Europe and America were or are in no way involved."[88] As was to be expected, Malinowski came back with a rebuttal rather similar in tone to his earlier debate with Mitchell. Hinting that Herskovits's comments were more name-calling than critique, Malinowski suggested that the opposition of "practical anthropology" to "the scientific study of acculturation" was intentionally manipulated to present the practical as *necessarily* unscientific. "Those of us who advocate 'practical anthropology' insist only on the study of vital, relevant, and fundamental problems. That such problems affect practical interests directly is not our fault. That a question does not become less scientific because it is vital and relevant will only be denied by one who imagines that academic pursuits begin where reality ends."[89] Debunking once again the image of the scientist as trapped in the laboratory, Malinowski's coy rhetoric—"don't hate me because I'm useful"—appeals to a rhetoric of social responsibility shared by a good many intellectuals of various political persuasions, even as the particular social formation to which it provides service may not be one that they all uphold. It is the same rhetoric as that employed by Kathleen Gough in her own advocacy of a politically "relevant" anthropology.

By suggesting that Malinowski was responding to the opportunities afforded by colonialism, I am reasserting the obvious and indisputable fact that anthropology as a discipline gained tremendously from the colonial project. Indeed, without its colonial conditions of possibility, the specific disciplinary trajectory of anthropology and the resultant ethnographic archive as we know it would hardly exist in its current form. In this sense, as Gough was to put it later, anthropology was certainly the "child of imperialism." But to say this is not to say much about the necessary politics or even the necessary

---

cause they have anything of scientific value to offer that could not already be gained from studying earlier contacts. It seems to me that although Herskovits is entirely correct to point out that culture contacts have always taken place, the difference in degree as well as kind of contact taking place in the period of high colonialism makes their study crucially different from earlier periods. To suggest that the focus on these changes is purely to be read as the corruption of science by "practical" interests seems rather misguided.

88. Herskovits, *Acculturation*, 32.

89. Bronislaw Malinowski, "The Present State of Studies in Culture Contact: Some Comments on an American Approach," *Africa* (1939): 38.

consequences of the discipline—ill-mannered or disreputable parents can certainly raise well-mannered and responsible offspring. The more thorny issue seems not to be anthropology's pedigree but rather the trajectory of its own development. What is called for then is a more local analysis of the various manifestations of anthropological work both in theoretical writings and in practical situations rather than a generalized judgment.[90]

Such a local analysis in the context of Malinowski shows that for better or for worse, the greatest source of energy for Malinowski was not, despite his appeal to fellow anthropologists for "relevance," the colonial project itself, or even, despite his often protectively sympathetic (even if verging on patronizing) defense of the native, the native himself, but rather the force of professionalism. In a private memo written in 1931, George Stocking tells us, Malinowski wrote that it was important for academic anthropologists to spend their time breeding young anthropologists "for the sake of anthropology and so that they in turn may breed new anthropologists."[91] This sense of ultimate responsibility not to the colonizer, or to the colonized, but to the discipline itself is present albeit in a different guise in the same response to Mitchell that we have been examining. In a telling remark Malinowski writes: "I fully agree with Mr. Mitchell that the specialist is not enough, that we do not want academic men meddling in colonial politics, any more than I should like Mr. Mitchell to take over my chair in anthropology. . . . Because the specialist, if he is to remain a specialist, obviously cannot become an amateur administrator, or planter, or missionary. His is a full-time job, and not a sinecure at that."[92]

If Malinowski's final loyalty was neither to the colonizer nor to the colonized but to his intellectual and professional work, then one could argue that, ironically, his profession brought him not closer to a political involvement, as he himself professed, but rather worked to shelter him from the messy politics of everyday colonialism.[93] The choice of critical intervention without accept-

90. And such a localized analysis will provide a more messy and therefore more accurate picture of the workings of anthropologists under colonialism. The political valency of anthropology in such an analysis will be seen to shift from case to case.

91. Bronislaw Malinowski, "Res. Needs in Soc. & Cult. Anth.," draft memo, quoted in Stocking, "Maclay, Kubary, Malinowski," 54.

92. "Rationalization of Anthropology and Administration," 419–20.

93. George Stocking notes, "But while the power of scientific knowledge never lost its attraction to Malinowski, his somewhat opportunistic attempt to make it more 'practical' did not by any means represent a complete transformation of his anthropology. Moving towards the historical world,

ing an official position on either side is one that has often seemed compelling to progressive intellectuals,[94] and in the case of Malinowski it was crucial to sustain him in England. For this professionalism—which was also a pragmatism—was fostered, I would argue, not only by a Polish modernism that, as Jan Jerschina has suggested, emphasized the "social role of an individual in society and his significant participation in the course of history" but also by Malinowski's strong sense of his own homelessness.[95]

A Polish intellectual in exile from a nation without a State,[96] Malinowski attempted to make himself a home not so much in England as in the specific space of a growing discipline. If England to him was no more than a space to make a name and earn a respectable living, then the stark reality of such a conflation must have seemed even greater when the possibility later arose for him to return to Poland. For when Poland regained its territory after World War I, Malinowski was offered a teaching position at Jagiellonian University in Cracow, the city of his birth. It was an offer Malinowski declined, feeling that his

---

Malinowski's anthropology remained imperfectly historical. Trumpeting its utility for colonial establishment, it nevertheless distanced itself from the exercise of colonial power. Proclaiming its 'deromanticization,' it left plenty of room for the romantic impulse to operate in the space it created for ethnographic research" ("Maclay, Kubary, Malinowski," 65).

94. See Edward Said, "Gods That Always Fail," in *Representations of the Intellectual* (New York: Vintage, 1994), 103–21, for a discussion of such a political position.

95. Jerschina, "Polish Culture of Modernism and Malinowski's Personality," in Ellen et al., *Malinowski between Two Worlds,* 130. In addition to placing Malinowski in the culture of Polish modernism, we may also place him in the Polish legacy of thinking about the social role of the scientist. I quote at length from Jacek Kurczewski in this regard, for his historical discussion on this sheds important light on Malinowski's own aspirations of making Anthropology into a Science. "According to the social pattern then prevailing (nineteenth century), the eminent scientist was a social leader, with social authority based on his knowledge and genius, but independent in his political, moral and religious views. . . . A citizen scientist was above all expected at that time to care for the needs of the lowest and poorest classes. Those who educated the countryfolk, established schools and banks for the peasants, prevented begging in cities through development of proper jobs and hospitals were greatly applauded; and the hero of Positivism, John Stuart Mill was worshipped for vindicating human rights, universal suffrage and women's liberation" ("Power and Wisdom: The Expert as Mediating Figure in Contemporary Polish History," in *The Political Responsibility of Intellectuals,* ed. Ian Maclean, Alan Montefiore, and Peter Winch [Cambridge: Cambridge University Press, 1990], 78). Malinowski says of his homelessness: "I am very far from being proud of being a citizen of the world, but I am one and now cannot help being that. . . . I told you how homeless and detached I feel and shall feel everywhere, even in my own country" (quoted by his daughter Helena Wayne (Malinowska), in the foreword to a collection of essays on Malinowski's Polish heritage (Ellen et al., *Malinowski between Two Worlds,* xiv).

96. The idea of the Polish nation predates its formation as a state in the post–World War I period. Before the war, the territory of Poland was partially under Austrian and Russian control.

work could better flourish in England, but it was a decision that continued to trouble him. In a letter of 1928, six years after the decision, Malinowski was to refer to it as his "renegacy to Poland."[97] If it was a sense of betrayal that Malinowski felt toward Poland, then I would argue that this was not the result of any absolute loyalty to England itself. Rather, as many intellectuals in exile, Malinowski retained in England a sense of otherness, a sense of difference, even while aspiring toward and indeed achieving a most prominently central position in his own academic discipline. To be sure, any study of Malinowski's letters and other writings shows that he was extremely interested in prominence for himself and his students, both in terms of intellectual status as well as career and professional success, but his ultimate passion remained the intellectual pursuit of culture and difference itself. Read in this light, Malinowski emerges not so much as yet another "dead white male" of the tradition of anthropology but rather as a peculiarly interesting ex-colonial subject, an outsider to the English academy—making it, as Michel de Certeau would put it, "habitable."[98]

Professionalism, then, has been the subtext of my own reading of Malinowski, and in contrast to the oftentimes negative connotations of the term in contemporary critical discourse, professionalism in my account is, if not a virtue, certainly not a sin. The workings of professionalism are to me worthy of study in their own right because they increasingly seem to me, not only in the case of Malinowski but also in the case of more contemporary migrant intellectuals, to be at the core of the geographical negotiations that such subjects must of necessity undertake. Yet professionalism is oftentimes thought to be the enemy, especially in the left-liberal academy in which many such intellectuals reside. Although mindful of the critique of professionalism offered by cosmopolitan intellectuals such as Edward Said,[99] I think its almost jingoistic

97. Quoted by his daughter Helena Wayne (Malinowska), in Ellen et al., *Malinowski between Two Worlds*, xv.

98. Michel de Certeau's metaphor of a text that is like an apartment that is made "habitable" by the renter is particularly appropriate here (see *The Practice of Everyday Life* [Berkeley: University of California Press, 1984], xxi). In the process of making England and the English academy "habitable" for himself, Malinowski, I suggest, similarly brought in a perspective from the outside, which was to make a permanent mark on the discipline. Although much more interesting work remains to be done on Malinowski's Polish background, a good place to start is Ellen et al., *Malinowski between Two Worlds*.

99. See Edward W. Said, *Representations of the Intellectual* (New York: Pantheon, 1994), for a discussion of the pitfalls of professionalism. Although Said is critical of "professionalism," it is important to note that no one would disagree with his position if "professionalism" were so narrowly defined

devaluation in the academy is unfortunate. Here I am in agreement with
Bruce Robbins, who suggests that intellectuals on the left should acknowledge that it is precisely the profession and the academy that have sustained
their political aspirations and that intellectual and professional achievements
are not things to be embarrassed by.[100] In the case of anthropologists like Malinowski, the resistance that they often faced from those more directly involved in colonial administration and settlement should indicate that,[101]
whether we can today recognize it or not, they must have been doing *something* to upset these colonial agents, and whatever it was that they were doing
to so upset them was ultimately backed by the growing authority of a profes-
sionalized discipline.

Richard Fardon has pointed out that discussions of Malinowski, although
waning by the 1970s, resurged in the 1980s (and one might add the 1990s), presenting him as a mythical and occasionally deified figure.[102] This new Malinowski, suggests Fardon, has decreasing resemblance to Malinowski the man,
and increasingly appears as a personification of a political position or value.
The possibility of such a move is of course ever present in any account that
tends to conflate a whole discipline or field of study into a single person as op-

---

as he defines it in these lectures. "By professionalism I mean thinking of your work as an intellectual as something you do for a living, between the hours of nine and five with one eye on the clock,
and another cocked at what is considered to be proper professional behaviour—not rocking the
boat, not straying outside the accepted paradigms or limits, making yourself marketable and above
all presentable, hence uncontroversial and unpolitical and "objective" (74). If this be professionalism, then indeed let's get rid of it. Unfortunately, however, Said seems to disregard the fact that
academic professionalism works precisely to privilege those who "rock the boat." Said's own *Orientalism* was precisely such a gesture of rocking the boat, a project that was neither uncontroversial
nor apolitical, and it was precisely that work more than any other that placed Said as a prominent
figure in the professional academic marketplace.

100. "In the face of the right's offensive, it is no longer possible to deny that something palpably
grounded in reality, something realized and accomplished, exists for the right to attack, and the left
to defend. All this public recognition, however critical, is forcing left intellectuals to acknowledge
what they have often not wanted to acknowledge: their own cultural and institutional *achievements*" (Robbins, ed., *Intellectuals: Aesthetics, Politics, Academics* [Minneapolis: University of Minnesota Press, 1990], x).

101. Mitchell was not the only administrator to voice dissent. A rather self-important and condescending rebuke of anthropologists was also offered by Lord Raglan. See Lord Raglan, "Anthropology and the Future of Civilization," *Rationalist Annual* (1946): 39–44; and Lord Raglan, "The
Future of Social Anthropology," *Man* (May–June 1943): 58–60. This latter piece also generated a
few angry responses.

102. Richard Fardon, "Malinowski's Precedent: The Imagination of Equality," *Man* 25.4 (December 1990): 573.

posed to reading it as a collective culture. Thus, for instance, a more complex awareness of the state of the field in the late 1920s would also pay attention to the weakening positions of evolutionists such as Elliot Smith, and to corollary developments in other contexts, particularly the increasing influence of a very different strain in anthropology—the Boasian school of American anthropology. Although such an expansive project would be the subject of a full booklength study (or several), my particular focus on Malinowski is driven precisely by Fardon's observations. Malinowski tends today (more than ever before) to become either glorified by some (who think he was almost singlehandedly responsible for one of the greatest methodological innovations in anthropology—participant observation) or denigrated by others (especially those who rightly take him to task for his diary entries that display some of his pejorative attitudes and rather reckless behavior toward the various "natives" he studies).[103] Could he have foreseen this fate when he once wrote, "Rivers is the Rider Haggard of anthropology, I shall be the Conrad"?[104]

If Malinowski was quite consciously attempting a Conradian selffashioning, then it is clear that circumstance if not sheer will has rendered the comparison quite worthy.[105] Polish émigrés both, they both became the central figures in their respective métiers, Conrad's *Heart of Darkness* arguably being the single most-cited text of "British" modernism, Malinowski's functionalism and methods of "participant observation" becoming the most innovative aspects of "British" anthropology. And if their own works exhibited traces of their outsideness, as I argue for Malinowski and others have argued

103. See Bronislaw Malinowski, *A Diary in the Strict Sense of the Term* New York: Harcourt, Brace and World, 1967); for a critical reading of portions of the diary see Marianna Torgovnick, *Gone Primitive: Savage Intellects, Modern Lives* (Chicago: University of Chicago Press, 1990), 227–43.

104. Quoted in Raymond Firth, ed., *Man and Culture: An Evaluation of the Work of Bronislaw Malinowski* (New York: Routledge, 1957), 6.

105. One of the most provocative comparative readings of Malinowski and Conrad appears in James Clifford's essay titled "On Ethnographic Self-Fashioning: Conrad and Malinowksi." Clifford's essay provides a careful close reading of Malinowski's *Diary in the Strict Sense of the Term* in the context of Conrad's *Heart of Darkness*. Despite all the tropological similarities, allusions, and willful emulation of Conrad in Malinowski's works—to which Clifford's reading does great justice—Clifford somewhat mysteriously concludes (contrary to the overwhelming evidence in his own essay) that anthropology "is still waiting for its Conrad" and that "Malinowski was not the Conrad of anthropology" (96). Baffled as I am by Clifford's conclusions, my own reading of Malinowski as a Conrad figure is intended to extend his exegesis rather than repeating it. See Clifford, "On Ethnographic Self-Fashioning: Conrad and Malinowski," in *The Predicament of Culture: Twentieth Century Ethnography, Literature, and Art* (Cambridge: Harvard University Press, 1988), 92–113.

for Conrad,[106] then perhaps it is an allowable delight for the deconstructionist to observe, here as elsewhere, that at the origin there is difference—that the so-called master's voice is in fact always already the voice of the other, that purity, even at the origin, is a mythical fable.

Yet it is important to note that it is neither functionalism nor the method of participant observation that has gained center stage in most contemporary readings of Malinowski. Rather, it is the publication of Malinowski's Trobriand diary and the two volumes of his letters to his wife, Elsie, that has cast a decisively negative shadow on his work.[107] It is in this context that Malinowski and Conrad bear an uncanny resemblance. For if, as Chinua Achebe suggests of the latter, Conrad's liberalism is such that it "condemned the evil of imperial exploitation but was strangely unaware of the racism on which it sharpened its iron tooth,"[108] then one could plausibly make the same claim about Malinowski. Critical of British imperialism, Malinowski was not himself immune to racism and was often prone to make, albeit in the privacy of a diary or a letter, remarks that to our own sensibilities seem exceedingly offensive. But herein I believe lies the importance of Malinowski (or for that matter Conrad) to a student of culture—for what he shows us is a configuration of political positions that seem so alien to our own that even while we ourselves may reject them, we must, after reading Malinowski, do so with the recognition that our own configurations too must seem contingent and not natural to societies other than our own.[109]

It is in the context of such considerations that I have read Malinowski. My

---

106. Edward Said writes, "What makes Conrad different from other colonial writers who were his contemporaries is that, for reasons having partly to do with the colonialism that turned him, a Polish expatriate, into an employee of the imperial system, he was so self-conscious about what he did" (*Culture and Imperialism*, 23). See also Geoffrey Galt Harpham, *One of Us: The Mastery of Joseph Conrad* (Chicago: University of Chicago Press, 1997) for a nuanced reading of Conrad in the context of his Polish background.

107. Helena Wayne, ed., *The Story of a Marriage: The Letters of Bronislaw Malinowski and Elsie Masson*, 2 vols. (New York: Routledge, 1992).

108. Chinua Achebe, "An Image of Africa: Racism in Conrad's *Heart of Darkness*," in *Heart of Darkness: An Authoritative Text, Backgrounds and Sources, Criticism*, ed. Robert Kimbrough (New York: Norton, 1988), 262.

109. Thus, for instance, the question seems to be—how can one be a racist and an anti-imperialist at the same time? We often assume in the late twentieth century that to be racist is to be imperialist and conversely, to be antiracist is to be anti-imperialist. What the likes of Conrad and Malinowski teach us is that such configurations of political positions that seem so obvious to our own political sensibilities are often contingent and not natural alliances.

own characterization of Malinowski is intended to see him in a rather different light from which he has traditionally been seen. An ex-colonial intellectual traveling to a major European metropole, a cultural and linguistic outsider aspiring and espousing a professional ethos in order to find himself a "home," a figure whose very centrality in the discourse of British anthropology belies its supposed status as the authoritative "master discourse" of a Western European modernity, Malinowski remains an enigmatic figure, if not of a "frustrated radical,"[110] then at least of an ambivalently progressive liberal.

"Rabbits Turned Poachers," or Anthropology in Reverse

In a remarkable passage examining the epistemological condition of the anthropologist, Claude Lévi-Strauss notes: "While often inclined to subversion among his own people and in revolt against traditional behavior, the anthropologist appears respectful to the point of conservatism as soon as he is dealing with a society different from his own."[111] If this is an accurate characterization of the epistemic status of traditional anthropological practice in which the values of the anthropologist's own society are held at bay while the society being studied is favorably presented, then how do the political valences of the anthropologist shift when the anthropologist is one of the "natives" in a colonial situation?[112] How, in other words, does the disciplinary habitus of the

110. The term is Wendy James's, who suggests that we may think of anthropologists working in colonial conditions as "reluctant imperialists" or as "frustrated radicals." See Wendy James, "The Anthropologist as Reluctant Imperialist," in Asad, *Anthropology and the Colonial Encounter,* 41–69.
111. Lévi-Strauss, *Tristes Tropiques,* 383.
112. I use the term *native* anthropologist in accord with the conventional usage of this term in the great majority of anthropological literature. In this sense a "native" anthropologist is any anthropologist who chooses to study his or her own culture—this would include an Indian anthropologist studying aspects of Indian culture or an American anthropologist studying American culture. The problematics of equating a whole culture with a nation is of course one of the limits of this definition, as is any reflection of internal differences within even the most narrowly defined culture-group. Yet the term remains a useful tool for distinguishing between the levels of remove of the traditionally Western anthropologists and the local ones. The term *indigenous* anthropologist could well be substituted here by those for whom the term *native* has negative connotations. Since words do not contain intrinsic or essential meanings but only meanings and connotations defined by their usage, and since furthermore the term *native* and the associated concept of "nativity" do not seem to me to be any more compromised than the alternative term *indigenous* (one could ask "indigenous" to what? just as one could ask "native of what?") I have retained their usage here. Yet, out of deference to those readers who may still worry about the negative connotations of the word, I have followed the convention of bracketing it within quotation marks.

"native" anthropologist confront the dual demands of retaining skepticism toward her "own" society while casting in a favorable light the society studied (which is also her "own")? In which societal space does such a "native" anthropologist revolt, and in which space instead does she uphold cultural tradition? How does the choice of studying anthropology affect the "native" subject's political stance vis-à-vis her own culture?

Jomo Kenyatta, who was later on in life to become the first president of the independent state of Kenya, was one such "native" anthropologist, and a look at his anthropological work may help us address some of these issues. Born around 1894 in a Gikuyu farming family in central Kenya, Kenyatta was educated at the Presbyterian Church of Scotland Mission. He moved to Nairobi in his twenties to take up a minor post in government service but was soon to find himself increasingly immersed in political activities. As Kenya changed status from being a British protectorate to an official colony in 1920, the colonial state began to take greater measures to enhance the benefits of white settlers. Increasing alienation of African land, decreasing wages, and proposed legislation of increased "hut" taxes led to the formation of the East African Association in 1921. Kenyatta became an active member of this association until it was banned by the colonial state, its leaders being arrested and deported. A new organization consisting of younger Africans, primarily Gikuyu, was formed, and it was on the behalf of this organization (the Kikuyu Central Association, or KCA) that Kenyatta went to England in 1929. His mission was to be a political advocate of the Gikuyu—to demand the return of Gikuyu lands, to argue for the support of schools independent of mission affiliations, to call for greater representation of indigenous Africans on the legislative and municipal councils, and to repeal the increasing burden of the hut tax.[113] With the exception of one brief return to Kenya in 1930, Kenyatta stayed in Europe until 1946, visiting among other places Denmark, Sweden, Norway, and the Soviet Union. If not professionally engaged in anthropological work in each of these countries, Kenyatta's travels did take place in the context of his own increasing interest in anthropology, an interest that was most formally marked by the seminars he attended at the London School of Economics in 1936. His teacher at these seminars was Bronislaw Ma-

---

113. For a concise history of the political organization and demands of the Gikuyu at this time, and also for the repressive measures of the colonial state, there is perhaps no better account than that of Kenyatta himself. See Jomo Kenyatta, *Kenya: The Land of Conflict* (London: Panaf Service, 1946).

linowski, and the lesson Kenyatta was to learn was the lesson of function-alism.[114]

Facing Mount Kenya, Kenyatta's major accomplishment in the context of Malinowski's seminars, is one of the earliest anthropological works written by a Gikuyu about the Gikuyu.[115] In the preface, Kenyatta establishes his own authority—both scholarly as well as experiential—in order to authenticate the work. Here the ethnographic authority traditionally construed as derived from "having been there" is extended to include a further moment: "I know because I am." Insider knowledge becomes in this ethnography the locus of privilege, and accordingly, Kenyatta writes in a space-clearing gesture:

> My chief object is not to enter into controversial discussion with those who have attempted, or are attempting, to describe the same thing from outside observation, but to let the truth speak for itself. I know that there are many scientists and general readers who will be disinterestedly glad of hearing the Africans' point of view, and to all such I am glad to be of service. At the same time, I am well aware that I could not do justice to the subject without offending those "professional friends of the African" who are prepared to maintain their friendship for eternity as a sacred duty, provided only that the African will continue to play the part of an ignorant savage so that they can monopolize the office of interpreting his mind and speaking for him. To such people, an African who writes a study of this kind is encroaching on their preserves. He is a rabbit turned poacher.[116]

If there is here a strong note of antagonism toward the "professional friends of the African" whether they be colonial officers, missionaries, or even, one must add, non-African anthropologists, then this antagonism is more particularly an antagonism toward the dominant inventions of Africa. Such inventions,

---

114. It is very likely that Malinowski had Jomo Kenyatta in mind when he wrote: "The African is becoming an anthropologist who turns our own weapons against us. He is studying European aims, pretenses, and all the real and imaginary acts of injustice. Such an anthropology is no doubt mutilated and misguided, full of counter-prejudices, and charged with bitter hostility. It is often blind in its intransigence and sweeping in its wholesale indictment. But it cannot be ignored by the man of science; and it would be better if the practical man did not treat it as a joke or as an insignificant and minor excrescence" (*Dynamics of Culture Change in Africa,* 59).

115. Jomo Kenyatta, *Facing Mount Kenya* (New York: Vintage, 1965). The book was first published in 1938.

116. Ibid., xvii–xviii.

fears Kenyatta, have been insufficiently challenged by Africans. His own ethnography, written from an "internal" perspective, would seek to correct this imbalance and read the Gikuyu not as ignorant, heathen savages but rather as a people with a culture, having their own sense of values and autonomy.[117] What better discourse than functional anthropology to draw such a picture? What other discourse could as compellingly present a social system functioning perfectly well until the advent of an alien and repressive force?

Looking over the table of contents of *Facing Mount Kenya,* one would hardly note its political import. Organized as per ethnographic convention, the chapter headings and their order could well be replicated in a great number of contemporary ethnographies: "1. Tribal Origin and Kinship System"; "2. The Gikuyu System of Land Tenure"; "3. Economic Life"; "4. Industries," and so on—all these construct an image of the Gikuyu as a perfectly well-integrated society. As such, Carolyn Martin Shaw notes, Kenyatta's political treatise has often been subsequently read as a transparently simple text, mined only for its ethnographic "data."[118] To read it as such, however, is clearly to miss its import, which among other things is, as Simon Gikandi has suggested, to engage in a counterdiscourse of nationalism.[119] This counterdiscourse, Gikandi rightly points out, is heavily implicated in, and often derivative of, the colonial discourse it critiques. While borrowing categories from the discourses of colonialism, nationalist rhetoric such as Kenyatta's attempts to subvert these discourses, not so much by presenting an alternative picture of how things really were but how things could have been. In this sense Kenyatta's discourse of nationalism, too, is an "invented" discourse of a mythical past and oftentimes utopian future, and it may well be read, as Simon Gikandi suggests, as one of the founding texts of the literary tradition of the Kenyan

---

117. Kenyatta's project of countering the prejudices of colonialist discourse, however, was bound to remain unsuccessful, given the vested interests of the colonial project. As an example of precisely such prejudice, consider the following quotation from a book review of *Facing Mount Kenya:* "In the chapter on Religion the introduction of Kikuyu texts as subjects for discussion should not be taken as indicating the existence of a formal creed or set of definitions. To the reviewer they suggest efforts of the author himself to express what he conceives to be the beliefs of his people. The Kikuyu in general are singularly unable to give any coherent or reasoned account of tribal beliefs and customs" (A. R. Barlow, review of *Facing Mount Kenya, Africa* [1939]: 114).

118. Carolyn Martin Shaw, *Colonial Inscriptions: Race, Sex, and Class in Kenya* (Minneapolis: University of Minnesota Press, 1995), 131.

119. Gikandi, "On Language, Power, and National Identity: The Project of African Literature" (paper presented at the Language and Identity in Africa Symposium, Program of African Studies, Northwestern University, 29–30 April 1989).

"national romance" later to be developed by writers such as Ngũgĩ wa Thiong'o.

If Gikandi's provocative reading of Kenyatta's text suggests that the conventional reading of *Facing Mount Kenya* as no more than a "description of Gikuyu culture" is limited,[120] if not misguided, then we should remember that the political valence of the book was certainly not lost on its original audience. A 1939 review of the book written, interestingly enough, by one of Kenyatta's former mission school teachers suggests, for instance, that "the facility with which Kenyatta, the ethnographer, merges into Kenyatta, the general secretary of the Kikuyu Central Association, makes it difficult to decide whether his book should be viewed primarily as a scientific study or as a vehicle for propaganda."[121] Yet another reviewer, Dr. H. R. A. Philip, wrote in 1938: "The author glories in shame and parades that which is indecent, and this in the name of science. How contrary to the Spirit of true Christianity. . . . here surely is an aspect of the conflict with the 'unfruitful works of darkness' that the young Kikuyu Church is engaged in."[122]

Anticipating the anger that the book would generate in the colonial community both at home and in Kenya, Malinowski wrote an introduction to the book in which he praised it for its scholarship and objectivity.[123] Kenyatta, Malinowski suggested in this introduction, wrote to a large extent without "any passion or feeling,"[124] and if indeed he did exhibit a bias, then it was not African bias, but rather a European one. Although many commentators have read this statement of Malinowksi's to be an indictment of Kenyatta's methodological Eurocentrism, I would argue that it is instead yet another instance of Malinowski's rhetorical skill. For what better way to soften Kenyatta's unsympathetic reader than to seduce him with the promise of "objectivity," lack of undue African passion, and European bias on the part of Kenyatta? What better way to assure Kenyatta a readership than to suggest that he had indeed ac-

120. Shaw, *Colonial Inscriptions*, 131.

121. Barlow, review of *Facing Mount Kenya*, 115.

122. Philip, *Kikuyu News*, September 1938, 175–76, quoted in *The Myth of "Mau Mau": Nationalism in Kenya* ed. Carl G. Rosberg Jr. and John Nottingham (New York: Meridian Books, 1966), 134.

123. This claim of scholarship and objectivity was often echoed by Kenyatta's supporters. One such supporter was C. L. R. James, who wrote in his review of the book that "even an unscientific reader can see the scrupulously scientific approach, the order, the method, the objectivity" ("The Voice of Africa," *International African Opinion* 1.2 [August 1938], 3).

124. Bronislaw Malinowski, introduction to *Facing Mount Kenya*, by Jomo Kenyatta (New York: Vintage, 1965), x.

complished a major feat by suppressing his justified anger in the interests of science? And what better political tribute than to outline, as does Malinowski, the reasons for such justified anger on the part of Africans such as Kenyatta?[125]

To be sure, no one was fooled when the book first appeared into thinking that Kenyatta's was a dispassionate voice or one devoid of feelings.[126] Rather, the book was read as politically motivated through and through even to the point at which it was brought up in Kenyatta's Mau Mau trial much later in the 1950s. Here, in the case of the "Queen against Kenyatta and Others" the question of Kenyatta's credibility was raised vis-à-vis some of the pronouncements in the book. Thus, records Montagu Slater, "a passage was read from *Facing Mount Kenya* criticizing European oath rituals such as 'kissing the Bible and raising hands' as meaningless to Africans. (Kenyatta's) answer was he was writing of non-Christian Africans."[127] Further, Kenyatta was questioned about his own practices of polygamy and whether he subscribed to the views of the Gikuyu that he had undertaken to describe.[128] What is ironic about the

125. Thus Malinowski launches a critique of the disintegration of society, Western as well as African, during the onslaught of modernity. "For, to quote William James, 'Progress is a terrible thing.' It is terrible to those of us who half a century ago were born into a world of peace and order; who cherished legitimate hopes of stability and gradual development; and who now have to live through the dishonesty and immorality of the very historical happenings. I refer to the events of the last few years which seem to demonstrate that Might is Right; that bluff, impudence, and aggression succeed where a decent readiness to co-operate has failed" (Malinowski, Introduction, ix).
126. Statements such as the following on Kenyatta's part would not have left any doubt as to the politics of his ethnography among its readers: "Instead of advancing 'towards a higher intellectual, moral and economic level,' the African has been reduced to a state of serfdom; his initiative in social, economic and political structure has been denied, his spirit of manhood has been killed and he has been subjected to the most inferior position in human society. If he dares to express his opinion on any point, other than what is dictated to him, he is shouted at and black-listed as an 'agitator.' The tribal democratic institutions which were the boast of this country, and the proof of tribal good sense, have been suppressed. Oppressive laws and ordinances, which alone engross the monopoly of thought, of will, and of judgment, have been imposed on the African people" (*Facing Mount Kenya,* 190); "The harmony and stability of the African's mode of life in political, social, religious and economic organisations, was based on the land which was, and still is, the soul of the people. The first step which the European civilising missions took to disorganise the Africans in order to exploit and oppress them, especially in South and East Africa, was to take away the best African lands. This is one of the evils of European civilisation that has found its way to the great African continent, and one which past, present and future generations will never forget" (204–5).
127. Montagu Slater, *The Trial of Jomo Kenyatta* (London: Secker and Warburg, 1955), 161.
128. "Q: Looking back in it does it still represent your views on the Kikuyu tribe? A: The book cannot necessarily be a guide during my whole life. Q: Have you changed your opinions since then? A: The book is not my opinion as such—but it represents the habits and customs of the Kikuyu people. . . . Q: Do you practice polygamy? (Counsel for Defence objects that polygamy is not one

prosecution's questioning in this trial is that in an otherwise detailed interrogation of Kenyatta intended to demonstrate his alleged relationship with the violence of the Mau Mau, there is a curious absence of a discussion of a key moment in his ethnography.

This key moment, which seems to have drawn very little subsequent commentary, is the moment of a fable. Before taking a look at this narrative moment, however, it is necessary to understand its location in the ethnography. The fable appears toward the end of Kenyatta's chapter titled "The Gikuyu System of Land Tenure." Here, Kenyatta spends a considerable amount of energy detailing eight different kinds of traditional property rights through which land can be owned and inherited. The chapter is indeed the political backbone of the entire treatise, since its point is to counter the British invention of the Gikuyu as having communal land rights. The invention of land rights as "communal" allowed the British to acquire Gikuyu lands without adequate compensation, even though the lands they were acquiring were, by principles of Gikuyu land tenure, the private property of individuals. The establishment of land tenure as based on a system of *private* property was therefore the crux of the Gikuyu-British conflict, and Kenyatta's chapter was one of the major articulations of the Gikuyu position on the matter.[129] It is toward the end of this politically charged chapter, then, that Kenyatta tells the story of the friendship between the elephant and the man.

"Once upon a time," the story goes, "an elephant made a friendship with a man."[130] One day there was a heavy thunderstorm, and the man took shelter in his hut while the elephant begged him to let him put in his trunk so that he may shelter it. The narrative plot henceforth would be perfectly familiar to any colonized Gikuyu: when the man agrees to share the hut with the elephant, he soon finds that the elephant has inched all the way in, and the man himself is

of the charges and is overruled) Q: Do you practice polygamy? A: Yes, but I do not call it polygamy" (quoted in Slater, *Trial of Jomo Kenyatta*, 159–60).

129. There is an irony here that is not often noted. White settlers in Kenya and other antagonists of Kenyatta often attempted to discredit him by calling attention to his visits to Moscow and Siberia and suggesting that Kenyatta was unduly influenced by the "Communists." Although the influence of Communism on Kenyatta, and particularly on the pan-Africanist movement emergent among his associates in Britain, is certainly not negligible, it is nevertheless the case that in actuality the charges here are being reversed. In other words, with respect to the issue of land rights, Kenyatta is the one arguing for the prevalence and importance of "private" ownership, and he is accusing the British precisely of a "communist" ideology that reads precolonial Africa as devoid of any sense of private property.

130. Kenyatta, *Facing Mount Kenya*, 47.

left out in the open. The two friends have an argument, and soon enough their altercation reaches the ears of the king of the jungle, Mr. Lion. Mr. Lion arrives on the scene, intending to resolve the matter, but the elephant, a high minister in the jungle kingdom, assures the king that it is only a minor quibble, and that he can rest assured of peace. Mr. Lion orders the establishment of an Imperial Commission to look into the matter and turning to the man remarks: "You have done well by establishing friendship with my people, especially with the elephant who is one of my honorable ministers of state. Do not grumble any more, your hut is not lost to you. Wait until the sitting of my Imperial Commission, and there you will be given plenty of opportunity to state your case" (48). Pleased by the promise of a fair judgment, the man awaits the commission, only to find that the elephant has appointed all his friends (Mr. Rhinoceros, Mr. Buffalo, Mr. Fox, Mr. Alligator, etc.) to sit on the commission. The man protests and "ask(s) if it was not necessary to include in the Commission a member from his side. But he (is) told that it (is) impossible, since no one from his side (is) well enough educated to understand the intricacy of jungle law. Further, . . . as they were gentlemen chosen by God to look after the interests of races less adequately endowed with teeth and claws, he might rest assured that they would investigate the matter with the greatest care and report impartially" (49).

As is to be expected in this loaded colonial allegory, the commission not only finds in the elephant's favor, but individual members also follow suit and occupy every new hut that the man builds for himself. Finally, angered by the workings of the elephant and his friends, the man decides to take his revenge. Early one morning, when the huts occupied by the jungle lords are already undergoing decay, the man goes out and builds a much larger hut. Sure enough, the jungle lords all come over to occupy the hut, but while in it, each one begins to argue for his own right to the hut. "While they were all embroiled together," writes Kenyatta, "the man set the hut on fire and burnt it to the ground, jungle lords and all. Then he went home, saying: 'Peace is costly, but it's worth the expense,' and lived happily ever after" (51).

Literally the final sentiment in this highly significant chapter, it is surprising that the story received little attention in Kenyatta's cross-examination. For although the story itself cannot of course be taken as any indication of Kenyatta's own involvement with the Mau Mau, it does seem to suggest that violence may be the only option available to the disenfranchised Gikuyu. But if such a case could have been made by the lawyers for the prosecution, then an attentive defense counsel could well have reminded the court that Kenyatta had already testified that while he had faithfully recorded the "habits and customs" of his people in his ethnography, it could not be taken to be an accurate reflection of his own personal beliefs.[131]

This imaginary court exchange returns us then to some of the questions with which we began our reading of Kenyatta. How are the political positions of the "native" anthropologist interpellated in his text? Can such an anthropologist selectively retain a skeptical distance from some of the values of his own culture, even while he describes them on their own terms? Or is such a writerly position necessarily one of cultural conservatism? The tensions surrounding these issues are nowhere greater than in Kenyatta's discussion of clitoridectomy, to which we now turn.

The sixth chapter of Kenyatta's book, although titled "Initiation of Boys and Girls," is almost exclusively devoted to an account of clitoridectomy and its cultural history. If male initiation is backgrounded in this chapter, it is clearly because of the centrality of clitoridectomy in Kenyan political history at the time of Kenyatta's writing. Briefly put, the history involved the continued attempts of the missionaries to put an end to the practice and the continued resistance to such change on the part of some of the Gikuyu. Although the tensions involved precipitated throughout the 1920s, it was in the late 1920s and early 1930s that the tensions escalated. Kenyatta presents an outline of this history and suggests that at this time "children of those who did not denounce the custom"—the wording here is important—"were debarred from attending missionary schools."[132] Furthermore, the missionaries decreed that only those who "denounced the custom" (126) would be entitled to teach in missionary schools. Many Gikuyu protested by leaving the mission churches and by calling for the formation of independent schools.

Referring to this chapter in Kenyatta's book, Carolyn Martin Shaw claims that although Kenyatta had early on in life been "pro-choice" on matters of clitoridectomy, he was soon to change his position. "It was not until he was introduced to functionalism that he so proudly heralded clitoridectomy as the underpinning of Kikuyu society. Before both politics and functionalism began to work on him," writes Shaw, "Kenyatta had said that he was personally opposed to clitoridectomy, but also against the government and missionaries using threats and force to abolish the practice."[133] Although I agree with the

---

131. See footnote 128.
132. Kenyatta, *Facing Mount Kenya*, 125.
133. Shaw, *Colonial Inscriptions*, 64.

great majority of Shaw's critique of the gender blindness of Kenyatta, I wonder whether this particular formulation does not grant too much agency to functionalism itself. If Kenyatta seems to present clitoridectomy in a favorable light in this chapter, surely it has more to do with his own resistance to colonial intervention of any kind than to do with a functionalist disposition?[134] And furthermore, to return to the question with which we began this discussion, can we absolutely attribute to Kenyatta himself the point of view that he attributes to the Gikuyu? Surely Kenyatta's account is more a response to the "threats and force" used by the government and missionaries to abolish the practice than a reflection of any personal conviction of the benefits of the practice?

Jeremy Murray-Brown, Kenyatta's biographer, notes the following exchange between a Scotsman and Kenyatta regarding the issue of clitoridectomy:

(Q:) "I gather that, speaking generally, you say that mutilation is a bad thing. Then if it is a bad thing, why should not the Church do its best to get it abolished by every means in their power? — that is why the Church exists."

(A:) "I put it in this way, to sum it up in a nutshell, their way of looking at it is that the way of gradual conviction is to be preferred to that of a direct attack by means of spear and shield."[135]

Furthermore, Murray-Brown notes that when Kenyatta was confronted with the issue of the colonial legislation of clitoridectomy, he sent a statement to the colonial office:

I would respectfully draw your attention to the fact that any attempt to coerce my people by "force majeure" will have the very opposite of the desired effect as it causes my people to attach attenuated importance to the maintenance of this custom.[136]

What these statements suggest is that Kenyatta was aware that the crisis over clitoridectomy and indeed its deployment by the KCA and the Gikuyu as a ral-

134. Certainly the functionalist orientation would have led Kenyatta to put his faith in cultural autonomy, but it is the political project afforded by the lived experience of colonialism itself rather than the theoretical paradigm that seems to me to be the ultimate driving force behind Kenyatta.
135. Jeremy Murray-Brown, Kenyatta (New York: E. P. Dutton, 1973), 164.
136. Ibid., 140.

lying cry against the British was in fact the result not of a spontaneous resurgence of Gikuyu tradition but rather a direct result of British repression. Take away the repression, allow for indigenous autonomy, and the practice, Kenyatta seemed to believe, would disappear. In this sense, the increased cultural value of clitoridectomy was ironically not the pure product of the Gikuyu but rather the product of British intervention. Much of this sense, I argue, remained with Kenyatta even during the writing of his ethnography, and rather than seeing him as being blinded by functionalism into defending clitoridectomy, I see him as offering a cultural explanation of the practice from the point of view of the Gikuyu while offering a historical critique of its colonial conditions of possibility.[137] In other words, if there is a shift in emphasis between the earlier Kenyatta and the Kenyatta of *Facing Mount Kenya*, then I would argue that this shift is not one between a pro-choice position and one that embraced clitoridectomy. Rather, it is a shift of emphasis between a "pro-choice" position on an individual level ("each woman should decide the matter for herself") to a "pro-choice" position on a collective level ("each culture should decide such matters for itself").

And yet to recognize this, of course, is also to recognize the danger inherent in any move made from the level of the individual to the level of the collective. For in the shift in emphasis there is also the possibility of the loss of an individual's control over her own destiny. It is in this sense that a position, radical vis-à-vis the colonizer, can turn itself against individual members of the community. For in such a situation, a woman, say, who chooses not to participate in the custom, is no more just the social outcast or rebel of yesterday, but indeed a traitor to the community and its emergent nationalist sensibility. A local practice becomes appropriated into a newly defined semiotic order, gains momentum, and threatens to control ever more than before the lives of those associated with it. In many cases, history has shown us, the lives affected most by the inventions of such nationalist traditions are those of women, and it is here that nationalist discourses, functionalist or otherwise, often expose their limitations. We turn in our next chapter to a consideration of precisely such an invention.

---

137. To further make my claim that Kenyatta was never comfortable with clitoridectomy itself as a legitimate cause for agitation, we may note that in an otherwise complete historical account of Gikuyu grievances and demands that Kenyatta wrote in 1946, clitoridectomy itself does not make even a minor appearance. (In other words, Kenyatta was specifically excluding the right to practice clitoridectomy from Gikuyu demands). See Kenyatta, *Kenya*.

CHAPTER 3

Colonial Self-Fashioning and the Production of History

Institutional Knowledges and Disciplinary Truths

In the last chapter, I presented a case for the reevaluation of the political critique of cultural anthropology based on a reading of three specific anthropologists. My argument was that although the postcolonial critique of anthropology was an important moment in coming to terms with an often paternalist discipline, a closer look at the lives and motivations of individual anthropologists warrants a revised and more tempered recasting of the discipline. To be sure, my examples were chosen to portray very specific aspects of dimensions of the discipline—I chose to look at Edwin Smith not only because he was one of the most cited legitimators of the discipline but also because he most saliently portrayed the necessary, and perhaps in the final analysis necessarily flawed, humanism on which the anthropological project was based. I chose Malinowski not only because he is by all accounts the father of functionalist anthropology but also because a consideration of his own subjectivity, professional positioning, and rhetorical savvy give lie to any critique that assumes epistemological naïveté on the part of colonial anthropologists. Finally, I chose Kenyatta not only because he was one of the first Africans to explicitly use the discourse of functional anthropology in his project of nationalism but also because in doing so he effectively challenged both the existing colonial archive on the Gikuyu as well as the postcolonial assumption that nothing good can come of anthropology.

I want to emphasize that although other examples might well be (and perhaps ought to be) mustered to present anthropology in colonial Africa in a different light—perhaps even in the most negative light—it is nevertheless by way of examples that the discussion of colonial anthropology will best proceed. It is in fact the assumption of a foundational politics that has most driven the radical critique of the discipline, and as I suggested in the first chapter on the discourses of rationality, this assumption is problematic. The politics of a discipline, episteme, or a theory are to be read in their local negotiations and contingent practices. This is where we must part with the poststructural refusal of the role of the human subject. It is human subjects who provide the point of contact between disciplinary demands on the one hand and ethical, political, and social demands on the other. And it is only by paying careful attention to how such human subjects negotiate these multiple demands that any sense of a political practice may be maintained. If I seem to have played my cards such that anthropology has emerged in my account in a manner more sympathetic than palatable to some of us, I have done so merely to provide the possibility of a narrative counter to the one with which we are more familiar. But my ultimate stake is not rescuing anthropology from the critics—it is rather to assert that whatever we may want to make of the politics of anthropology, we must read it at the various specific moments at which it entered the lives of subjects on both side of the colonial divide. It is only if we do so that we can recognize that no discipline is all-consuming and no episteme impervious to the threat of its unthought.

With such an emphasis on the importance of the subject, I turn now to a consideration of the Tiv historian Akiga Sai. My choice of Akiga is, again, a calculated one, and thus I do not present him as a "representative" African colonial subject. Indeed, Akiga is far from representative; if anything, by virtue of his social position in his own society, he is rather privileged. I read him, then, as one voice among several others that is available to us today and that has the virtue of richly articulating the dynamics of indigenous beliefs about religion, gender, politics, and the monetary economy. These articulations powerfully render Akiga's text as one of the more important dangerous supplements of the colonial archive. Reading his text, we get a fresh perspective not only on how some African subjects such as Akiga Sai negotiated colonial modernity but also of the various "otherings" that were necessitated by such self-fashionings.

If anything could remotely resemble a large factory for the production of knowledge about Africa in the anglophone colonial world, the most likely candidate would be the International Institute of African Languages and Cultures set up in London in 1926. With Lord Lugard as its chair, and Diedrich Westermann and Henri Labouret as its directors, the institute played a major role in setting the agendas for Africanist research and also in the dissemination of Africanist knowledge. In the original charter presented in the first issue of the institute's journal *Africa,* Lugard claimed that the institute would be "an entirely non-political body."[1] Nevertheless, it not only would be concerned with "scientific study" but also would aim "towards bringing about a closer association of scientific knowledge and research with practical affairs." The institute's task would be to "discover how the investigations undertaken by scientific workers may be made available for the solution of pressing questions that [were] the concern of all those who, as administrators, educators, health and welfare workers, or traders, [were] working for the good of Africa." To enable such a project, Lugard established several avenues for collaborations, discussions, and meetings between members of the institute and colonial officers, educators, missionaries, and so on, but more importantly for our purposes here, he sanctioned two series of publications—"one under the general title of African Studies and the second under the general title of African Documents." "In the first series," Lugard wrote, "will be included studies by experts, as these become available, dealing with the range of subjects which fall within the purview of the Institute. The second series will consist of brochures or texts written or dictated by Africans, preferably in their own language and translated into a European language. Such texts may include stories, songs, dramas, riddles, proverbs, historical and other traditions, descriptions of social institutions and customs, myths and religion in its every aspect" (4).

It is of course easy for us today to read Lugard's agenda and be annoyed by some of its assumptions. For instance, leaving alone all the ramifications of "the good of Africa," we may ask how Lugard could claim almost in the same breath that the institute was "nonpolitical" and also interested in becoming an ally of colonial agents. What could "political" have meant to Lugard if this was "nonpolitical" activity? Furthermore, what were the implications of the two-tiered system of publications initiated by the institute? Note that the "experts" on Africanist knowledge in this scenario were all in fact white Europeans with perhaps an occasional American, and no Africans could be experts even if the

1. Frederick Lugard, "The International Institute of African Languages and Cultures," *Africa* 1.1 (1928): 4.

object of study was their own culture. The works of Africans would only be classified as "documents" produced in the form of brochures or texts, whereas the works of the "experts" would be "African studies." And, as is to be expected in such a hierarchized system, the research priorities would lie in the scholarly studies while the publication and dissemination of the African documents would, Lugard writes, depend on "whether the funds at (the Institute's) disposal (would) permit of a venture of this nature" (4).

African, indigenous knowledge, then, is seen as supplementary, almost a coda, and indeed presented as such in the individual quarterly issues of the institute's journal for a good number of years. There, after the "scholarly" work that occupies the first couple of hundred pages, is found a two- or three-page section called "The Voice of Africa." Here the native gets to speak, but usually only sings for us, tells us a few stories about hares and lions, or entertains us with a few words of proverbial wisdom. The "Voice of Africa" is there mainly for our entertainment, a convenient break between the scholarly articles we have just read and the book reviews and bibliographies that are yet to come, whose function is to encourage us to open the doors of our studies and to go out and explore the vast terrain of African studies.

It is important never to forget this situation, not only because it speaks to the ways in which institutions authorize some people as opposed to others (and precisely *who* is privileged changes from time to time) but also because they effectively legitimate certain *kinds* of discourses as opposed to others. What we see here is not just an inability to conceive of Africans as scholars of their own cultures but also an inability to see discourses such as poetry, drama, and myths as themselves constituting a form of cultural study. At most, such discourses may be seen as useful raw material, data from the "native" perspective to complement the more "objective" perspective of scholarly histories, archaeologies, linguistic analyses, and so on. The possibility that these discourses may, in and of themselves, through a logic comprehensible within their *own* order, be able to speak to the everyday lives and concerns of not only the people who propagate them but also the outsiders who study them is a possibility that goes unrecognized and unexplored.

The text that will be of primary concern in this chapter is one that would have been part of Lugard's "African Documents" series had the series ever fully materialized. *Akiga's Story: The Tiv Tribe as Seen by One of Its Members* was published by the institute in collaboration with Oxford University Press and included a preface by one of the Institute's directors, Diedrich Westermann. The text was originally written around 1935 in Tiv by a man called Akiga, who, according to Rupert East, the translator of the text, "was the first of his tribe to come directly under European influence."[2] This is explained by the fact that the first Europeans to arrive in Tiv country were the missionaries of the Sudan United and Dutch Reformed Church who came to the village of Akiga's father, Sai, in May 1911. Sai was the senior elder of his clan, and after many discussions with the missionaries he allowed his son Akiga to be employed by them. Akiga, then, was one of the first to be converted to Christianity and to learn to write in Tiv. Akiga writes, "It was while I was wandering round through every part of Tivland, preaching the Gospel of Jesus Christ, and at the same time seeing and hearing the things of Tiv, that the idea of this 'History' took shape in my mind. So I began to ask, and to look, and to delve into everything concerning the Tiv people." And further, "It has been my constant prayer that God would help me to write this book, in order that the new generation of Tiv, which is beginning to learn this New Knowledge, should know the things of the fathers as well as those of the present generation. For everything that belongs to the Tiv is passing away, and the old people, who should tell us about these things, will soon all be dead. It makes me sad to think that our heritage is being lost, and that there will be none to remember it" (2).

Akiga's "story," then, is most resolutely a history, and one of its aims, as will become evident in our reading of it, is to be critical of colonial intervention. It does not take too much effort to hear, even in this short quotation, Akiga's ambivalence and resistance to the kinds of changes that he sees taking place around him. Akiga recognizes that the institution that he is so much a part of, and indeed so much a product of, the institution of the Church, is an important propagator of the "New Knowledge" that is effacing the old. Nevertheless, the irony that it is precisely the moment of evangelism that becomes the scene of his own history lesson does not escape him. Christianity gives with one hand what it takes with the other. And it is in the midst of this give-and-take that Akiga's subject position and his narratorial "self-fashioning" become worthy of study. Akiga must engage in a doublespeak in order to pass the test of "appropriateness" not only on the part of his community but also on the part of his Church mentors and his translator and editor, Rupert East. And furthermore, if this doublespeak must address all these various constituencies, then perhaps more importantly it must on occasion also address his own hybrid self. Thus if we detect occasionally contradictory assertions in Akiga's

---

2. Akiga Sai, *Akiga's Story: The Tiv Tribe as Seen by One of Its Members,* ed. and trans. Rupert East (London: Oxford University Press, 1939), 1.

text, we must read them not as lapses but rather as the efforts of a multiply marked subject attempting to appropriate these various strands into a workable and meaningful account of his own life.

If Akiga is constrained by the political and discursive demands of the colonial space in which he finds himself, Rupert East, it must be remarked, is also constrained. As a government officer responsible for the Education Bureau, he must also censor what may offend English readers and only translate those sections that are "relevant."[3] Working from within a discursive and ideological tradition in which the only reason for listening to the native voice is to attempt an understanding of a generic native "mentality" and "native point of view," East quite easily rejects from his translation most of the specifically "historical" accounts. He writes, "Akiga set out to write a History of the Tiv. He has not succeeded in this, because the Tiv, like most African tribes, have no history in our sense of the word. But he has given an account, from the native point of view, of the events of recent years, and particularly of the effects of contact with European culture. He has also achieved his main object of recording the dying traditions of his people for the benefit of posterity. The book must not be judged as an anthropological treatise, but as a contribution to the newly born African literature" (6).

Insisting that Akiga's text is neither a history nor an anthropology but closer to fiction, East participates in a denigration of Akiga's native voice in a manner analogous to Lugard. Were there any doubt as to the hierarchical nature of the distinction between these disciplines and the "newly born African literature" in which East places Akiga, one need only read East's qualifier, in a different context, on the potential of African languages in scholarly study. Introducing an essay titled "Imaginative African Literature" in the journal *Africa,* East writes, "It is unlikely for many years to come that it will be possible, or desirable to adapt African languages to the teaching of the more technical branches of knowledge, which *belong to a higher stage of education;* the following remarks, therefore, apply chiefly to pure literature."[4] It would be fair to say then that for East, Akiga's contribution, written in an African language, can only be that of a lower order of knowledge, nontechnical and, indeed, nontheoretical. Instead of recognizing Akiga's stylistic choice of incorporating dra-

---

3. East writes in his introduction: "But for obvious reasons it has been necessary to keep personalities out of the English version, and names of government officers have therefore been omitted, or replaced by the titles of their appointment" (Sai, *Akiga's Story,* 7).

4. Rupert East, "A First Essay in Imaginative African Literature," *Africa* (1936): 351; my emphasis.

matic events, proverbs, and rumors as integral tools of his own historical consciousness, East insists on reducing the text to "mere" literature.

If there is a blind paternalism in East's rhetoric, we will encounter more of the same in his extensive annotations and marginalia accompanying Akiga's text. If we are tempted to critique East, however, I would argue that the point of our critique should not be to blame East for being quite deaf to some of the explicit criticisms that Akiga provides, or for including sections of the original text that Akiga wanted left out from the translation, or for being excessively supportive of the practices and policies of the colonial administration. To blame him for these things would be radically ahistorical on our part—for, in many ways, just as Akiga is constrained in the forms of his critique, East too is an actor in a larger social structure that puts him under relative constraints.[5] To be sure, there is a great asymmetry in the play of social structure and individual agency (to return to a central problem in social theory) between that of a colonized Tiv subject and a colonial Education officer. But to be unwilling to recognize the constraints of social structure on colonial agents themselves is to grant them a limitless individual agency no more and no less false than the conversely completely passive, agencyless native subject of what we may call the pre-Scott era.[6] Retaining a healthy skepticism for East's editorial interven-

5. The notion of "*relative* constraint" is important in my analysis, since it productively points to the fact that the hierarchies of institutions play into the possibility of instigating change. Situated at the center of British anthropology, the relative constraints on Malinowski are minimal—he can move the discipline with him; situated as an officer relatively low in the colonial administrative hierarchy, the relative constraints on Rupert East are greater. Institutional (and discursive) change when individually directed seems often to come from above—from people who already have positions of authority and who bank on that credibility to instigate change. Resistance from below, which as I suggest in footnote 6 serves to put a check on domination from those with authority and power, only works effectively when it emerges as a collective project.

6. I refer here to the work of James Scott, whose *Weapons of the Weak* (New Haven: Yale University Press, 1985) and *Domination and the Arts of Resistance* (New Haven: Yale University Press, 1990) were among the most important theoretical contributions to the study of resistance. Scott posits the existence of a "hidden transcript" that exists in conjunction with the more "public transcript" traditionally studied by social theorists. The "hidden transcript" developed and enacted by the dominated is a mechanism for resistance and may erupt both in the form of a large-scale rebellion or in more controlled and limited everyday forms. Even though technically not the first (see, for instance, Michael Crowder, ed., *West African Resistance* [London: Hutchinson, 1971]; A. B. Davidson, "African Resistance and Rebellion against the Imposition of Colonial Rule," in *Emerging Themes of African History*, ed. T. O. Ranger [Nairobi: East African Publishing House, 1968], 177–88), Scott's work is important not only because it provides substance to theories of resistance but also because it goes further in inviting a consideration of the limitations on the agency of the oppressor. Such a move, it seems to me, has not yet been adequately made by students of colonialism.

tions, let us here be grateful to him for making available, despite his problematic choices of what to include and what to exclude, a text that was subsequently (to the best of my knowledge) never published in the original Tiv.[7] But we must nevertheless be willing to express our dissatisfaction with the stark distinctions that the European Africanist tradition, of which East was a part, made between fact and fiction, science and literature in the early twentieth century.

Ever since the publication of Hayden White's *Metahistory,* indeed ever since the Barthes of "Historical Discourse,"[8] the role of language and tropes in historical narration has been a prominent concern for historians and literary critics alike. The distinction between the "historical" and the "literary" is necessarily put in question once it is recognized that in every text we may read traces of its historical articulations but always through the mediation of the literary, that is, of language. Raymond Williams reminds us that at least until the fifteenth century, the English language did not necessarily distinguish between histories and stories. "In early English use, history and story (the alternative English form derived ultimately from the same root) were both applied to an account either of imaginary events or of events supposed to be true."[9] It appears that it is only with the growth of science as the dominant paradigm that history begins to acquire its objectivist face (but, of course, it keeps silent about the histories of non-European peoples) and continues its quest for progress and universal truths. In this moment of high modernity, then, history must represent itself as authoritative by recourse to its scientific visage. But if such an alliance is a relatively recent invention, like Foucault's Man, it too is now dying a sure death.[10] After two world wars signifying the "crises" of Western civilization, and after the emergence of alternative histories of "the people without history,"[11] Western historians are increasingly beginning to rethink the appropriateness and plausibility of providing objectively true, to-

---

The unspoken assumption of colonial critiques continues to be that the individual colonizer's agency is almost limitless. This rings false to any student of colonial biographies, memoirs, and other texts. Students of colonial and postcolonial studies should not allow such agency in the context of the colonizer to remain undertheorized.

7. Original Tiv manuscript is in Ibadan. Publication has been proposed but not yet materialized.

8. See Hayden White, *Metahistory: The Historical Imagination in Nineteenth Century Europe* (Baltimore: Johns Hopkins University Press, 1973); Roland Barthes, "Historical Discourse," in *Introduction to Structuralism,* ed. Michael Lane (New York: Basic Books, 1970), 145–55.

9. Raymond Wiliams, *Keywords* (London: Oxford University Press, 1976), 119.

10. Michel Foucault, *The Order of Things* (New York: Vintage, 1973), 303–87.

11. See Eric Wolf, *Europe and the People without History* (Berkeley: University of California, 1982).

tal accounts. If this tendency toward "partial truths" and "local knowledges" is a mark of emergent disciplinary knowledges in the contemporary West, it is in many ways a product of the extradisciplinary knowledges produced during the colonial encounter.[12]

My reading of Akiga's text is meant to be placed within this context of an emergent and as yet experimental historiography, a context that David William Cohen and E. S. Atieno Odhiambo call the "production of history."[13] A focus on the production of history is a focus on how historical knowledge is constructed, invoked, debated, utilized, trafficked, or withheld by various competing or colluding agents in specific sociohistorical contexts. By its very nature, this field of practice is polysemic, tentative, always hearkening elsewhere even when pronouncing its own local claims. In contrast to more traditional historiography, it is interested not so much in "what really happened" as in how various participants and observers experienced the happenings and shared those experiences. With respect to Africa it recognizes the fact that a great majority of these "experiences" were articulated outside the purview of the colonial and scholarly gaze and is therefore alert to resulting silences and absences. And in cases in which specific accounts were made, it attempts to be vigilant to bodies and spaces that were covered up or covered over by such accounts, whether they were those produced by the colonizers or the colonized. In its reading of "colonial self-fashioning" this emphasis on the production of history remains particularly alert to how colonized subjects, should they choose to share their opinions and experiences with the colonizers, must, in an unequal economy of knowledge, wrench their experiences into the discursive forms of the latter. For such subjects the production and dissemination of knowledge has meant, as V. Y. Mudimbe has suggested, working "within the 'intelligence' of the Same."[14] But this process of epistemic translation has not been a politically vacuous one—for it is precisely through the process of being

12. On "partial truths" and "local knowledges" see Clifford Geertz, *Local Knowledge: Further Essays in Interpretive Anthropology* (New York: Basic Books, 1983), 19–35. I have often thought that the idea of the "fragmentation" of subjects, the contingencies of beliefs, and the pragmatist usability of theoretical positions was the dominant "cultural moment" of the colonial encounter, not only on the part of the colonized but also of the colonizers. The "breakdown of grand narratives" was a feature of the colonized subject's life very much in the moment of the encounter of a Western modernity. But this "postmodern" condition *avant la lettre* was in many ways more troubling and painful than some of its more recent Western manifestations.

13. David William Cohen and E. S. Atieno Odhiambo, *Burying SM: The Politics of Knowledge and the Sociology of Power in Africa* (Portsmouth, N.H.: Heinemann, 1992).

14. V. Y. Mudimbe, *The Invention of Africa* (Bloomington: Indiana University Press, 1988), 43.

such translators that many colonial subjects found a way to distinguish them-selves from the "uneducated" natives. As Gayatri Spivak has suggested, in or-der to be heard at all, subaltern voices have had to play by the rules of the disci-plinary and institutional game, but in doing so they have also ceased to be "subaltern" in any meaningful way.[15] In coming to terms with these pro-cesses, this project shares the goals and efforts of fellow scholars such as the Comaroffs who attempt to study the "colonization of consciousness and the consciousness of colonization" at various sites of the Euro-African colonial encounter in South Africa.[16]

To pursue such a project, one may well pay attention to the multiple stories of the colonial encounter that we can discern in Akiga's text. I begin with an event described in that text that provides us with ways to think about some of the stakes involved in maintaining sharp distinctions between fact and fiction, truth and lie, reality and illusion. This event is doubly important in our proj-ect, first for its presentation of the Anglo-Tiv colonial encounter, and second for its coded critique of Western historical discourse and the latters' ideal of objectivity. It is a key moment in Akiga's text, not only because it attempts to record an important moment in the colonial history of the Tiv but also be-cause, by foregrounding the essentially contested nature of historical writing, it quietly corrodes Akiga's own authority as a writer of an authoritative na-tionalist history.

On Truth and Lie in a Colonial Sense

There is a section in Akiga's text that tells the story of two brothers, Saama and Oralai. One day, when Saama was returning to his own village from Akwana, he decided to rest for the night in the village of Ibumun. During the night he passed away, and his brother Oralai was called to come and bury him. Akiga's text reads as follows:

> After Oralai had buried him, word was brought to Tordwem that it was he who had killed his brother Saama.[17] When Tordwem heard this, he sent a

15. See Gayatri Spivak, "Can the Subaltern Speak?," in *Marxism and the Interpretation of Cultures*, ed. Cary Nelson and Lawrence Grossberg (Urbana: University of Illinois Press, 1988), 271–313.

16. Jean Comaroff and John Comaroff, *Of Revelation and Revolution: Christianity, Colonialism, and Consciousness in South Africa*, vol. 1 (Chicago: University of Chicago Press, 1991), xi.

17. Tordwem is the chief of the clan. The accusation here is that Oralai has killed his brother by re-course to *tsav*, which in this context can be likened to witchcraft. Tsav, according to the Tiv, is a

policeman to seize Oralai and bring him to his village. Tordwem and the elders asked Oralai why he had killed his brother. Oralai protested that he had not killed his brother, and that his accusers were lying. He said, "I am much distressed by the death of my brother, and feel his loss deeply. Why do you add to my grief? There were only two of us, and why should I kill Saama, to be left alone in the world?" Tordwem and the elders told him not to tell deliberate lies. But if he persisted in denying that he was guilty, they said that Agishi, his section head, should go with him and a policeman to open up the grave. For if it were indeed Oralai who had killed his brother, the corpse would not be there; but if he had not killed him, they would find the body in the grave. . . .

So Chief Agishi set out with the policeman and the *ugwana*,[18] and Oralai, who was accused of killing his brother. When they arrived at the grave they stood round it in a circle, while some one took a hoe and opened it up. When they had opened it they saw the dead man, Saama, inside, as plain as could be, and quite untouched. "You see?" asked Oralai. "Is this not Saama lying in the grave?" When he said this, Agishi slapped him across the mouth. "Don't tell lies!" he said. "Saama is not in the grave." "Good Heavens!" cried Oralai. "You can all see Saama as well as I can." The policeman and the *ugwana* started to beat Oralai, telling him to stop lying, and filled in the grave again with the body inside. They brought Oralai bound before Tordwem. Tordwem asked them what they had seen, and they all replied with one voice that Saama was not in the grave. Thereupon, since Oralai again asserted that he was in the grave, and they strongly affirmed that he was not, Tordwem sent some more of the elders to go back with them, and open up the grave again.

So they rebound Oralai, and set off. They again dug up the grave and saw Saama in it, and Oralai again said, "You see? There is Saama in the grave." But they replied, "Don't talk nonsense. You're a confirmed liar. We do not see Saama in the grave." At this Oralai's heart began to fail him. They came back to Tordwem, and he asked them, "What did you see this

---

physical growth located around the human heart that gives a human being power over others. Tsav can be of both good and bad kinds, but it is clearly the bad tsav that leads to a murder. The practitioners of tsav-connected killings are the *mbatsav*, who are said to kill clan members and resuscitate their own power by eating their flesh. The actual existence or lack thereof of such practices is a question at the heart of the event extracted here.

18. Elsewhere Akiga refers to the *ugwana* as a kind of local mafia employed by the police to carry out their violent deeds.

time?" They said, "Saama is not in his grave." When Oralai made as though he would contradict they all shouted him down, saying that he was willfully lying. So he admitted that Saama was not in the grave. The chief asked him whether it was he who had killed him, and he said "Yes." Tordwem then asked him for what purpose he had killed him, and he answered that he had killed him to set right an *imborivungu*.[19] The chief said, "Who else was with you when you killed him?" He said that beside himself there was an older man called Agbega. So Tordwen told his scribe to write down, "Oralai has killed his brother Saama, assisted by Agbega." When this had been done they told Oralai, "Since the scribe has put it in writing the matter is closed. Wherever you go, from now on you must say exactly these words and no others, namely that it was you and Agbega who killed Saama to set right an *imborivungu*. If you say anything different from what has been written in the book the white man will not spare you, for the written word cannot lie."[20]

The story does not end there. Agbega is brought in for questioning, and he denies having anything to do with the "murder." But his own son Dauda alleges that he saw his father and Oralai carrying Saama's flesh on the night of the murder. Agbega, realizing that he cannot prove his innocence, agrees to lead the policemen to his hut where he says he has kept the imborivungu. He enters the hut alone, the police waiting outside, and stabs himself with an arrow. His dying words are "Agishi, come, take me and bury me. Dauda, my son, has killed me. May he live happily." Thereupon the general consensus is: "Now there is no doubt that he was guilty. He was afraid that the white man would kill him, so he killed himself instead" (287).

I tell this rather long story not just because it is the stuff of which good drama is made but more importantly because it allows us to get to the heart of several issues that arise when we study the past. What do we make of this story? And, more importantly, what did the various participants and observers associated with the event make of it?

The story occurs in Akiga's text in a discussion of *tsav*, which according to Tiv tradition is an actual physical growth around the human heart. Tsav is what gives a person power over others, and although it need not necessarily be

---

19. This is a human bone, which as a part of the paraphernalia of the mbatsav is said to have ritualistic powers and is used to "set the land right."

20. Sai, *Akiga's Story*, 284–86.

a negative force, it may well be used to cause harm to others.[21] Every Tiv death is associated with tsav either through the volition of another possessor of tsav (one of the *mbatsav*) or by the violation of a taboo associated with tsav by the victim himself. This is rooted in the Tiv belief that although the cause of death may be natural, it must be willed by a supernatural force.[22] In the case of a death through the volition of another (as is the accusation made against Ora-lai), the belief is that the mbatsav responsible for the death gather together after the burial and exhume the body so that they can "eat the flesh" and thereby strengthen their tsav.[23] Thus Saama's grave is opened up to determine whether or not he was killed by the volition of another (in this case Oralai and Agbega) or whether instead he died because he was himself a possessor of tsav who had violated a taboo.

If we are to follow the narratorial voice of Akiga, then it is clear that the story is about the fabrication of a nonevent, that of one brother killing another by means of tsav. Since, according to Akiga, Saama's body is very much in the grave, we could read it as a story of how the written word can indeed lie, and how it can, through force and perseverance, claim to be true. But surely this narrative is only an exaggerated example of Nietzsche's famous dictum that "Truths are illusions which we have forgotten are illusions"?[24] For in the most direct way, our story is precisely about the creation of a "truth" that is given legitimation ultimately, in one instance, by the task of writing and in another by death—or, rather, suicide. Thus the Derrideans among us might say that ironically, truth resides here, not at the moment of presence (i.e., "I was there and I saw the body" or "I was there and the body was gone") but rather in its dangerous supplement, writing and death. Once written, the chief tells Ora-lai, he cannot contradict the testimony—for the written word cannot lie; suicide, bringing the final closure on the life of the accused, becomes the surest sign of guilt.

21. I am aware of the abuses of the "ethnographic present" in anthropological writings. In my paraphrase of Akiga's text I have chosen to retain his tense here, but the historical changes associated with tsav will shortly become evident in my analysis.

22. Thus, for instance, Akiga explains: "A man may be shot in the chest, and the bullet enter the heart, but if the *mbatsav* have not already killed him by night, and decreed that he shall afterwards be killed by a bullet from a gun, he will not die" (Sai, *Akiga's Story,* 251).

23. There is no evidence available that suggests that cannibalism was practiced among the Tiv. It may be more appropriate to read this as a symbolic gesture rather than a literal one.

24. Friedrich Nietzsche, "On Truth and Lie in a Nonmoral Sense," in *Philosophy and Truth: Selections from Nietzsche's Notebooks of the Early 1870's,* ed. and trans. Daniel Breazeale, Atlantic Highlands, NJ: Humanities Press, 1979), 84.

The force of the written word, and the Tiv association of writing with the white colonizer, is a recurrent motif in Akiga's story. For instance, early on in his treatise Akiga describes the difficulty of interviewing Tiv elders with a goal toward transcribing folklore and other traditions. The elders, Akiga suggests, are suspicious of any attempts at such transcription, since written knowledge itself is seen to be of value only to the white colonizers and not to the people themselves. Given the fact that the white people are most definitely among the Tiv only for a temporary stay, why share this knowledge with them?[25] Further, such openness, the elders believe, can only lead to colonial interference with native practices. "Others think," writes Akiga, "when you ask them something and they see you write it down, that you are making a report to give to a government official, who will increase their tax."[26] Later on in the text, when Akiga describes the functioning of the native court system, it becomes all the more clear why the elders are suspicious of writing. In the early days of colonial administration, Akiga writes, the British district officer required the Tiv staff-chiefs to keep a tally of the cases they tried in the native tribunals (393–97). Under this system, the chiefs did little legal work and left it to the local policemen and other subordinates to handle the disputes. The policemen took it upon themselves to pass judgment and indulged in a great deal of sexual and economic exploitation. Since sticks were used as tallies, an exaggerated number of sticks could be sent to the British as evidence of a lot of activity in the native tribunals. The British, we are told, later substituted money for the sticks, and since money began to be used as a tally, it created the possibilities of income generation. At this stage, the chiefs became involved, for now they saw a potential to extract money from the people under the guise of following the orders of the colonial administration. Akiga writes that when the British officers came to learn of the massive extraction of money, they substituted, for the money, scribes who were to record the proceedings of the cases and pass them on to the district officers. The chief and the elders of the tribunal council were now held in check by the predominantly younger scribes. "One would say to the chief: 'I know everything about writing. If you try any tricks with me, I shall write a letter to the white man, and he will depose you at once'" (394). In such a context in which the young scribe, "who knew all about writing, and even spoke the white man's language," became "the European's own man" threatening the traditional authority of the elders (394), it is no surprise

25. Note the implicit nationalist aspiration here.
26. Sai, *Akiga's Story*, 3.

that the elders viewed the power and authority of writing with suspicion and dismay.[27]

But perhaps the compelling link between this last writing scene and the one that records Oralai's guilt is not so much their common location in the colonially sanctioned native jurisprudence as it is the manner in which they so clearly give lie to the notion that the written word cannot lie. When the scribe threatens to write a letter to the white man if things don't go quite according to his tastes, it is clear that he need not traffic only in "truth" to do so. In Oralai's story, methods of ascertaining truth-value such as repeatable observations[28] "confirming" Oralai to be a liar (see passage above) do not necessarily lead to a "truer" perspective on Oralai's actions. What they do point to is not so much truth as they do power, not so much what really happened as what is authorized as the story of what really happened. If these stories are compelling allegories of the production of history, we need not read them simply as demoralizing stories of human interest compromising the truthfulness of historical accounts, but rather as invitations to always read "total" or "objective" accounts as partial or perspectival ones and "empirically verifiable truths" as always open to interpretation.

If truth is, as Akiga here reminds us, very much a product of our own situatedness, and if what has hitherto passed as truth is likewise a condition of what Foucault reads as both institutional ("exterior") and discursive ("interior") controls,[29] then it is all the more necessary to reimagine the conditions of the productions of what is read as "history." Terence Ranger, commenting on the "gravely flawed" knowledge produced by the colonial legacy of social science in Africa, writes:

> It seems to me that the historian has three things to do in this situation. The first is to study more deeply the ways in which the knowledge produced by colonial social science has been corrupted by the circumstances

27. When the white colonial officers heard about the potential abuses of the scribes, they encouraged the chiefs to use their traditional authority to impose sanctions against the younger scribes. On hearing this the elders said, "The white man is trying to fool us. He wants to entice us into beating the scribes, and then to depose us. Because the scribes and the white man are all one; the scribe can write, just like a European. We are not going to be so stupid as to lose our chiefdom like this!" (395–96).

28. I am thinking here of the scientific method and its reliance on repeatable results of experimentation as a criterion for truth-validity.

29. See Michel Foucault, "Discourse on Language," in *The Archaeology of Language*, trans. A. M. Sheridan (New York: Harper and Row, 1976), 215–37.

in which it developed. The second is to realize that once one has established the falsity of a proposition one cannot just dismiss it from further historical consideration. A good part of the historian's task in reconstructing twentieth-century African change is to record the multiple misunderstandings that worked. African innovations based on misapprehensions distort past reality but become part of present reality; so too do anthropological constructs. The third task—and obviously the most difficult—is to strive towards a more humane and less flawed knowledge, a truer picture of Africa.[30]

Ranger's proposal is suggestive because it underlines the role that narratives, whether historically accurate or not, actually begin to play in people's lives. Ranger warns us not to discard and ignore these stories but rather to attempt to understand how these "misapprehensions" of the past may have become part of the present reality. Ranger, it seems to me, is right on target here, except perhaps for the fact that he wishes to retain the historian's prerogative to be in search of a "truer" or more accurate picture of Africa. And incidentally, this "truer" picture, almost by definition, Ranger seems to imply, will be "more humane." So the final reflexive turn, the one in which the historian may turn the mirror on himself or herself, by questioning the possibility of a supposedly unperspectival "truth" itself, is never made. If it is indeed the case, as Ranger suggests, that people do not always live lives that are, shall we say, "historically correct," and if it is indeed the case that they tell stories to themselves about their pasts that are more useful than truthful, then, as historians, wouldn't nuancing the ideal of truth, indeed be the more "humane" way?

Consider in this context the 1952 essay by Laura Bohannan, "A Genealogical Charter," which in many ways is an essay ahead of its time.[31] After describing the importance of genealogical knowledge in the everyday life of a Tiv person, Bohannan explains that such knowledge is always contextually produced. There is no value placed by the Tiv in knowing a genealogical charter in the abstract, for the sake of just knowing it; it is rather to be utilized as a sanction and confirmation of particular relationships in the present. According to Bohannan, the Tiv do not doubt that it is possible to construct a *true* genealogy, and that as such it is something knowable. Yet this abstraction—the "true" ge-

30. Terence Ranger, "From Humanism to the Science of Man: Colonialism in Africa and the Understanding of Alien Societies," *Transactions of the Royal Historical Society*, 5th ser., 26 (1976): 137.
31. Laura Bohannan, "A Genealogical Charter," *Africa* 22.4 (1952): 301–15.

nealogy—is not based on the same criterion of validity used by Europeans: the criterion of internal consistency. The criterion used by the Tiv remains that of contingent usability. Thus even when writing threatens to create and regulate genealogical "truths" and "lies," Bohannan suggests that in moments of crisis, such as in the impending death of an elder man, competing genealogies continue to circulate.[32]

Is there a moral here for those of us interested in studying the past? Is it just that we should be skeptical not only of oral documents but also of written documents, and not read them as markers of objective truth? That would be a lesson far too banal, and in any case unnecessary, since no historian works so uncritically. Most historians are careful enough to look at many different sources, of various kinds—oral, written, archaeological—before they set about writing their histories. But what they may not do, and this is the important point, is question, along with Laura Bohannon, whether their criteria of validity, criteria such as those of "repeatability" (sometimes understood as "verifiability") and "internal consistency," are necessarily the appropriate criteria given the contingencies of the cultures they study.[33] Clearly, as Bohan-

---

32. Laura Bohannan writes: "For example, one man of great influence, a government chief, is dictating to his scribe the genealogy of the larger segments of Tiv and that of the smaller segments which are under his influence. He believes sincerely that his genealogy is correct; his influence and his fame for knowing things is so great that few dispute it. He himself says that he wants it written down because his son—a man of less influence—may not be believed when, after his father's death, he quotes that same genealogy. Certainly during a recent illness of the old man, alternate genealogies favouring other lines sprang up overnight. With his recovery they disappeared" ("Genealogical Charter," 314).

33. Another example that speaks to this is Paul Bohannan's translation of a chapter of Akiga's text left untranslated by Rupert East. In the notes on this chapter, "The 'Descent' of Tiv from Ibenda Hill," *Africa* 24.4 (1954): 295–310, Bohannan writes (and I quote extensively): "As translator of Akiga's chapter, I want to state that it is my opinion that the incidents and stories collated by Akiga do not have any essential correlation with chronology or what we would call history. Tiv elders, who tell these stories, do not make such correlations—the primary image is spatial, not chronological. Tiv do not, with any degree of agreement, correlate any particular story with any particular individual or lineage—or, by extension, any particular time. Were we to assign any sort of historical significance to these myths, we should be adding a dimension which is lacking for the men who tell them. The presence and disposition of Tiv are adequate to prove their truth to Tiv. They are not so to us. . . . I should, however, like to assure Akiga and those of his countrymen who are literate or educated—to whom the historicity to these stories matters—that I am not calling their myths and stories false. Perhaps I can best explain it to them by saying that the stories are *mimi* (true) but not *vough* (precise and verifiable). I have sought to establish the basis of their truth: Akiga's account is sociologically rather than historically true" (309).

non suggests, what counts as a "valid" or "true" statement (and by extension valid or true "history") varies from one culture to another, and it is this recognition that makes one wonder about who and what is left out in Ranger's "truer picture."[34]

Resistance, Agency, and the Practice of Everyday Life

However, the story of Oralai's ordeal is still incomplete. Akiga informs us that it was this very incident that led to the end of the anti-tsav movement called *Haakaa,* which was in effect the product of Tiv and British colonial collaboration.[35] As a decisive moment in the development of British attitudes toward Tiv beliefs, we must ask, what was the significance of this event in the eyes of the colonial officers? As Akiga himself asks of the British at the end of this narrative: "What can have been their views about it?"[36]

We may get some sense of the British view of this event through the account written by the British district officer at Wukari, Captain Emberton. On receiving the case from Tordwem, Emberton decided to investigate it further himself:

34. In other words, it is important to recognize that the relative uses to which historical knowledge is put varies from culture to culture. And this means that the value put on historical discourses themselves will vary across cultures. Some societies, for instance, may choose various contemporary rituals as legitimating practices where others may use historical claims. The often awkward gesture, "we had a history too," while still necessary (as in the case of some of my own work here), risks embracing—at times uncritically—the supposedly unquestioned superiority of historicism as a form of knowledge at all times, in all places. Put in terms of some current theoretical concerns, the suggestion being made here is that it is important to recognize that slogans such as Fredric Jameson's "Always historicize!" falter precisely at the moment when they proclaim themselves as transhistorical imperatives. For a further consideration of this claim, see Robert Young, *White Mythologies: Writing History and the West* (New York: Routledge, 1990), 102. For an interesting discussion of this in another African context, see the introduction to Samuel Josia Ntara's *History of the Chewa* (Wiesbaden: Franz Steiner Verlag, 1973), xii.

35. For further historical accounts of anti-tsav movements in general and the Haakaa in particular, see Paul Bohannan, "Extra-Processual Events in Tiv Political Institutions," *American Anthropologist* 60.1 (February 1958): 1–12; David Craig Dorward, "The Development of the British Colonial Administration among the Tiv, 1900–1949," *African Affairs* 68.273 (1969): 316–33; Dorward, "Ethnography and Administration: A Study of Anglo-Tiv 'Working Misunderstanding,'" *Journal of African History* 15.3 (1974): 457–77; Richard Fardon, "Sisters, Wives, Wards, and Daughters: A Transformational Analysis of the Political Organization of the Tiv and Their Neighbours. Part 1: The Tiv," *Africa* 54.4 (1984): 2–21.

36. Sai, *Akiga's Story,* 289.

I have now seen Saama's corpse and have no doubts whatsoever that it has NOT been tampered with at all. None of the limbs has been severed and the flesh shows only the signs of normal decomposition. I showed it to all the witnesses who told the previous story to us and they agree that all the flesh is there complete, but persist that the *mbatsav* have the power of reconstructing the body. [Oralai][37] now says that he did not eat the flesh and had no dealings with [Agbega] whatever. He was, he says, beaten and made to say that he was responsible for Saama's death by the District Head. Personally, I think he probably was trying to become an initiate. . . . I think that Saama died a natural death but as [Oralai] was known to have had a difference with him, he was accused of being concerned in it. [Agbega]'s suicide is said to be due to fear instilled into him by the District Head and by the fact that his son had turned against him and given evidence against him. Dauda, son of [Agbega], now says that he did not actually see the flesh brought home by his father and [Oralai], but only thought it was flesh.[38]

Emberton's view, written as a letter to a fellow officer and government anthropologist, Captain R. C. Abraham, assures the presence of the body and confirms that the witnesses now agree to seeing it. Further, it manages to elicit from Oralai his plea of innocence and the story of the fabrication, showing as I suggested earlier, that the written word can indeed lie. Yet, significantly, Emberton retains an ambivalent stance toward the prevalence of tsav (as in his entertaining of the possibility that Oralai was trying to be initiated into the mbatsav) and is quite uncertain about the precise valence of the witnesses' claim that the mbatsav can reconstruct the body. His ambivalence leads to the correspondence between the district officer and the anthropologist and to a further investigation of the matter by the latter.

The anthropologist Abraham, pursuing his own interrogation, also confirms that Saama's body has been untouched, that Oralai had accepted guilt only in the face of exceeding torture, and that Agbega's death is the combined result of fear of violence and the dismay of being falsely accused by his son. Downplaying the telling social struggles to which this event speaks, Abraham reads it as no more than the exemplification of the Lévy-Bruhlian claim about

37. In Abraham's text, the names are transcribed as "Arayi" for Akiga's "Oralai" and "Agbega" for Akiga's "Agbega." I have retained Akiga's transcriptions here to avoid confusion.
38. Letter to R. C. Abraham, in *The Tiv People,* R. C. Abraham (Lagos: Government Printer, 1933), 98.

the prelogical nature of the native mind. Thus for Abraham, "as the Tiv recognize no form of natural death apart from sorcery or poison, all were convinced that [Oralai] was guilty and *so strong was this conviction* that when the body was exhumed, no less than fourteen individuals, *against the evidence of their senses,* were certain that the body had been dismembered and the burial-cloth removed; the concrete evidence of vision had no weight against their inner conviction."[39] Abraham's Tiv, then, are caught within their own social myths and symbols to the point where they just cannot be empiricists good enough to distinguish between realities and illusions.

If the British official response to tsav is one of watchful ambivalence, Akiga's response is more skeptical. Not believing in the supernatural power of the tsav himself, Akiga must nevertheless be able to account for it. It is no surprise that Akiga discovers what his Western counterpart, the social anthropologist, has also recently discovered[40]—the power of a functional explanation. If Abraham has taken the path of a certain symbolic anthropology that attempts to account for beliefs on their own terms, Akiga, instead, chooses the functional explanation of tsav, which reads it as a mechanism of social control. But unlike the functional anthropologist who downplays the self-conscious agency of individual actors within a society in using or inventing traditions for specific social purposes, Akiga insists on foregrounding these inventions. Thus, for Akiga, tsav accusations are well-calculated mechanisms of societal control, levied against people who are seen to pose a threat by gaining excessive power, by others who already have such power (i.e., chiefs), or by those who stand to gain the protection and support of the white colonizers (i.e., younger men employed by the British, etc.) The accusations, Akiga claims, hold ground only because of the actual or potential threat of violence levied against the accused by the accusers and the agents of the colonial officers. Ironically, then, in Akiga's schema, tsav occurs only when an anti-tsav movement catches on, and such latter movements occur when political tensions rise to the point where a social upheaval demands an enforced check on undue individual power. At this point in the text (and this will change later), unlike Abraham, Akiga does not regard the Tiv as numbed in their senses because of their overwhelming beliefs, but rather as astute individuals who go along with the familiar signs that they have learned to read and manipulate in order to survive the troubled world in which they live. However, when the times do

39. Abraham, *Tiv People,* 100; my emphasis.
40. That is, in the 1920s and 1930s.

get unbearable, they do question the practices and ask: "Why is it supposed that the chiefs themselves are not *tsav*? Is it only we that are *tsav,* who are not chiefs?"[41] It is in times such as the current colonial ones, claims Akiga, that anti-tsav movements have arisen most prominently. The colonial rise of tsav movements suggests, then, that they are less the products of a primitive past than the products of an uncertain contemporary modernity.

The distance between Abraham and Akiga is not just the distance between two interpretive styles—one foregrounding collective representations, the other underlining the political contexts of beliefs. It is rather the more fundamental difference between reading the Tiv as passive, ahistorical, and mystical emblems of pure alterity, on the one hand, and reading them instead as historically sensitive, politically astute manipulators of knowledge in an unequal colonial order, on the other. As such, the two perspectives mark competing evaluations of colonial realities—one exhibiting the anxieties of an incomplete colonialism, the other, at least at this point, recognizing in precisely such gaps the articulation of what Michel de Certeau would call native "strategies" of resistance.[42]

If the stark distinction being made here between religious belief and resistance strikes most of us today as being problematic not least because of its questionable assumptions about the modalities of resistance, we will soon see that Akiga too is worried by it. Indeed, Akiga's text wavers on this issue to the point where some of his natives end up looking increasingly like Abraham's— engulfed so deeply in a mystical world that they cease to be calculating, ratio-

---

41. Akiga continues: "If any accusation connected with the *mbatsav* were brought against a chief, the other chiefs gave evidence in his favour, and he was acquitted. Nor was anyone *tsav* who was a favourite of the chief" (Sai, *Akiga's Story,* 284).

42. Michel de Certeau distinguishes between what he calls "tactics" and "strategies" of resistance by focusing on their differential relationship with the existence of a "proper" locus from which they are carried. Thus he writes, "A strategy assumes a place that can be circumscribed as *proper* and thus serve as the basis for generating relations with an exterior distinct from it (competitors, adversaries, 'clienteles,' 'targets,' or 'objects' of research.)"; "A tactic insinuates itself into the other's place, fragmentarily, without taking it over in its entirety, without being able to keep it at a distance" (de Certeau, *The Practice of Everyday Life,* trans. Steven Rendall [Berkeley: University of California Press, 1984], xix). In the context of colonial cultures this distinction, however, gets somewhat blurred. On the one hand, tsav practices, as Akiga suggests, are ways to manipulate the colonizer's space as represented by the legal and other bureaucratic machines. In this sense they are "tactics." On the other hand, tsav is also a way to establish precisely that proper space of alterity that de Certeau calls for in his discussion of "strategy." I hope it is clear that in the context of colonial politics this paradox is more than one of semantic choice.

nal agents. Akiga remains troubled by this fear, for he has not yet found a way to imagine a third space of agency, a space between that imagined by Abraham's symbolic interpretation and that by his own functionalism. In this third space, agency would appear in the more dispersed calculations and manipulations of interests and desires, in the relative weighing of ethical orders and political choices, in the traffic between one's own traditional habitus and the call of modernity that so poignantly characterize the practice of everyday life. But in the absence of such a conceptualization of agency, and writing, as his is a protonationalist account, Akiga finds it necessary to insist on foregrounding here the self-conscious resistance practices of his people.

Thus trickery and lies, which in most European accounts of the African unequivocally display the inferior moral lot of the native, become in Akiga's history native strategies of coping with precolonial as well as colonial everyday life. Akiga notes that theft is a shameful crime among the Tiv and was historically always so, whereas "telling lies, on the other hand, was always considered a fine thing."[43] Hence the dictum: "O man, never speak the truth. If you do, you will not escape the sword. A man should be quick to answer" (344). Akiga's text is rich with moments of intentional trickery in the face either of violence or some other potential threat, as for instance, the Tiv practice of placing the red juice of the *ikpine* tree on traveling women who, appearing wounded, would be left alone by the men of the neighboring villages.[44] Or else the story of the chief of Ukan, who, faced with a difference of opinion with his fellow Tiv elders in front of the white man, "affected to stagger right in front of the white men, as though he were about to fall on his face, in order that the white man should think him unwell and refrain from plaguing him with questions."[45] Or again, the story of Abaivo, a Tiv man employed as a police officer by the colonial government, who gets Chief Yaakur to corroborate a fictitious story about Abaivo's power over the mbatsav, the story being a calculated attempt to bring him respect and authority among the British and other fellow Tiv (280–81).

If these are individually motivated strategies of dealing with colonial insti-

43. Sai, *Akiga's Story*, 344.
44. This is a particular reference to the institution of "Marriage by Capture" in which men of an enemy village would lie awaiting women travelers in order to take them as permanent hostages (and forcefully marry them). Akiga suggests that the greatest enemy of the Tiv, the Mbaiyongo, would not touch women who were crippled, hurt, or otherwise wounded. Hence the "trickery" involved here (see Sai, *Akiga's Story*, 137).
45. Sai, *Akiga's Story*, 163.

tutions, more collectively devised mechanisms are also at work. Akiga writes, for instance, of the "slaughter-slab": "The Tiv originally knew nothing of a slab for cutting up human flesh; they always said that the *mbatsav* found a big tree, bent it down to the ground and cut up the meat on its leaves. But when the *Haakaa* came, Ukum started the idea of the slaughter-slab" (281). This new invention, suggests Akiga, became a convenient way to respond to colonial authorities who demanded, under the threat of violence, that the person accused of engaging in tsav bring forth the associated paraphernalia. In such a context, it was easy to make a "slaughter-slab" from old blankets and strips of cloth and hand it over as the evidence that was required.

Also associated with the supernatural world of tsav was the Tiv recourse to "swearing by the *Swem*." *Swem*, referring to a hill sacred to the Tiv, was traditionally represented by a little pot filled with ashes, wood, and other ritually significant objects.[46] Taking an oath by the Swem was historically considered by the Tiv the last recourse in the trial of a "hard case," leaving the justice to the power of the Swem, who would surely punish the wrongdoer. But, says Akiga, "the reason that the *Swem* is so popular amongst the Tiv today is because through it they can obtain acquittal when they appear before the white man, and not because they have any faith in it as a time-honored institution."[47] If the Swem "has become nothing but a means of escape from justice," (223) as Akiga puts it, it has ironically become so not because the Tiv believe in it but instead because the British do. If this classic Tiv example of what Eric Hobsbawm and Terence Ranger have called the "invention of tradition" is a remarkable commentary on the negotiation of everyday life in a colonial context,[48] it is no less insightful for exposing the mocking reading of white colonial justice:

> When a man is summoned to court on account of a crime which he has committed, his people, who know perfectly well that he is guilty, give him every encouragement. "When you go," they say, "keep on telling the same story. Whatever charge they bring against you, deny it. Don't contradict yourself. With the white man's justice it is merely a matter of keeping on saying the same thing and you get off. And if they dress the *Swem*

46. See Sai, *Akiga's Story*, 219, and discussion of *Akombo*.
47. Sai, *Akiga's Story*, 223.
48. See Eric Hobsbawm and Terence Ranger, eds., *The Invention of Tradition* (Cambridge: Cambridge University Press, 1983).

and tell you to swear on it, swear. Don't be afraid. We, your people, are your *Swem*. Only we can kill you."[49]

The problematic ethical stance of a historian who has chosen to expose his fellow Tivs' willful manipulation of the British is not lost on Akiga. "Tiv chiefs and judges know (of the manipulation), but they will not speak of it openly in such a way that a European would understand. And if any one were so to disclose the true state of affairs, they would not be pleased with him, for to them it is a way by which they can save themselves from the white man" (223). If "traitor" is too strong a word to describe Akiga here, it is perhaps only so if we read him to be a shrewd writer who, in order to convey the Tiv mockery of what they perceive to be the British obsession with consistency, must escape Rupert East's censure by somehow locating it within the sanctions of British decorum. In this reading, then, Akiga's exposition of the Tiv mockery of the British is coded not so much as radical critique but as a good-humored indulgence on the part of a native informant who ultimately stands with the British.

A Christian Ethic

But perhaps there is yet another ethical calling to which Akiga is responding. Could this exposition of the Swem oaths be the result of a Christian ethic seeking to dethrone "false" Gods? Could it be a Christian conscience that pricks even as it recognizes the resistance potential of lies?

What we have at work in Akiga's text is a troubled consciousness. In its protonationalist and anticolonial moments, this consciousness wishes to foreground and celebrate a politically calculated resistance strategy that draws on the Tiv belief in tsav. But even as it reads the resurgence of Tsav as mere manipulation on the part of the Tiv, it silently worries about the potential hold of tsav belief over the minds of some of the agents. In other words, if there is a will-to-resistance in the protonationalist moment, it is disrupted by the dangerous supplement of traditional belief itself.

Consider the fact that although the majority of Akiga's chapter on tsav presents the practice from a traditional ("internal" would be begging the question in this context) Tiv point of view, this discussion is prefaced by a Christian Akiga dismayed by the "surface" thought and learning of his people

49. Sai, *Akiga's Story*, 223.

whose "knowledge of material things (cannot) penetrate to their immortal souls" (240). It is this un-Christian knowledge that Akiga sees as leading to the fear of the mbatsav, which "has taken hold on the people like a persistent and incurable disease" (240). What we have here, then, is a subtle, but for Akiga a necessary, qualifier on the earlier account of Tiv manipulation—if tsav belief is being used as resistance, Akiga must admit that only some people are self-consciously using it as such, and there may still be those others who remain "incurably" tied to the beliefs.

If the implications of this acknowledgment are in the immediate context most pertinent to the anxieties of a recently converted colonial subject, then they are no less important for the light they shed on our understanding of resistance practices. The questions that Akiga's circuitous readings pose are fundamental to any study of resistance: What does it mean to have "agency"? Can one be an "agent" without willing it? Does resistance have to be consciously conceptualized *as* resistance for it to operate as such? Does *belief* in a ritual or a witchcraft practice undermine its resistance potential?

In effect, here is a historian unable or unwilling to read resistance in tsav *as* tsav. In other words, for Akiga, tsav has resistance potential despite the beliefs and practices surrounding it, not because of them. Left out of the analysis, as a result, is, for instance, the possibility of any serious consideration of tsav as a critical religious discourse about the dangers and abuses of "power"— "power," we must remind ourselves, being the most literal translation of the word *tsav*.[50] Again, although there is some discussion of how the category of "tsav" itself is not rigid in Tiv history but rather has evolved to gather increasingly negative associations, the significance of this is never developed. The very rich bodily metaphors associated with tsav, and the recourse to these metaphors in the context of discussing the deterioration of the larger social body (the "spoiling of the land" by the white man), is similarly sidestepped.[51] Fi-

50. On this, and some of the other potential avenues suggested in this paragraph, see Adrian Campion Edwards, "Seeing, Believing, Doing: The Tiv Understanding of Power," *Anthropos* 78.3–4 (1983): 459–80.

51. See Jean Comaroff, *Body of Power, Spirit of Resistance: The Culture History of a South African People* (Chicago: University of Chicago Press, 1985), 116–18, 201–2, for a suggestive account along these lines. To those who may accuse me of verging on the "ahistorical" here by seemingly wanting Akiga to be a Bourdieu-like "practice-theorist," some important qualifiers are necessary. First, it is not my aim to "fault" Akiga but rather to show how a functionalism that must gain its own identity by radically opposing itself to a symbolic reading will necessarily fail to imagine this third space. Second, even if one were to fault Akiga for not imagining this space, such a demand would be a mistake not because of his earlier temporal position (for that would imply a problematic teleology

nally, the structural analogies between the tsav rhetoric of flesh-debts and the practices of interclan exchanges of brides is left open.[52]

The unwillingness to pay serious attention to the internal logics of the religiosity of native practice is a characteristic that Akiga shares with other nationalist and radical historians.[53] In a powerful critique of radical historiography in the Indian context, Ranajit Guha reads on the part of radical historians a similar "disdain for the political consciousness of the peasant masses when it is mediated by religiosity."[54] Focusing on one such account that foregrounds the manipulation of religion by the rebelling leaders of the peasantry, Guha writes that it displays the "failure of a shallow radicalism to conceptualize insurgent mentality except in terms of an unadulterated secularism. Unable to grasp religiosity as the central modality of peasant consciousness in colonial India, [it] is shy to acknowledge its mediation of the peasant's idea of power and all the resultant contradictions. [It] is obliged therefore to rationalize the ambiguities of rebel politics *by assigning a worldly consciousness to the leaders and an otherworldly one to their followers making of the latter innocent dupes of crafty men.*"[55]

This is not the occasion to rehearse the many persuasive accounts that have since been offered to understand religion and rituals as resistance practices.[56] It is sufficient to note in our consideration of Akiga's narrative that if Guha's

---

for theoretical insights and explanations), nor because of his native position (for that would imply a problematic ethnocentrism that only sanctions the nonnative anthropologist to imagine such spaces), but rather more simply because it would proceed from the uncritical assumption that the kinds of explanations (such as "practice-theory") that seem to work for many of us in the Anglo-American academic spaces today would of necessity be useful to Akiga himself. I discuss this issue further a few paragraphs below.

52. Very little work seems to be done along these lines in the Tiv context. For now it is sufficient to note Richard Fardon's reference to the ward-sharing groups among the Tiv as "those who eat one *ingol.*" See Fardon, "Sisters, Wives, Wards, and Daughters," 10.

53. See Fanon's skepticism of traditional religious practices (which he calls the "magical superstructure") in nationalist liberation (*The Wretched of the Earth,* trans. Constance Farrington, preface by John-Paul Sartre [New York: Grove Press, 1968], 54–55).

54. Guha, "The Prose of Counter-Insurgency," in *Culture/Power/History: A Reader in Contemporary Social Theory* ed. Nicholas B. Dirks, Geoff Elay, and Sherry Ortner (Princeton: Princeton University Press, 1994), 362.

55. Ibid., 363; my emphasis.

56. See, for instance, Jean Comaroff, *Body of Power, Spirit of Resistance;* Jean Comaroff and John Comaroff, eds., *Modernity and Its Malcontents: Ritual and Power in Postcolonial Africa* (Chicago: University of Chicago Press, 1993); Martha Kaplan, "Meaning, Agency, and Colonial History: Navosavakadua and the *Tuka* movement in Fiji," *American Ethnologist* 17 (February 1990): 3–22.

radical historian is disdainful of religion as the modality of a peasant consciousness, then Akiga, the Christian historian, is also uneasy about its implications. Just as the radical historian is almost disappointed with the peasants for not being able to act on a fully secular class-based consciousness, Akiga too feels awkward about validating a political practice based on a set of beliefs he himself has shunned.

In suggesting that Akiga's text displays a tendency similar to that observed by Guha, I do not intend to slight Akiga's powers as a cultural historian. That kind of slighting would be appropriate to a different kind of project, which sought to dismiss a competing claim in order to advocate its own. My own aim here is not so much to advocate any such alternative account as to present a reading of how a Tiv colonial historian could produce a history of his people — as resisting agents — even as history itself was continually producing him, as a Christian.

If Christianity thus marks Akiga's skepticism, its narrativization takes the classical form of a story of conversion. When he was a young boy, Akiga tells us, he was considered to have an inordinate amount of tsav by the elders around him. Even though he himself knew that most of the events that his observers attributed to his tsav were no more than everyday events such as his leaving the house to relieve himself at night,[57] Akiga found himself forced to accept the public role thrust on him. If he were to protest, he would not be believed, and he quickly learned that he could capitalize on people's fears of the tsav by just acquiescing with the belief.[58] One day Akiga was questioned by his brother Hilekaan as to what he saw when he went out the previous night. His brother was dissatisfied with truthful responses and beat him for any response that did not confirm an association with tsav. So Akiga turned round the story as though it were the work of mbatsav. "'I will tell you the truth,' he said. 'What I saw last night were the owls of the *mbatsav*. There were two of them, and they had indigo cloths wrapped about their bodies'" (245).

The autobiographical moment is significant, not only as yet another exposition of the fabrication of a story in the face of violence but also as a moment of self-reflection. And this self-reflection, we gather from what we know about the production of the text, caused Akiga some unease—Rupert East, in his editorial commentary, informs us that having written in the original manuscript

---

57. This is a reference to the belief that members of the mbatsav gather together to carry out their deeds at night.
58. Sai, *Akiga's Story*, 242–45.

about these childhood experiences and his later adult lack of belief in tsav, Akiga wished ultimately to retract these confessions from the final version. Despite Akiga's explicit request to delete this confession, East decides to retain it "in fairness to [Akiga] himself and his teachers" (236) so that the published account may bear the trace of Akiga's newly found Christianity.

Diedrich Westermann insists in the preface that Akiga is the ideal man to write such a book because of his working "on the border-line of the old and the new" (vii). For Rupert East, Akiga is the perfect "halfie" subject, "one half of him bound up with the loyalties due to his (Christian) calling, the other half identified with the inner life of his own tribe. . . . He does not therefore record the practices and traditions of his people from the standpoint of a detached observer, but as part of his own mental experience" (4). But what Akiga's Western interlocutors ignore here are all the painful contradictions of a hybrid subject, at once skeptical of the beliefs of his people and desirous of speaking to and perhaps even for them.[59] Of a subject, in other words, who must praise the form of resistance of his people, but not necessarily the content of their beliefs.

If Akiga must deliberate on whether to include these paragraphs of disavowal, his deliberation is not merely a stylistic one but rooted in the very struggle to speak as a Tiv. For indeed this confession locates Akiga "elsewhere" in a position that he himself recognizes as being on the outside. He attempts at one point to make this position into a virtue by suggesting that the perspective of the outsider may be a privileged one: "So it is that the man who stands close to the house cannot see in what manner the roof is crooked. It is only when he goes back and stands some distance away from it that he gets a true view, and can tell the builders how to set it straight."[60] But such exteriority, Akiga recognizes, cannot be an absolute one. One thing he learns as a child is that he gains authority on the knowledge of tsav only through a public belief in his powers of tsav, and the same holds true of his history of the Tiv. Considering the fact that these "stories" of the tsav that he propagates as a child are, by his own account, a bunch of lies that nevertheless, given his alleged author-

---

59. It is important to emphasize the pain here. As R. Radhakrishnan suggests in a different context, although postmodern, metropolitan versions of hybridity are "characterized by an intransitive and immanent sense of *jouissance*," Akiga's colonial hybridity is an "expression of extreme pain and agonizing dislocations." See R. Radhakrishnan, "Postcoloniality and the Boundaries of Identity," *Callaloo* 16.4 (fall 1993): 753.

60. Sai, *Akiga's Story*, 240–41.

ity as tsav, are read as true,[61] we may surely hear in them the echoes of the courtroom scribe. The richness of Akiga's text is evident here in the remarkable irony that constructions of authority in which being and truth are reduced to the same are put into question precisely at the moment in which such an authority is being invoked. Writing a text that must speak both to the Tiv as well as to the white onlookers, Akiga recognizes that he must learn the arts of a colonial self-fashioning that engages both the centripetal and the centrifugal. Thus, if exteriority is a privileged space, so is interiority. As though to remind himself of these confusing privileges—which are also demands—Akiga admonishes the younger generation: "And do you, however great your knowledge may be, remember that you are a Tiv, remain a Tiv, and know the things of Tiv; for therein lies your pride. Let us take heart. The old mushroom rots, another springs up, but the mushroom tribe lives on."[62]

It is in such seemingly paradoxical attempts to locate himself both inside and outside that Akiga experiences a colonial modernity. Intervening in a world that is increasingly becoming interconnected, Akiga is caught between cultures, is vulnerable to being rendered "inauthentic" in each.[63] As such, he displays all the ambivalent qualities of a modern subject. "To be modern," writes Marshall Berman, "is to live a life of paradox and contradiction. It is to be overpowered by the immense bureaucratic organizations that have the power to control and often destroy all communities, values, lives; and yet to be undeterred in (one's) determination to face these forces, to fight to change the world and make it (one's) own. It is to be both revolutionary and conservative: alive to new possibilities for experience and adventure, frightened by the nihilistic depths to which so many modern adventures lead, longing to create and to hold on to something even as everything melts."[64] The irony for Akiga, as for so many Christian converts in colonial Africa, is that modernity, in his case, is not participating in Berman's vision of a relatively secularized "nihilistic" form of a technological society, but rather in one that is resolutely

---

61. "When I realized that every one admired me for my *tsav*, I was much flattered, and began to tell people all sorts of lies about the *mbatsav*. In this, moreover, I was never contradicted. They said I was so full of *tsav* that anything that I said about the *mbatsav* was not to be doubted" (Sai, *Akiga's Story*, 244).

62. Sai, *Akiga's Story*, 4.

63. For an elaboration in another context, see James Clifford, "The Pure Products Go Crazy," in *The Predicament of Culture* (Cambridge: Harvard University Press, 1988), 11.

64. Berman, *All That Is Solid Melts in the Air* (New York: Penguin, 1982), 13–14.

religious.[65] The space between the "revolutionary" and the "conservative" is one between two sets of beliefs, both of a religious order, and perhaps the greatest difficulty for the colonial subject thus located is to work out their necessary alignments in the struggle to "fight to change the world and to make it (one's) own."

Where Have All the Women Gone?

Let us return to the case of Saama and Oralai once more. In his discussion Captain R. C. Abraham notes the following as Oralai's confession:

> I asked Saama to give me his sister in order that I might give her in marriage and with the proceeds, obtain a wife for myself. Saama refused, so I went to our grandfather Agbega who was an old man, and asked him to help me; he said he would put Saama out of the way and I could then take possession of the girl.[66]

The case under discussion, then, revolves around the body of a woman. It is a case, as Gayle Rubin would put it, concerning the "traffic in women,"[67] an instance in which the lives of women become a matter between men. If Akiga omits this detail from his account of the case that was responsible for the end of the Haakaa, it is not because he is unaware of its significance. Indeed, at another point in the text, in the midst of the discussion on tsav, Akiga writes: "Most commonly it is over the question of a woman that an elder bears a

---

65. A brilliant example of such a stance is presented in the essay "The Modern Life of the East African Native" written by H. M. T. Kayamba, one of the first Africans to write in the journal *Africa*. In this essay, Kayamba echoes many of the themes and opinions we find in Akiga's text, one of which is the importance of Christianity for Africa. Like Akiga, Kayamba is skeptical and critical of colonial capitalism and the materialism it engenders, and sees in Christianity a possible solution for the dilemmas of the modernizing African subject. "Civilization" in the following quotation is to be read as the secular part of colonialism: "It is to be wished that foreign relations, especially Christianity, will always precede civilization. The result of civilization on paganism is very destructive, but without bestowing anything good in its place. This can only be done by Christian religion. The state of the African without religion is dangerous. However educated or civilized he may be, without religion his condition is worse than that of a pagan" (Kayamba, "The Modern Life of the East African Native," *Africa* [1932]: 54).

66. Abraham, *Tiv People*, 97.

67. See Gayle Rubin, "The Traffic in Women: Notes on the Political Economy of Sex," in *Toward an Anthropology of Women*, ed. Rayna R. Reiter (New York: Monthly Review Press, 1975), 157–210.

grudge against a youth and bewitches him, or because a younger man has se-duced one of his wives."[68] What then are we to make of this omission? How do we read this nameless sister of Saama, at once reduced and magnified to a function—an exchangeable Woman?

To recognize, along with a whole generation of deconstructive critics, that the greatest insights of a text may well lie in its blindnesses, its aporias, its gaps and its silences—to recognize this—is to be alert to the absent presence in Aki-ga's text of women. How do women function in Akiga's account? And how do they speak to us and to him? To listen to their muted voices, we need to enter the complexly intertwined yet intricately woven narratives of gift and ex-change, credit and debit, purity and danger, domination and resistance pre-sented by Akiga. These narratives are also narratives about locating the Tiv Woman in the midst of a changing world, or rather, as in the case of Akiga, gauging the changes in the world by tracing the various locations of the women.

In his section "Concerning Women" Akiga lists the virtues of the Tiv women of the past. The Tiv Woman of Akiga's account is also, like Saama's sis-ter, reduced to a function, not in this case as a potential body to be exchanged but instead as a "good wife" or a respectably raised daughter. Like so many masculinist accounts, the discussion of men in Akiga's chapter tends to read men as leaders, as politicians, as members of a larger polis, whereas the women are placed in the more domestic space of the home, whether that of the father or that of the husband. Thus, on listing the traditional hard daily chores of Tiv women, Akiga concludes:

> This is what good wives used to do in the past. With the cotton spun for him by his wife a man might weave cloths, and with these buy many cat-tle. Sometimes a poor man would become rich entirely through his wife. Another virtue possessed by the women of former days was that when the men were sitting talking they would never open their mouths unless they were asked. But the women of today will interrupt their menfolk in the middle of a sentence, whether their opinion has been asked or not. The Tiv say that women nowadays are on a complete equality with men, and the country has gone to the dogs (310).

If wifely virtue is to be traditionally found in hard labor intended to raise the fortune of one's husband, and in such obsequious behavior as not speak-

68. Sai, *Akiga's Story,* 246.

ing unless asked to, then the dangerous sign of "modernity" is the newfound articulateness of the women. This articulateness, we may assume, is most oppressively felt by the men, who, in line with conventional representational strategies, are referred to here by Akiga as "the Tiv." If it is instead the Tiv *men* who say that the country has "gone to the dogs," one can only wonder what the women, or at least some of the women, are saying.[69] *Some* of the women is important here—for even as we attempt to understand Akiga's experience of modernity as the experience of women suddenly challenging their husbands, we must also take him up on the revealing slippage in the phrase "good wives." Would it not be fair to assume, then, that this qualifier "good" bespeaks a different kind of wife, erased from Akiga's memory—the "bad" one—who, to go along with the teleological narrative, was always already "modern" in her traditional space, always already able to interrupt her husband? And likewise, could we not find, if Akiga would give them more narrative space, some women among his contemporaries who had not quite embraced the seemingly liberating moment of modernity?[70]

While keeping these questions open, we must ask, what further "signs of the times" are the women displaying? An important sign of change, suggests Akiga, is in the realm of the aesthetics of the body. What were originally

69. The point I am making is not new, but important enough to be repeated. Over and over again in the anthropological literature one encounters descriptions of the Tiv being one of the most egalitarian African ethnic groups. Although to a certain extent this may be true, it always behooves us to ask: who is left out of this "egalitarian" scenario? See, for instance, Bohannan, "Extra-Processual Events in Tiv Political Institutions," 1–12; Dorward, "Development of the British Colonial Administration among the Tiv, 316–33; Dorward, "Ethnography and Administration," 457–77; Edwards, "Seeing, Believing, Doing," 459–80.

70. We learn to make such distinctions from Chandra Talpade Mohanty's important critique of the tendency of some Western feminist writing to subsume all women in the third world into the rather homogenous category of "third world women." Thus, in such scholarship, she writes, "a homogenous notion of the oppression of women as a group is assumed, which, in turn, produces the image of an 'average third world woman.' This average third world woman leads an essentially truncated life based on her feminine gender (read: sexually constrained) and her being 'third world' (read: ignorant, poor, uneducated, tradition-bound, domestic, family-oriented, victimized, etc.)" (Mohanty, "Under Western Eyes: Feminist Scholarship and Colonial Discourses," in *Third World Women and the Politics of Feminism*, ed. Chandra Talpade Mohanty, Ann Russo, and Lourdes Torres (Bloomington: Indiana University Press, 56). As Mohanty suggests, to go by such an invention of women in the third world is not just to be simply ethnocentric but also to miss out on the real effects of internal differences such as those of education, class, status, motives, beliefs, and various political locations in the lives of such women. In our own case then, we must remain mindful of such divisions before postulating any theories of "Tiv women."

bodily markings for ethnic identification and pride are now being used as fashion statements. The most significant of these changes is one called the "Nail," introduced by a young man who had seen it while "traveling in foreign parts with a white man's loads."[71] The various facial scars that went under the name of the "Nail" became popular among the young men, perhaps because the women, according to Akiga, were increasingly seeking out men with such scars. "They do not like men with raised marks, because they carry symbols of the past" (45). Thus the "modern" Tiv women, suggests Akiga, by refusing to marry the older men with the older markings, are causing havoc in the land. And this mark of modernity is not a relatively contained one, for it has influenced not just the young women but also the older ones. Thus, "A woman may have been married for a long time to a husband with raised markings, but leaves him on the ground that the white man has said that women must do as they wish, and she, for her part, does not wish to have a husband with a lumpy face" (45).

Once again for Akiga, tradition is marked and indeed experienced as a time when all the women were "good" obedient wives, and modernity the exact negation of such an experience—that is, a time when all the women, young and old, are rebelling against the elder men for apparently frivolous reasons such as the pursuit of fashionable body markings. "It is the modern Tiv women who have caused all these troubles, and many others like them, to come upon the land of Tiv," writes Akiga (48). But it is important to note that just as "tradition" is experienced here both as that which is *prior* as well as that which is *pure,* modernity too is conversely experienced, as that which is *later* as well as that which, coming from the exterior, is *impure.* If what Akiga and the elder men are confronted with is a modernity, it is importantly a *colonial* modernity in which the white colonizers are implicated. The general sentiment of the elder men is well articulated in the rebuke of one elder to his rebellious wife: "Look at the way you women are ruining the country! Aren't you pleased that the white man has given you claws to scratch with!" (318).

If the white man has given the Tiv woman "claws to scratch with"—and we may add, "tongues to lash out with"—he has done so by passing a law banning exchange marriages.[72] "For in as much as marriage by exchange has been replaced by the bride-price system, and a woman can no longer be given away in marriage forcibly, but only if she consents of her own free will, it goes badly nowadays with those who have raised scars on their faces."[73] This, then, suggests Akiga, is at the heart of the changing location of women in modernity and the single-most common cause of social tension and upheaval. Thus if the Tiv reliance on tsav is more a colonial rather than a precolonial phenomenon, it is intimately connected with the introduction of the "bride-price," or "dowry," by the British. Yet another colonial stereotype is on the verge of being exploded here insofar as the "bride-price" is recognized not as something authentically Tiv but as a Western imposition. Indeed, Akiga notes, the Tiv men claim that the white man, by introducing money into the marriage negotiations, has rendered women slaves (54).

It is important to recognize that if, as we saw in the discussion of tsav, Akiga's nationalism is tempered by his new missionary location, then the same mechanism is at work in his reading of the Tiv women. Although he may indeed be a champion of the virtues of the "good wives" of the past, Akiga does not look on the male traditionalists with favor. Thus, in line with his Christian leanings, Akiga criticizes the institution of polygamy as one that encourages the unequal treatment of wives, in which the husbands display partiality toward some over others (313). He criticizes the traditional practices of the inheritance of widows as institutions in which women were vulnerable to suffering (317). He notes with dismay that in the older times of exchange marriages, a young woman would have no say in whom she married: "Some women even stabbed themselves to death when they were given to an old man against their will; but in spite of all, the Tiv did not care" (166). Further, Akiga is careful to point out that the recent ban on such exchange marriages and the introduction of the "bride-price" is looked on favorably by most of the women and by the younger men. "The women say that this is the best thing the white man has done since he came. Instead of being slaves, they are now free women" (167), free that is, to marry the younger men of their choice who in turn can aspire to raise the necessary sum of money through their integration in the migrant economy. Thus, unlike in exchange marriages, the women can no more be forcibly exchanged, nor do the young men have to wait their turn, sometimes until a relatively old age, to acquire a female *ingol* to exchange for a wife.[74]

In the context of such internal generational splits among the Tiv, it is telling

---

73. Sai, *Akiga's Story*, 45.

74. An *ingol* is a woman (often a sibling) who is exchanged by the man with the guardian of his bride-to-be.

that Akiga conveniently omits the fact that the primary colonial advocates of the ban on exchange marriages in the Tiv context were not the colonial officers but rather precisely the missionaries among whom Akiga has himself found a home. Distressed by the moral dimensions of the older setup (which is also associated with polygamy),[75] anxious about the increasingly fluid sexual conduct among "unsettled" young male migrants, and desirous of marriages between young converts (who would be free to marry each other without the traditional exchange setup), the missionaries looked to the "bride-price" as a mechanism to empower the young men with access to the cash economy in their pursuit of brides. Discussing the ban on exchange marriages, the historian David Craig Dorward writes, "The South African Dutch Reformed Mission, which had been active in Tivland since 1911, also supported the (young men's) demand for 'dowry' marriages. Converts who joined the mission often could not obtain 'marriage wards' with which to secure Tiv wives. Thus exchange marriage was an obstacle in the way of evangelism."[76] Given this, it would be fair to suggest that the rhetorical emphasis that Akiga places on the disruptions caused by the Nail and by the women and by the white officers are clearly meant to shift the attention away from the Christians with whom he is himself associated. It is also, one might add, a mechanism to critique changes coming from the outside through colonial intervention and migration, without foregrounding the outsideness of the missionary institution itself.

We might say, then, that the complexities of Akiga's readings of Tiv women defy conventional categorizations. He is enthralled by the "good wives" of the past who do not challenge their husbands, but he is also critical of the traditional men who mistreat and abuse their wives. He is critical of the rebelliousness of the "modern" woman, yet he is sympathetic to her liberation from a traditional patriarchy. He is critical of the workings of colonial capital and especially the migrant economy, but he remains impressed by the Christian humanist dispositions that, in his colonial context, accompany it. Without ever allowing the women to fully speak for themselves in any unmediated way, Akiga's text becomes a performance of ventriloquism. If in such moments of

75. This is a problematic invention on the part of the missionaries, since, although polygamy is certainly associated with indigenous cultural sanctions rather than Christianity, at one point Akiga tells us that polygamy is more of a contemporary phenomenon than a precolonial one. "In former times the Tiv did not have so many wives as they do to-day. Most of them had one wife. A very important man or a chief may have two" (Sai, *Akiga's Story*, 313). Only with the contemporary association of prestige with polygamy, suggests Akiga, has the practice increased.

76. Dorward, "Development of the British Colonial Administration among the Tiv," 325.

Akiga's text we are tempted to imagine the revolutionary nature of the unspoken and unrecorded consciousness of his fellow Tiv women, we must be cautious and tentative about our constructions. As feminist historians who study African societies and their colonial encounters have often reminded us, the advent of colonial domination, and in particular the imposition of various monetary taxes resulting in predominantly male migrant labor, meant that the women who were left behind in the villages often had to struggle harder to make ends meet.[77] Wage labor in urban colonial Africa, while leading to hybridized "structures of feeling" among Africans that were articulated in such phenomenon as prestige-value associated with urban work and a corollary demeaning of "village work," rarely ever provided enough to sustain either the traditional needs of the rural families or the newly created demand on the part of rural or migrant Africans for Western commodities. To hear in the voices of the Tiv women only a sense of elation and liberation, as Akiga occasionally seems to, is to embrace uncritically one of the most important legitimating myths of colonialism: the myth, to paraphrase Gayatri Spivak, of white men saving black women from black men.[78] Yet while recognizing its limits, in the spirit of an "affirmative deconstruction," we may still continue to imagine those voices at least as "theoretical fictions" that "entitle" and motivate our project of reading.[79] For our task is not just to attempt to unearth these past

77. On this point and other relevant historical notes on the location of women in the transition from precolonial to colonial economies in Africa see, for instance, Ifi Amadiume, *Male Daughters, Female Husbands* (London: Zed Books, 1987); Kathleen Staudt, "Women's Politics, the State, and Capitalist Transformation in Africa," in *Studies in Power and Class in Africa,* ed. Irving L. Markovitz (Oxford: Oxford University Press, 1987); Linzi Manicom, "Ruling Relations: Rethinking State and Gender in South African History," *Journal of African History* 33 (1992): 441–65; Belinda Bozzoli, "Marxism, Feminism, and South African Studies," *Journal of Southern African Studies* 9.2 (April 1983): 139–71; and the essays collected in the following three edited volumes: Women in Nigeria, eds., *Women in Nigeria Today* (London: Zed Press, 1985); Sharon B. Stichter and Jane L. Parpart, eds., *Patriarchy and Class: African Women in the Home and the Workforce* (Boulder, Colo.: Westview Press, 1988); Jane L. Parpart and Kathleen Staudt, eds., *Women and State in Africa* (Boulder, Colo.: Lynne Rienner Publishers, 1989).

78. See Spivak, "Can the Subaltern Speak?" 297.

79. One such limit is being aware of our presumptuousness in assuming that we can fully understand the location of such subjects. Criticizing such gestures, Michel de Certeau writes: "With respect to the possessed woman, the primitive, the patient, demonological discourse, ethnographical discourse and medical discourse effectively assume identical positions: 'I know what you are saying better than you'; in other words, 'My knowledge can position itself in the place whence you speak'" (de Certeau, *The Writing of History* [New York: Columbia University Press, 1988], 250). For "affirmative deconstruction" and "theoretical fictions" see Gayatri Chakravorty Spivak, "Sub-

voices, to render them audible, but just as importantly to understand the nature of their audibility within their own contemporaneity and the nature of their subsequent silencing in written accounts.

To register the double-edged problematics surrounding the audibility of women in nationalist narratives, we may turn to the text's stark critique of colonial intervention. Akiga suggests that it was the workings of colonial capitalism that led to the increased occurrence of sexual diseases such as gonorrhea among the Tiv. Although the disease existed among the Tiv before colonial times, Akiga tells us it spread more rapidly because of increased contact between the Tiv and foreign peoples. "But when the white man came, the Tiv began to travel about and mix with the Chamba, Dam, Hausa and Akporo peoples, amongst whom the disease was rife, and not only to mix but also to intermarry with them."[80] The rise of migrant labor, suggests Akiga, was also responsible for increased promiscuity and prostitution, and thus both the moral and the physical fiber of the Tiv community was weakened.

Akiga's critique is quite persuasive, particularly his move to demonstrate how the supposed sexual promiscuity and excess of the African, so significant a trope in the racist colonial imagination, is more a *product* of colonial practices than a vestige of a primitive past. This move, along with others such as his insistence that tsav is more a colonial phenomenon than a precolonial one, or his similar demonstration of the colonial context of the bride-price, is the major rhetorical strategy in Akiga's critique of colonialism. Yet, in this particular context of a discussion of women, it is important to read the differential ways in which the critique functions. For here the point of Akiga's critique is a singular one—he wishes to show that in areas of culture contact the women have stopped producing as many children as they used to in the past, and families have decreased in size. The rural areas, on the other hand, continue to procreate at the precolonial rate.

If you have read the novel *The Joys of Motherhood* by Buchi Emecheta, or the few available oral histories of African women living under colonialism, or even some of the historical or ethnographic literature that focuses on such women, you will want to ask whether these decreasing family units with women "complain(ing) of internal pain" (355) after having given birth to one or two children are not perhaps as much an effect of a changing consciousness

altern Studies: Deconstructing Historiography," in *Selected Subaltern Studies* ed. Ranajit Guha and Gayatri Chakravorty Spivak (Oxford: Oxford University Press, 1988), 12.
80. Sai, *Akiga's Story*, 354.

as they are of physical duress.[81] Clearly one need not, indeed one must not, undermine the real significance of the spread of sexual diseases through the workings of colonial capital.[82] But is there also a space, perhaps, which Akiga is unwilling or unable to grant, for a rising consciousness among women, especially those in contact with the rapidly expanding colonial public sphere, of the desirability of a smaller household? To be sure, we need not necessarily think of such a consciousness as singularly revolutionary, for it may be no more than an accommodation to the demands of yet another, albeit differently constraining system—that of colonial capital.[83] Yet it is important

81. So, for instance, Belinda Bozzoli's claim that historians have paid little or no attention to the domestic struggles in which African women were engaged, both in precolonial as well as in the changing colonial times, is relevant here. Discussing the southern African context, Bozzoli writes about the transition to a migrant male economy: "The sudden imposition upon *women*, not 'the family' of full responsibility for the maintenance of a social system under increasing and devastating attack, must surely have involved some conflict, some vast social, moral and ideological reorganisation" ("Marxism, Feminism, and Southern African Studies," 146). One such ideological reorganization, I am suggesting, is the relative value placed on childbearing as opposed to other social functions and demands. If we are interested in women's negotiations of the changes demanded by colonialism, we need to take, as Akiga cannot, such reorganizations into account. For a compelling narrative on such changes see Buchi Emecheta's ironically titled *Joys of Motherhood* (New York: G. Braziller, 1979).

82. Although more work needs to be done on the spread of venereal diseases and their impact on childbearing in the Tiv context of this period, Carol Summers's article, "Intimate Colonialism: The Imperial Production of Reproduction in Uganda, 1907–1925" *Signs* 16.4 (1991): 787–807), provides a useful analysis of such a phenomenon. Particularly relevant is Summers's discussion of the missionary position on the matter, including its inventions of African morality and its attempt to set up a "Maternity Training School" to teach African women how to be "good" mothers. For an interesting parallel anxiety about the productive capabilities of European women in colonial spaces, see Ann Laura Stoler, "Carnal Knowledge and Imperial Power: Gender, Race, and Morality in Colonial Asia," in *Gender at the Crossroads of Knowledge,* ed. Micaela di Leonardo (Berkeley: University of California Press, 1991), 51–101. Finally, Nancy Rose Hunt's "'Le Bebe en Brousse': European Women, African Birth Spacing, and Colonial Intervention in Breast Feeding in the Belgian Congo," *International Journal of African Historical Studies* 21.3 (1988): 401–32, although focusing on aspects of childrearing different from my own, provides a refreshing reading of the colonial anxieties about African childrearing in the Belgian Congo.

83. Again, the issues here are complicated. The dominant narrative is that colonial capital, interested in sustaining an African workforce, was as concerned as the Africans about the declining birthrates in the early part of the century in many parts of Africa. Although the archival literature suggests that this is true, I argue that it is inappropriate to read this demand as the singular demand placed on women by the changing economies. Thus, for instance, some women, attempting to migrate to town to provide services such as beer shops for the predominantly male workforce, were being incorporated into the colonial economy in a rather different way. Further, such new roles would have shifted their own perceptions of the traditional childbearing role ascribed to them.

to note that although Akiga can read the agency of the "modern" woman in most cases, when it comes to what is traditionally rendered the most crucial function of the woman—childbearing (the reproduction of the community)—he is blind to any possible resistance to a patriarchal tradition. Modern woman in this account can rebel in all sorts of ways except in refusing to produce children. If in the case of the ideology of tsav the question "What if they really do believe in it?" makes a Christian Akiga uneasy, here the question "What if she does not wish to have many children?" is not even allowed to be asked. Childbearing itself is essentialized into the very Being of Tiv women—neither the "traditional" nor the "modern" woman can be allowed to escape this duty. But Akiga himself knows that even as he is emphasizing the unquestionable values of childbearing, these very values are being questioned by the younger Tiv. Elsewhere in his text Akiga disapprovingly notes: "Nowadays a man will give anything to marry a pretty woman, even though she may not be able to bear children at all, so that every one may say what a handsome wife he has got. The old idea is not considered as it used to be; in these days it is looks that count."[84] If there *is* any agency here, it is located not among the women but among the men who are seen to prefer beauty to progeny. And in defiance of his own observation about changing norms, Akiga is compelled to insist that if a woman does not produce children, she not only is the subject of communal rebuke but is also, most importantly, "herself . . . never happy" (312).[85]

Money, Writing, and "Primitive" Economics

If the dangers of pursuing beauty as opposed to (re)productivity are prevalent in Akiga's text, they speak to a larger social concern with the loss of depth,

84. Sai, *Akiga's Story*, 112.
85. We may contrast Akiga's position here with the way in which childbirth becomes associated with patriarchical (rather than maternal) desire in the eyes of some women in other literature. Thus, for instance, in her book *Valenge Women*, E. Dora Earthy suggests that the women she studied had self-induced abortions "to vent spite upon the husband" (Earthy, *Valenge Women* [Oxford: Oxford University Press, 1933]). Likewise, Maria Rosa Cutrufelli notes a similar observation among women of the former Belgian Congo and quotes a woman from Ponthierville as saying that abortion is performed "by women who married unwillingly and now refuse to produce children to the benefit of their husbands or their families" (Cutrufelli, *Women of Africa: Roots of Oppression* [London: Zed Press, 1983], 140). Finally, S. M. Molema, in his study of the some of the Bantu communities of South Africa, writes about traditional Bantu women of the past: "Bantu women had

meaning, and value. Superficiality, commercialism, and impersonal relations are seen by Akiga to disrupt the previously "organic" relationship of the people to each other and to their land. The "pretty" woman serves in Akiga's text as the ultimate metaphor of such change, and it is by following the trail of this "pretty" woman, not this time through his own text but through a much-circulated Tiv story generated during the colonial period, that we may gain some perspective on this process of change.

The story is about a poor farmer named Amagu, who, through hard work and thrifty habits, manages over the years to save a decent sum of money. One day, just as he is counting his money, his neighbor Orliam arrives and requests a loan for a bride-price. Amagu refuses, suggesting that he himself would soon need the money to get remarried. Fearing Orliam's greed, however, Amagu gets anxious about the safety of his money, whereupon he is advised by his elders to go to the city and deposit the money in a white man's bank. Determined to ensure the safety of his savings, Amagu goes to the city of Makurdi for the first time and is awestruck by its sights. Eventually, he comes upon a woman in the marketplace, "the most beautiful woman he had ever seen." He is seized by the desire to marry her and asks her the name of her father so that he may approach him with the bride-price. The woman accepts, and Amagu sets off to her father's village, where he meets a villager. On learning Amagu's intentions, the villager warns: "My friend . . . do not act in such haste. The woman is beautiful but her beauty is a snare. She is evil and will not bring you happiness. Do not marry her." Amagu disregards the warning and marries the woman and takes her home. He buys her the best of things and gives her the choicest meats. But he soon finds that his wife cheats on him, that she is a thief, a liar, an unkindly aunt to his nephews, and above all, a wife who has prepared for him no food. Amagu wishes to discipline her, but finds that his heart melts in the presence of her beauty. When his gentle rebuke does not engender any change in her behavior, he takes her back to her father's home and demands a return of the bride-price. Her father refuses to return the money and advises him to send her to the market where he first found her. Amagu is saddened, and the villager who had earlier warned him delivers the story's moral: "When you pay so much for a wife, especially if she is beautiful,

---

none of the *new-fangled ideas about having only a limited number of children*" (Molema, *The Bantu: Past and Present* [Edinburgh: W. Green and Son, 1920], 127; my emphasis). What I am asking here is how, in these various instances, do we account for the shifting consciousness of the women?

it is only wise to take your time and find out about her character and behavior first, before you jump into marriage."[86]

I introduce this story here not only because it speaks so "beautifully" to Akiga's own anxieties about the young men's choice of beauty over (re)productivity but also because it allows us to return once again to the case of Saama and Oralai. The story merely repeats the same structure of anxieties and the same preference for presence found in that earlier episode. For what more is "money" here than a surrogate for that same fear which accompanied the arrival of "writing?" If writing is feared to be that tyrannical force that reduces presence itself to marks on a page, to a "dead" mode that insists on lethal "closure," then in this story, it is money that takes on this force. The moral of the story is not so much (or not only) about the uselessness of the beautiful, but more significantly about the closure established by the money economy. If the written word presents itself as one that cannot lie, then the money economy presents itself as one that is open to no negotiation. A "testimony," once written, cannot be changed; a "woman," once married in this new economy, cannot be returned.

A study of Akiga's chapter titled "Marriage and Tribal Organization" foregrounds precisely such readings of the newly regulated bride-price. Thus, for instance, Akiga notes a debate between a man who claims that he was so handsome that he could get married by virtue of his looks alone and not by recourse to a bride-price payment. His opponent on the contrary says that he was so rich "that he did not have *to keep going backwards and forwards* for the same thing. He merely paid out the money and was rid of the matter, so that he could turn his attention to something else."[87] If what is foregrounded here is the ability of money to establish "closure" to a marriage deal (this time supposedly in a manner favorable to the suitor), then what is quite consciously being opposed here is the earlier system in which a marriage exchange was considered incomplete until children had been born (102). In such a prior exchange situation, the bride was always "on loan" until she had produced children, and in case children were not forthcoming to a particular bride but were already born to the woman who had been exchanged in her place, then

---

86. "The Beautiful Wife," in *Tales Tiv Tell,* ed. Harold Bergsma and Ruth Bergsma (Ibadan: Oxford University Press, 1969), 9–14. This story, reproduced in a textbook meant for students in "Years 1–4 of Nigerian secondary schools," is followed by three study questions: "(1) How did Amagu get his money?; (2) What did Amagu see in Makardi?; (3) Did he use his money wisely?" (14).

87. Sai, *Akiga's Story,* 154; my emphasis.

talks would resume between the families about finding a way for each to have a fair share of the progeny. In such a system, then, much to the irritation of the colonial authorities, marriage exchanges were always open and were subject to renegotiation at later dates. The entry of money and the bride-price was meant to encourage somewhat clean-cut transactions with no further negotiations regardless of issues surrounding childbirth.[88]

In addition to being responsible for closure, "money" has other equally consequential attributes. In Rupert East's commentary we learn that the traditional system of exchange marriage strategically reconciles the patrilineal and matrilineal principles by insisting on a symbolic "transposition of personalities" between the exchanged women. East writes, "The essence of the idea is that the wife who is introduced into the group takes the place, in a very real sense, of the daughter of the family. She not only acts as her deputy, but for the purpose of bearing children, actually *becomes* the woman for whom she has been exchanged."[89] In this form of exchange—an exchange of plenitudes (an exchange unmediated by the "dead" form of "money")—there is room for a hierarchy: a true-sister exchange marriage is read as the purest form of such marriage, with exchanges of other female relations being secondary. When "money" enters the picture, not only does it establish "closure," but by introducing a secondary system of signification that in turn assumes the stance of a great equalizer, it disrupts such nuanced valences in the marital economies.

Akiga's reading of the entry of "money" among the Tiv is significant because it echoes the dominant motif surrounding this issue throughout the colonial library. In this account, money disrupts not just a particular economic space but indeed the entire ethos of a community. Listen, for instance, to the anthropologist Bruno Gutmann's almost poetic sense of the loss of such ethos, the loss of such presence: "For money is the most dangerous of all substitutes which take the place of real goods and values. Long habit has blinded us to its fatal working. The African who has passed through in a day the change in men's lives which has been wrought by money, sees more clearly the misery that it brings with it. He sums up the terrible process: 'the shilling takes the place of the brother.' Money dissolves the organic relations between men, and where a man would make demands upon his fellow man's physical and personal strength which could be repaid by nothing less than an obliga-

---

88. For some of the potential consequences of these different systems on the lives of women, see Rubin, "The Traffic in Women," 205–6.

89. Sai, *Akiga's Story*, 101; my emphasis.

tion to a similar service in return, money steps in, and in place of a human being puts a dead medium of exchange, which lets him pay his debt by giving the other man a minimum share of his fortune and enables him to use men's services without thanks or personal obligations."[90] Although many of the effects described here—as Akiga confirms—are undeniably real, the anthropologist's (colonial?) nostalgia, which quietly turns to the African to teach "us" about our own loss, repeats the troubling trope of the noble savage. In doing so, it insists on inventing the African space as a primordial, pre-economic space, where everyone helped each other through the sheer goodness of their hearts (again the noble savage), without any economic calculations whatsoever. In such a sharply divided world, "they" have symbols (or at most "symbolic capital") while in our own fallen state, "we" have economy.[91] But as Pierre Bourdieu has persuasively shown, the distinction between the "symbolic" and the "economic" tells more about the "ethnocentric naivities of economism" than it does about any essential difference in the practices.[92] By refusing to acknowledge Bourdieu's claim that "the theory of strictly economic practice is simply a particular case of a general theory of the economics of practice" (173), we lose any opportunities to learn how it is that "symbolic capital, a transformed and thereby *disguised* form of physical 'economic' capital, produces its proper effect inasmuch, and only inasmuch, as it conceals the fact that it originates in 'material' forms of capital which are also, in the last analysis, the source of its effects" (178).

In the context of our discussion of writing, if money and writing share many of the same attributes, it would be fair to proceed with a critique of the mythology of "money" along the same lines of our earlier critique of the mythology of "writing." In other words, if one lesson of the case of Saama and Oralai was precisely the deconstruction of the absolute binarism—Literate/Preliterate—then would it not suggest also a similar questioning of the polarity Monetary/Premonetary? Such a reading would allow us to overcome an ethnocentrism similar to the one Derrida noticed in Lévi-Strauss, except in our case, transferred to the space of the "economy."

90. Gutmann, "The African Standpoint," *Africa* 8.1 (1935): 7.
91. This "we" refers to those who align themselves with the community of the ethnically distant anthropological observer. It is also the "we" of the modern colonial subject attempting to write a history, which as Michel de Certeau reminds us, is inevitably a task of distinguishing between an earlier "they" and a contemporary "we."
92. Bourdieu, "Structures, Habitus, Power: Basis for a Theory of Symbolic Power," in Dirks, Eley, Ortner, *Culture/Power/History*, 173.

Derrida, let us recall, suggests that Lévi-Strauss's somewhat nostalgic reading of the entry of writing among the Nambikwara risks being at once ethnocentric and misguided in failing to recognize the originary violence of naming and of the logic of the "proper" that exists prior to the native's famous writing lesson.[93] The process of naming, based as it is in the concept of *différance*, is an *arche*-writing, suggests Derrida,[94] since it already carries within it the trace of a structure of writing. In other words, Derrida would have us focus not on the marks on a page but rather on the structuring principles behind such marks. Since such structuring principles always already exist in the so-called preliterate societies, the distinction "preliterate"/"literate" becomes problematic.

Just as the structure of writing is always already in place in an oral culture, it is important to recognize that the structure of the monetary, understood here as the convertibility and circulation of value from one medium to another, is also prevalent in cultures normally read as "premonetary."[95] Consider, for instance, Akiga's discussion of the form of marriage called *kem*. "Although at the beginning the Tiv had only the exchange form of marriage, after a time they saw the *kem* system practiced by foreigners (Chamba) and began to adopt it."[96] In this system, a man interested in a prospective bride would start showering her parents with gifts. "If he killed some small creature he took it to the girl's mother, or if he got some farm produce he would give this. When the farming season came round, he went to hoe a farm for his future mother-in-law. At that time, when there was not much property, these were the only kinds of payment that were made. Finally he picked a mushroom and gave it

93. See Jacques Derrida, *Of Grammatology,* trans. Gayatri Chakravorty Spivak (Baltimore: Johns Hopkins University Press, 1976), 101–40.

94. See also Derrida's essay, "Différance," in *Margins of Philosophy,* trans. Alan Bass (Chicago: University of Chicago Press, 1982), 1–27.

95. There is, of course, a rich literature, associated primarily with the work of Karl Polanyi, on the relevance of terms such as *money* in the discussion of precapitalist societies. See, for instance, "The Semantics of Money-Uses," in which Polanyi makes a conscious connection between monetary systems and writing systems (Polanyi, *Primitive, Archaic, and Modern Economics: Essays of Karl Polanyi,* ed. George Dalton [Boston: Beacon Press, 1968], 175–203). See also Barbara Herrnstein Smith, *Contingencies of Value* (Cambridge: Harvard University Press, 1988), 125–49 for a related analysis and other relevant citations. For a more specifically African contextualization, see Paul Bohannan, "Exchange and Investment among the Tiv," *American Anthropologist* 57.1 (1955): 60–70; Bohannan, "The Impact of Money on an African Subsistence Economy," *Journal of Economic History* 19.4 (December 1959): 491–503.

96. Sai, *Akiga's Story,* 125.

to the mother. This concluded the affair, and he was given the girl to take away with him" (125). To be sure, Akiga insists that for the marriage to be fully ratified, a woman would have to be forthcoming in exchange at a later date, but the important point here is that the structure of the "monetary" is already in place. For what we have here, in essence, is not just a set of gifts taking the "place" of a woman, but also the workings of a credit-based economy.[97]

To continue with such a line of questioning, we must recognize not only the structure or the form of the monetary within supposedly premonetary societies but also how the supposed effects of this alien system are in fact processes already at work in the prior economy. When Akiga suggests that the elder Tiv men blame the advent of money for their own loss of control over the marital economy, he is of course referring to the relatively greater access of the younger men to the cash economy and consequently to the younger women. But what is striking about this connection is the fact that it forgets the real changes in the marital economy already in place in Tivland, particularly through the *iye* system. Frustrated by having to wait for a long time to inherit a woman to exchange in a marriage, the young Tiv men and women had already begun to engage in a different type of marriage—"an honorable marriage by capture"[98]—in other words, a marriage by elopement. The existence of such a marriage, although it was reluctantly sanctioned by the elder men, cautions us against putting too much emphasis on "money" itself as that which either liberated the women or that which was the ultimate triumph over the elder men.

To suggest all this is not to suggest that Akiga's presentation of the experience of "writing" or of "money" by the Tiv is any less significant for our understanding of Tiv history. For if we read this story as one not of the a priori authority of writing, or of the essential difference of a monetary economy, but rather of their coming-to-being-experienced as such, then it may better position us to appreciate the concrete historical processes through which such forms begin to colonize the consciousness of the Tiv. Because they are instruments of colonial domination, such forms like Bourdieu's "disguised" form of the symbolic are experienced as alien, as radically different from anything the Tiv may have had, as authoritative, as true, as the mark of civilization itself not necessarily because they are such, but because they must seem such in order to

97. Indeed, the ideas surrounding the "contract" and its nullification, and ideas surrounding "debts," consistently emerge in Akiga's text.
98. Sai, *Akiga's Story*, 141.

function in the workings of colonial hegemony. Thus a critique of such forms must attempt to relearn their status in the colonial framework and question how they continue to be treated in colonial discourse.[99]

History, Colonial Critique, and an Ambivalent Modernity

In the words of Michel de Certeau,

> The historian is no longer a person who shapes an empire. He or she no longer envisages the paradise of a global history. The historian comes to circulate *around* acquired rationalizations. He or she works in the margins. In this respect the historian becomes a prowler. In a society gifted at generalization, endowed with powerful centralizing strategies, the historian moves in the direction of the frontiers of great regions already exploited. He or she 'deviates' by going back to sorcery, madness, festival, popular literature, the forgotten world of the peasant, Occitania, etc. all those zones of silence.[100]

With these remarks as a commentary on what I have attempted to do here, I bring to a close my reading of *Akiga's Story*. I hope this reading will work for some, and perhaps even encourage a few to read, teach, and write about this brilliant but little-known text. Yet it would surely come as no surprise if my reading were to offend others and evoke censure. To clarify what it is that I have been trying to do, I offer here the following notes.

    1. In the dominant narrative of the evolution of African historiography in the twentieth century, the advent of oral history is seen as the major methodological innovation in the field. Thus when Jan Vansina popularized the methods of studying oral traditions as history in the late 1950s and early 1960s, he was working against the grain of a discipline that primarily relied on the

---

99. Thus, for instance, Kings M. Phiri writes, "In this whole discussion of colonial capitalism and the impact it had on African economies, however, one thing has tended to be neglected, which is the effort Africans made to cope with the world of capitalism and to become capitalists themselves. Indigenous capital accumulation was undoubtedly something which developed gradually in most parts of Africa; nevertheless, as Iliffe has pointed out, the process deserves to be studied and documented for it has been one of the most important factors shaping modern Africa" (Phiri, "African History: An Assessment and an Agenda for Future Research," *African Studies Review* 30.2 [June 1987]: 42).

100. Michel de Certeau, *The Writing of History* (New York: Columbia University Press, 1988), 79.

written word.[101] The oral testimony given by native Africans was subject to doubt because it was felt that it was manipulable, changeable, and thus unreliable as an archive of what had really happened. Those who defended oral history against such prejudices were joined by scholars from other fields like Ruth Finnegan who set about establishing the relative authenticity and historical value of certain forms of oral narratives.

The efforts of those engaged in this project have been integral in moving discussions of Africa from the earlier ethnocentrisms that claimed that "Africa has no history" or at best read Africa as a silent partner in the advance of European history. The legacy of those historians—such as Cheikh Anta Diop and Basil Davidson, who in the era of African nationalisms and independence created the conditions of possibility for a rethinking of some of the cultural glories of precolonial Africa within the disciplinary framework of history—is a legacy that is still with us today.[102] But perhaps it behooves us today to look elsewhere, to look differently, and indeed occasionally to look at ourselves and our practices, even while continuing to reconceptualize African pasts.

In a recently edited collection of texts written by domestic servants in the colonial Belgian Congo, the editor Johannes Fabian suggests that although he and his colleague Bruce Fetter knew of the existence of these texts for over a couple of decades, their significance was until very recently lost on them. He writes: "I think I can speak for both of us when I say that we conducted our research in a frame of mind which, although we felt immediately that there was something remarkable about this text, directed our inquiries among Africans above all to oral information. Occasional written statements by Africans were welcomed as supplements to that primary source. Things have changed so much since that it is difficult to believe, now speaking for myself, how strong and unquestioned the alignment of Western with literate vs. African with non-literate still was in our epistemological orientation."[103] The point I

101. See Jan Vansina, *Oral Tradition as History* (London: James Currey, 1985). For an entertaining, if occasionally polemical, account of the trajectories of African historical studies in the twentieth century see Vansina, *Living with Africa* (Madison: University of Wisconsin Press, 1994).

102. See among many others, Chiekh Anta Diop, *Civilization or Barbarism: An Authentic Anthropology* (New York: L. Hill, 1991); Diop, *The African Origin of Civilization: Myth or Reality* (New York: L. Hill, 1974); Basil Davidson, *The Lost Cities of Africa* (Boston: Little Brown, 1959); Davidson, *Old Africa Rediscovered* (London: Gollancz, 1959).

103. Johannes Fabian and Kalundi Mango, eds., *History from Below: The "Vocabulary of Eliza-*

want to make here by recourse to Fabian's autobiographical reflection is a simple one—although methods of oral history rightly deserve great respect for providing the intellectual backbone for much of the scholarship on precolonial as well as colonial Africa, we should not allow ourselves to be conversely skeptical of written documents, especially when they are authored by colonial African subjects. Akiga's text—a written document (and I daresay no less interesting to historians because it is a written one) is one among a few significant others that deserve greater attention than they have hitherto been given. The writings of the Yoruba historian Samuel Johnson, the Chewa historian and novelist Samuel Ntara, the Tswana historian S. M. Molema,[104] along with the histories by domestic servants in Elizabethsville recently made available through Johannes Fabian's collection, are others that similarly deserve to be read not so much for their "footnote value" (the purpose that Akiga's text most frequently serves in the scholarly literature) but as integral aspects of our historical and interpretive research.

2. In the context of a colonial archive that contains relatively few texts written by African authors, the tendency to read each and every such text as the voice of the community is perhaps understandable. Yet, for reasons that should be clear by now, such a move, despite its often benevolent motives, is dangerous in that it effectively silences "other others" in any given community. As I suggested at the beginning of the chapter, I have attempted to read *Akiga's Story* neither as "the representative text" of an authentic Tiv history nor as the paradigmatic register of colonial change. Instead, I have chosen to read Akiga as just one among many possible speakers and actors on the Tiv stage, one whose voice English-language readers are fortunate to have available to them today. The fact that Akiga was a male subject who was also one of the first to be directly influenced by Christianity was of course not incidental but integral to the fact that his voice found entry into the colonial archive. As such, Akiga is not a "representative" subject but rather an extraordinary one. If, then, I have found it useful to focus on religious belief and gender as important markers of Akiga's text, I have foregrounded them in order not to pro-

bethsville" by Andre Yav—Text, Translation, and Interpretive Essay (Philadelphia: John Benjamins Publishing, 1990), 165.

104. Samuel Johnson, *A History of the Yoruba* (1897; rpt., London, 1921); Samuel Ntara, *A History of the Chewa;* Ntara, *Man of Africa,* trans. and ed. T. Cullen Young (London: United Society for Christian Literature, 1934); Ntara, *Headman's Enterprise,* trans. T. Cullen Young (London: Lutterworth Press, 1949); Molema, *The Bantu.*

mote Akiga as a "representative" Tiv subject but rather to suggest his very specific colonial self-fashioning.

At the same time, it is important to recognize that his "extraordinariness" makes Akiga no less an interesting and important subject of study. For the need to justify every native voice as "the authentic voice" of a colonized community is itself a residual ethnocentricism that demands "representativeness" from others while it celebrates "uniqueness," "individuality," or "genius," among its own.[105] Furthermore, by recognizing the extraordinariness of an Akiga, it is important not to fall, as V. Y. Mudimbe rightly cautions us, in the racist division between the "bush" African and the "educated" one. The point is not that education or Christianity has in any way "disqualified" Akiga from speaking as a Tiv, as he himself sometimes fears. The point is simply that claiming "representativeness" for a particular perspective, whether that be of Akiga or of Saama's unnamed sister, seems today to be a move of dubious political or theoretical value.

3. Finally, if the claim of "representativeness" is a problematic one, I have also been cautious in my enthusiasm to render audible subaltern voices. I have followed Gayatri Spivak in recognizing that the inability to render accessible the consciousness of the subaltern is one limit of historical knowledge, but like her I have found it a necessary theoretical fiction that has motivated my own thinking about this project. Quite truly, I doubt that I would have spent as many months thinking about this text as I have, if it had not been for the imaginary voices I kept hearing even as I reread Akiga's story. To be sure, the exact nature and content of those voices is still ultimately unavailable to me today, and I am sure they will continue to energize me when I return to the text. What I can say with relative confidence from this reading, however, is that it has taught me the fruitfulness of being ever vigilant to the silences of the texts we study. One such lesson, for example, has been the centrality of societal constructs of gender throughout the social spaces I studied. In this sense my reading of the case of Saama and Oralai shares more with the genre of "thick description" advocated by Clifford Geertz than with the traditional methods of an event history. It was in the working out of this "thick description" that I began to see how the seemingly gender-free space of tsav is in fact crucially tied to issues surrounding the circulation of women and men's access to them. Gender, then, like Foucault's "Power," has appeared to me everywhere in Aki-

---

105. See Paul Radin's discussion of "primitive philosopher" in *Primitive Man as Philosopher* (New York: Dover Publications, 1957), xxi–xl.

ga's text, although in various localized forms. Although I have traced only some of its incarnations here, I hope that my reading has shown how an attention to gender dynamics in such a text is a matter not just of adding the subaltern women to Tiv history but also of substantially rethinking the very ways in which a protonationalist history such as Akiga's itself operates as a site of the production of gender knowledge.[106]

Although the questions of subaltern consciousness and subaltern resistance remain open ones, Akiga's text is productive in foregrounding the various prosaic ways in which such subalterns resisted, adjusted to, or even appropriated the various changes that colonialism engendered among and around them. In this sense, Akiga's history forces us to rethink the "local knowledges" at work in various colonial contexts. Rather than thinking of the history of the Tiv and of their contact with Europeans from the Eurocentric narratives of imperial history on the one hand, and the equally Eurocentric, if anti-European, globalizing narratives of "world-systems theory" on the other,[107] Akiga's text provides us a space to understand the local negotiations of the practice of everyday colonial life on the part both of the colonizers and the colonized. In particular, by demonstrating the differential effects of colonial capitalism on the lives of the young women as opposed to the older men, the text provides us with a richer reading of the multiple valences of its entry than is generally available through the more global narrative of a world-systems approach.[108] In this way, the text allows us, as Gyan Prakash puts it in another

106. See Joan Scott's *Gender and the Politics of History* (New York: Columbia University Press, 1988) for a very readable and sensitive account of such work in feminist history.

107. World-systems theory developed primarily by Immanuel Wallerstein, although based in an anticapitalist and anticolonial desire, has often seemed to give too much valence to the power of "capital" to unequivocally affect the lives of all colonial subjects. The world, divided in the Center, Semi-Periphery, and Periphery, in this theory appears too rigidly economically predetermined by the forces of Capital itself. Although it remains a useful reminder of the global dimensions of seemingly local events, it necessarily misses out on the nuanced inflexions of competing local interests, ideologies, and discourses. See Immanuel Wallerstein, *The Modern World System* (New York: Academic Press, 1974); Terence Hopkins et al., eds., *World-Systems Analysis: Theory and Methodology* (Beverly Hills: Sage Publications, 1982).

108. On this see also Gyan Prakash: "We cannot thematize Indian history in terms of the development of capitalism and simultaneously contest capitalism's homogenization of the contemporary world. Critical history cannot simply document the process by which capitalism becomes dominant, for that amounts to repeating the history we seek to displace; instead, criticism must reveal the difference that capitalism either represents as the particular form of its universal existence or sketches it only in relation to itself" (Prakash, "Postcolonial Criticism and Indian Historiography," in *Social Text,* nos. 31–32 [1992]: 13).

context, "a return to the history of colonialism without rehearsing the natu-
ralization of colonialism as History." It enables a "project of understanding
that delves into the history of colonialism not only to document its record of
domination but also to track the failures, silences, displacements, and transformations produced by its functioning; not only to chronicle the functioning of Western dominance and resistance to it, but to mark those (subaltern)
positions and knowledges that could not be properly recognized and named,
only 'normalized' by colonial discourses."[109]

109. Gyan Prakash, "Introduction: After Colonialism," in *After Colonialism: Imperial Histories and Postcolonial Displacements,* ed. Gyan Prakash (Princeton: Princeton University Press, 1995), 6.

Coda

It is with the reading of Akiga Sai, then, that I bring this book to a close, but this closure, as any other, must be held to be tentative, situational, and always open to censure. At the simplest level, my project has been to "read," in the critical sense, a whole range of Africanist discourse produced in the period of high colonialism in anglophone Africa. The "colonial library" that I have sought to read has included ideas of race, rationality, and their relationship to the educability of the African; the politics of engagement of professionals along with the pragmatic deployment of a disciplinary practice such as functionalism; and finally, the self-fashioning of a personal and protonationalist identity through the writing of a heavily gendered indigenous history. I have been guided by the desire to take discourses seriously—and taking them seriously has often meant reading them not merely for the content of their assertions but moreover for the nature of their entry and subsequent reception into the world. Emphasizing the rhetorical aspects of discourses rather than merely their mimetic ones has also meant that my project has often been as interested in the practices of discursive circulation as in the texts themselves.

At a certain level, then, this book is also an investigation of the limits as well as the possibilities of disciplinary knowledges in the context of colonial Africa. Each chapter in its earliest guise was conceived within the intrinsic parameters of disciplinary agendas even when I was engaging in the critique as a literary critic. Thus, for instance, the chapter " 'Race,' Rationality, and the Pedagogical Imperative" was originally conceived as a response to the canonical discussions of African "Rationality" as they often appear in postcolonial philosophical treatises. My basic point was simple—although Africanist thinkers have spent a lot of time and energy presenting histories of discourses on "rationality" in the context of anthropology and ethnophilosophy, they have completely ignored the dangerously racist work being done at the same time by certain eugenicists and hereditarians. The unwillingness to consider this work is partly because of the fact that the "rationality" debates have often forgotten their biological underpinnings. Postcolonial African philosophy has, of course, not been blind to the workings of racism—but as I suggest in this book, in the majority it seems to be content with pointing out the philosophical or ideological racism of thinkers like Kant, Hegel, Hume, or Lévy-Bruhl while leaving untouched the work of those engaged in making the case for a more scientific basis of racial differentiation. But isn't it ironic that philosophy, often considered by its practitioners to be a metadiscipline, a discipline able to engage with the production of almost any kind of knowledge, should ignore, in this case, the work of scientists just because they were using the rhetoric of "frontal lobe deficiency" rather than "rationality"? And is it not even more strange that students of Africanist philosophy could have so easily embraced Frantz Fanon without emphasizing that even while he was formulating a psychological theory of racism he was at the same time working to counter the work of exactly those actors in colonial Africa who were alleging a physiological basis for "race"?

If the debates in African philosophy were at the origins of the chapter "'Race,' Rationality, and the Pedagogical Imperative," it was the discipline of cultural anthropology and in particular the school of thought known as functionalism that interested me in the next chapter. I first came to the texts of African anthropology in the hopes of finding in them some of the contextual material that I thought would help me in my readings of contemporary African literature. Since I was eager to get a sense of the range of Africanist knowledge as well as a historical perspective on scholarly changes within the field, I decided to read through back issues of the journal *Africa* from the first issue in 1928 at least through 1960. In retrospect it is clear to me that it was this experience that got me thinking about academic disciplinarity in the context of African studies in the first place.[1]

1. As I mention in chapter 3, the journal *Africa*, published by the International African Institute, was in the colonial period the most important venue for publication of scholarship on Africa. As such, it is an excellent resource for studying competing academic disciplinary claims and interests as well as responses to these claims by the "practical man."

By the time I had undertaken this task, the "narrative" turn in anthropology had already taken place, and my simultaneous readings in poststructural and postcolonial theory meant that I was also drawn to the critique of ethnographic representation that was increasingly being offered by scholars influenced by literary criticism. Added to this mix of influences, I found myself engaging with reassessments of the role of the intellectual in public culture and was much taken by the renewed political sense of the "professional," as it was being offered by literary critics such as Stanley Fish and Bruce Robbins. I found particularly compelling Bruce Robbins's claim that professionalism, often feared or held in contempt by left-leaning intellectuals, was in fact even to those on the left a space open for appropriation.[2] As I read more in the colonial library and simultaneously engaged with scholarship on the politics of professionalism and disciplinarity, it became obvious that both the earlier "collaborationist" critique of anthropology as well as the later assertions about the "naive empiricism" of the discipline had to be revised: Not rejected outright but at least revised.

For starters, I noted the jarring contradiction between the fact that functionalism, which was alleged to be the anthropologist's contribution to colonial governance, was also at the same time being mobilized by a nationalist such as Jomo Kenyatta to counter precisely this colonial project. For the postcolonial critique of "collaboration" to have worked, it, of necessity, had to erase this effort of Kenyatta's. For to put Kenyatta's work back into the archive of anthropology would have meant a revision of the critique, a recognition that since disciplinary knowledges and methodologies are always subject to appropriation, the political agendas they may be used to support cannot always be calculated in advance. It was in this context that the notion of the "dangerous supplement" began to haunt my analysis. That which was hitherto "outside," hitherto "inferior," hitherto "invisible," when brought into the frame completely disrupted the shape of the colonial archive. This, it should be clear, was not a simple gesture of "add African and stir." Rather, it was an epistemic shift, from seeing disciplinary histories and methodologies as being purely "Western" to seeing them as being also shaped by "non-Western" desires, from seeing, if you will, the periphery in the center and the center in the periphery. It was also, at the same time, an invitation to consider the agendas of postcolonial critiques themselves. For what might it mean for a postcolo-

2. See Bruce Robbins, *Secular Vocations: Intellectuals, Professionalism, Culture* (London: Verso, 1993).

nial project to ignore, for the sake perhaps of presenting a coherent critique, a work such as *Facing Mount Kenya,* which is explicitly functionalist and also clearly nationalist? These questions, then, led me to suggest that colonial subjects such as Jomo Kenyatta and Akiga Sai when read within the colonial archive function as the dangerous supplements not only of the colonial library but also of our own postcolonial sensibilities.

But although Kenyatta's work was, for my purposes, the most important example of how disciplinary practices may be appropriated for political agendas that they have not earlier seemed to support, I thought it would be worthwhile to investigate at least provisionally what it was that these earlier discourses did indeed support. Edwin Smith's story of the Golden Stool, which provided a "mythological charter" for the discipline, was a story too good not to retell, and in it I saw all the attractions and all the necessary failures of liberal humanism. A good Christian, Smith seemed to believe sincerely that the truth shall set us all free, even though the truth he was writing about in this instance was the truth of anthropology. If only Europeans would understand Africans, their customs and their beliefs, the world would be free of unnecessary violence and evil. A noble dream—indeed, who can honestly say that they have never been swayed by it? But at its limits, outside the classroom, the church, or the library, it is clear that material interests—in land or labor—are not resolved by understanding alone. As Max Gluckman was to later put it, "Knowledge alone cannot make a moral policy, it can as easily serve an immoral one."[3]

This insight into the limits of scholarly understanding was not lost on Malinowski. Arguing passionately for a "relevant" anthropology, he seems to have been aware that colonial interest was not to be so easily overcome. Read carefully and with attention to their rhetorical strategies, Malinowski's writings suggest that his plea for "relevance" was not a plea for colonial collaboration as much as a casting of the anthropologist as a cautionary watchdog of the colonial enterprise. But here too he knew where the limits of his discipline lay, and ultimately he knew that if anthropology would not univocally support the colonial agenda, it could not univocally denounce and subvert it either. Thus the more urgently he pleaded for "relevance," the greater the ambivalence he felt about the relevance of his disciplinary project. If Malinowski grew to be one of the most influential advocates of professional anthropology, he

---

3. Gluckman, "Malinowski's 'Functional' Analysis of Social Change," *Africa* (1947): 105.

became so not despite these limitations but because of them. There is a cautionary note to be heard here, and it is a note to which I will return.

But there was yet another layer to Malinowski that hit close to home. As an "alien" worker myself in the U.S. academy (as INS has never ceased to remind me), and moreover as an academic whose sole sense of community in this country so far has been the academic community, I felt some level of empathy for Malinowski. His attempt to deal with his homelessness by making himself at home within the parameters of his profession was one that I could relate to. Malinowski's case demonstrated that if "professionalism" has increasingly provided a certain space of legitimacy for leftist critiques, it has also provided a space for outsiders to enter within the fold of the academy and to work to transform it from within. Even though he himself castigates the idea of professionalism, Edward Said remains such a model of an outsider who, through his remarkable professional accomplishments, has helped reshape the discipline of literary studies from within. It is no simple coincidence, then, that the more I thought through my reading of Malinowski and the importance of his outsideness to his accomplishments, the more my reading began to parallel Said's reading of Conrad. Said writes of Conrad that he knew that "your self-consciousness as an outsider can allow you actively to comprehend how the machine works, given that you and it are fundamentally not in perfect sympathy or correspondence. Never the wholly incorporated and fully acculturated Englishman, Conrad therefore preserved an ironic distance in each of his works."[4] This recognition of the privilege as well as the demands of outsideness was one that was shared both by the writer who is often seen to be the doyen of British literary modernism as well as by the father of functional anthropology. If, as Africanists, we must insist on reading Jomo Kenyatta today as one of the most significant "dangerous supplements" of the African colonial library, perhaps a closer attention to the Malinowskis and Conrads of the European library may suggest that this library was always already subject to difference even at its origins.

The logic of supplementarity works, however, in more ways than one. If Kenyatta proves to be the dangerous supplement of the anthropological archive, he does so by mastering its techniques, by getting it right, by, as the saying goes, attempting to use the master's tools to dismantle the master's house. By contrast, not being privy to academic disciplinary training as is Kenyatta, Akiga Sai instead presents us with a discourse that insists on its status as histor-

4. Edward Said, *Culture and Imperialism* (New York: Vintage, 1994), 25.

ical without being subjected to the disciplinary conventions of History. With Akiga, then, we encounter the limit of disciplinarity itself and the question it raises of the possibilities of extradisciplinary authority. If Akiga's text (and other texts like it written by colonial African subjects who were not professional historians) continues to lurk on the margins of the discipline of African history, what might it mean for us to insist on reading it as a central text of African history today?

To ask such a question is to be alert once again to the double context of supplementarity in which such a reading takes place. At one level, in reading texts such as Akiga's not so much as data to be used in footnotes but rather as important interventions in the construction of historical memory, we stand to learn much about the ways in colonial subjects responded to a surely encroaching western modernity. The point of these readings is not to ascertain whether a given subject had indeed managed to get the history "right." Rather, the point is to understand the complexities of the experiences and the competing demands and motives that informed the production of these histories in the first place. And as should be clear from my reading of *Akiga's Story,* a close attention to such competing demands and motives means also attempting to read into the narrative other voices that have been marginalized or erased. As much a reading of a text's silences as of its pronouncements, such a reading insists on the play of supplementarity in the text's own exclusions even as it hopes to correct the historical exclusion of the text from the larger colonial library.

But paying attention to the textual silences in the context of historical narratives is already to engage at the second level of supplementarity in which Akiga's text participates. For, if at one level, reading *Akiga's Story* helps us develop a better understanding of various local engagements with colonialism, then, at another level, it helps us confront some of the limitations and assumptions of our own contemporary scholarly practices. One such often unarticulated assumption is the view that if we are to find indigenous historical discourses in Africa during colonial times, we are best served by collecting oral histories. Although oral histories continue to play a crucial role in our understanding of precolonial and colonial Africa, a text such as Akiga's suggests that written histories are too fruitful to ignore. A second assumption we often make is that the critique of "objectivity" in historical interpretation is a recent, postcolonial, and postmodern phenomenon. But if we are to go by Akiga's text, written in the 1930s, we note that an indigenous critique of the "objectivity" of accounts, historical and otherwise, was already beginning to take shape among the Tiv. It is in these senses, then, that reading texts such as Akiga's helps us not only have a richer account of colonial practices but also critique the epistemologies of our own contemporaneity.

The postcolonial debates around African rationality and their erasure of scientific racism, the postcolonial critique of functional anthropology and its erasure of the appropriation of anthropology by a nationalist thinker, the postcolonial marginalization of histories written by Africans subject to colonialism—these are the specific discourses that *Subject to Colonialism* has most immediately sought to counter and challenge. Although almost exclusively concerned with studying colonialism in Africa, then, the book has in fact been driven by postcolonial agendas. It would be presumptuous to think that the agendas that have moved my readings will be ones shared by all. The richness of the archive suggests instead that there is plenty of room for many more readings and for new agendas.

To understand this is not only to understand the open-ended nature of this work, but more positively to take up its call for further readings in yet other understudied texts of the colonial library. For instance, although I have attempted to place in a central rather than marginal role the work of African subjects in this library, these subjects have both been male. To be sure, as is clear in my readings of Jomo Kenyatta and Akiga Sai, the writing of their texts is predicated on a very crucial negotiation of a gendered identity and an overwhelming preoccupation with women as the physical as well as symbolic conduits of culture. Yet what remains absent in my study is any account of how the thematic may have worked in the consciousness of contemporary African women subjects. Given the relatively few women's texts currently available in the colonial library,[5] a project of even a purely archival nature focusing on such writings would be a significant scholarly accomplishment.

But why, one may ask, should we direct our efforts today to such archival projects? Is the study of colonialism still worth pursuing as we leave behind the twentieth century? And what are the political stakes involved in presenting, as I have here, a postfoundational account of colonialism and colonial disciplinary practices? Further, as Ann Laura Stoler has recently asked, "How do

---

5. Most texts written by African women writers are from the postcolonial period. Some recorded oral histories exist and would be crucial for such study. (See, for instance, M. Smith, *Baba of Karo* [London: Faber and Faber, 1954].)

we tell the difference between a reappraisal of the colonial order of things as a politically engaged strategy and one that is a retreat from the political exegencies of the present, scholarship at a safe distance, a voyeurism of the past?"[6]

In his eloquent treatise, *Colonialism's Culture: Anthropology, Travel, and Government*, Nicholas Thomas suggests that we must continue to study colonialism in order to expose the "continuities between former colonialist ideologies and those that retain currency and dynamism in the present. . . . In the case of anti-colonial critique it is the *similarity* of the past and present that defamiliarizes the here and now and subverts the sense of historical progress."[7] The goal of colonial studies to Thomas is essentially one of demystification not only of the colonial past but also, more importantly, of the postcolonial present.

It is the desire for such demystification, argues Thomas, that has made scholars increasingly shift attention from the study of colonialism as a homogenous structure to the multiply mediated ways in which colonialisms entered the lived experiences of various subjects both in the colonies and in the metropoles. This more recent emphasis on ambivalence and inconsistency has often made anticolonialists uneasy because it has seemed at times to exonerate the colonial enterprise. But, argues Thomas, "an argument that draws attention to positive imaginings of colonialism in the discourses of the colonizers should not be mistaken for one that rereads the relationships and projects in positive terms. The aim is not to rehabilitate imperial efforts, but to understand how far and why they were (and are) supported by various classes and interest groups."[8] It is only when we take the contradictions and multiple mediations of colonialisms seriously that we can understand how colonial subjectivities were formed through processes of resistance and accommodation. Extending Thomas, we may add that to hold the ambivalences of the colonial archive up for analysis is not to substitute the violence of the gun with the violation of the text, but rather to ensure that "violence," so readily identified with the colonizer, does not get so taken-for-granted that in our accounts of colonialism its complex workings ultimately get erased.

This post-Manichean way of thinking about colonialism has recently seen support from a range of Africanist philosophers as well. These scholars argue

---

6. Ann Laura Stoler, *Race and the Education of Desire* (Durham: Duke University Press, 1995), 198.
7. Nicholas Thomas, *Colonialism's Culture: Anthropology, Travel, and Government* (Princeton: Princeton University Press, 1994), 21.
8. Ibid., 17.

that the binary model of thinking about colonialism has had the unfortunate consequence of reifying a singular oppositional identity in postcolonial Africa, an identity often mistaken as essential. Thus, for instance, D. A. Masolo writes,

> While the overarching political view of postcoloniality as an emancipatory movement is completely justified, a problem arises with regard to its two-pronged assumption, prevalent in most influential postcolonial texts: first that all formerly colonized persons ought to have one view of the impact of colonialism behind which they ought to unite to overthrow it; second, that the overthrow of colonialism be replaced with another, liberated and assumedly authentic identity. So strong is the pull toward the objectivity of this identity that most of those who speak of Africa from this emancipatory perspective think of it only as a solid rock which has withstood all the storms of history except colonialism. Because of the deeply political gist of the colonial/postcolonial discourse, we have come to think of our identities as natural rather than imagined and politically driven.[9]

If colonialism itself were seen to be a complex and messy process that touched the lives of African subjects in various ways, such postcolonial assertions of African authenticity, Masolo suggests, would be easier to critique. In a similar vein, Kwame Anthony Appiah, in his collection of essays titled *In My Father's House,* has critiqued precisely such an essentialist understanding of African identity and suggested that academics work, even if slowly and marginally, to help dismantle the discourse of "racial" and "tribal" differences and to expose its false claims to an originary African metaphysics.[10] And, finally, in his powerful essay "Towards a Post-Africanism: Contemporary African Thought and Postmodernism," Denis Ekpo writes, "The modern African mind appears to have definitely conceptualized its identity, its destiny, its past and present, in the horizon of a conspiracy theory, that is, in perpetual accusation of, opposition to and fight against, the West."[11] In expending all its energies in this direc-

9. Masolo, "African Philosophy and the Postcolonial: Some Misleading Abstractions about 'Identity,' " in *Postcolonial African Philosophy: A Critical Reader,* ed. Emmanuel Eze (Cambridge, Mass.: Blackwell, 1997), 285.

10. Appiah, *In My Father's House: Africa in the Philosophy of Culture* (Oxford: Oxford University Press, 1992), 179.

11. Denis Ekpo, "Towards a Post-Africanism: Contemporary African Thought and Postmodernism," *Textual Practice* 9.1 (1995): 126.

tion, such a project has failed to address in any meaningful way the demands of a postcolonial society. What is now called for, argues Ekpo, is not a continued reluctance to engage with the West but rather a willingness to engage with Western postmodern theories that may help "liberate the mind and discourse for newer, de-totalized, polycentric, and more useful interpretations of the African world."[12]

The project of demystification advocated by Thomas, Masolo, Appiah, and Ekpo is a project that I share, and I am especially taken by the attempts to historicize postcolonial identities and practices. It is in this sense that for me the study of colonialism is not, as Ann Stoler cautions us, a project of mere voyeurism, but rather an exercise that is politically motivated. And yet, as should be clear from my earlier account of how I came about working on these issues in the first place, the most immediate sphere of politics for me has been the domain of African studies itself. To say this is not to part company with those who productively attempt to bring together the discourses of the academy with extraacademic concerns, and it is certainly not to belittle their efforts. Rather, it is to acknowledge the fact that a great deal of work still needs to be done after the work of theorizing is over. Is that not after all the lesson we learned through our critique of Edwin Smith? If, as we said then, the truth alone shall not set us all free, then can we so eagerly believe today that the new, antifoundational truths will automatically set postcolonial Africans free? Or to put it in more concrete terms, will the new knowledge that African identities are historical and circumstantial in itself be sufficient to change much by way of the standard of living or of the civil liberties of contemporary Africans?

To ask such uncomfortable questions is not to cast an overly skeptical note on scholarly practices. It is only to recognize the possibilities as well as the limits of the scholarly enterprise. For if this book has suggested anything about the political efficacy of scholarly production, it is that it is ironically both over- as well as underdetermined. Exaggerated claims either on the side of academic "purity" on the one hand or academic "relevance" on the other are, in this scenario, both bound to fail. Just as we are today convinced that "purity" and "objectivity" are themselves politically loaded concepts, we cannot in all honesty fail to recognize that the notion of "relevance" is also bounded by competing political interests and claims. As scholars of Africa, and moreover as postfoundationalist scholars, I suggest we attempt not to ground a new politics on our antifoundationalist insights (for to do so would mean losing sight

12. Ibid., 129.

of the most compelling claims of the deconstructive enterprise) but rather, along with Malinowski, to continue to work toward accounts that seem "relevant" to us and our constituencies without being blind to the contingencies of "relevance" itself.

To say, then, that postfoundationalist thinking cannot by its own account ultimately ground a new political agenda is not only to make the claim I have often made about the contingent nature of theoretical appropriations, it is also to remind ourselves continually that the complexities of contemporary Africa demand more than sloganeering, and certainly more than academic accounts. As Appiah puts it, "Every time I read another report in the newspapers of an African disaster—a famine in Ethiopia, a war in Namibia, ethnic conflict in Burundi—I wonder how much good it does to correct the theories with which these evils are bound up; the solution is food, or mediation, or some other more material, more practical step."[13] But as he continues to note, theoretical accounts have indeed influenced African lives often in unintentional ways, and it is thus useful for academics to continue interrogating them. In some senses, as Malinowski might have noted, this is fortuitous, since trained as most of us are trained, situated in the academy as most of us are situated, providing accounts is indeed what we can most meaningfully do.[14] And although we can never be sure as to how our work will be appropriated and by whom, at least we can continue to do it with a certain modesty about its range of influence and, of course, do it in good faith.

13. Appiah, *In My Father's House,* 179.
14. By "most of us" I speak of the great majority of Africanists that I know who are employed in academic positions outside Africa and are primarily responsible for university teaching and research. Africanists in Africa, as my recent trip to South Africa suggested, often have a more direct access to extra-academic political agency even when they primarily work in the academic sphere.

Bibliography

Abraham, R. C. *The Tiv People*. Lagos: Government Printer, 1933.

Achebe, Chinua. "An Image of Africa: Racism in Conrad's *Heart of Darkness*." In *Heart of Darkness: An Authoritative Text, Backgrounds and Sources, Criticism*, ed. Robert Kimbrough. New York: Norton, 1988.

Allier, Raoul. *The Mind of the Savage*. Trans. Fred Rothwell. London: G. Bell and Sons, 1929.

Althusser, Louis. "Ideology and Ideological State Apparatuses." In *Lenin and Philosophy and Other Essays*. New York: Monthly Review Press, 1971.

Amadiume, Ifi. *Male Daughters, Female Husbands*. London: Zed Books, 1987.

Anderson, Perry. "Components of the National Culture." *New Left Review* (1968): 3–57.

Appadurai, Arjun. "Global Ethnoscapes: Notes and Queries for a Transnational Anthropology." In *Recapturing Anthropology: Working in the Present*, ed. Richard Fox. Santa Fe: School of American Research, 1991.

Appiah, Kwame Anthony. "Strictures on Structures: The Prospects for a Structuralist Poetics of African Fiction." In *Black Literature and Literary Theory*, ed. Henry Louis Gates Jr. New York: Methuen, 1984.

——. *In My Father's House: Africa in the Philosophy of Culture*. New York: Oxford University Press, 1992.

——, and Amy Gutman. *Color Conscious: The Political Morality of Race*. Princeton: Princeton University Press, 1996.

Arendt, Hannah. *The Origins of Totalitarianism*. 3 vols. New York: Harcourt Brace, 1951.

Asad, Talal, ed. *Anthropology and the Colonial Encounter*. Atlantic Heights, N.J.: Humanities Press, 1973.

Banaji, Jairus. "The Crisis of British Anthropology." *New Left Review* 64 (1970): 70–85.

Barlow, A. R. "Review of *Facing Mount Kenya.*" *Africa* (1939): 114–15.

Barthes, Roland. "Historical Discourse." In *Introduction to Structuralism,* ed. Michael Lane. New York: Basic Books, 1970.

"The Beautiful Wife." In *Tales Tiv Tell,* ed. Harold Bergsma and Ruth Bergsma. Ibadan: Oxford University Press, 1969.

Benn, Stanley I., and G. W. Mortimore. *Rationality and the Social Sciences.* London: Routledge, 1976.

Berman, Marshall. *All That Is Solid Melts in the Air.* New York: Penguin, 1982.

Berreman, Gerald D. "Is Anthropology Alive? Social Responsibility in Social Anthropology." *Current Anthropology* 9.5 (December 1968): 391–96.

Bhabha, Homi. *The Location of Culture.* New York: Routledge, 1994.

Biesheuval, Simon. *African Intelligence.* Johannesburg: South African Institute of Race Relations, 1943.

Boas, Franz. *The Mind of Primitive Man.* 1911. Rpt., New York: Free Press, 1965.

Bohannan, Laura. "A Genealogical Charter." *Africa* 22.4 (1952): 301–15.

Bohannan, Paul. "Exchange and Investment among the Tiv." *American Anthropologist* 57.1 (1955): 60–70.

———. "Extra-Processual Events in Tiv Political Institutions." *American Anthropologist* 60.1 (February 1958): 1–12.

———. "The Impact of Money on an African Subsistence Economy." *Journal of Economic History* 19.4 (December 1959): 491–503.

Bourdieu, Pierre. *In Other Words: Essays Towards a Reflexive Sociology.* Stanford: Stanford University Press, 1990.

———. "Structures, Habitus, Power: Basis for a Theory of Symbolic Power." In *Culture/Power/History: A Reader in Contemporary Social Theory,* ed. Nicholas B. Dirks, Geoff Eley, and Sherry B. Ortner. Princeton: Princeton University Press, 1994.

Bozzoli, Belinda. "Marxism, Feminism, and South African Studies." *Journal of Southern African Studies* 9.2 (April 1983): 139–71.

Brelsford, Vernon. *Primitive Philosophy.* London: John Bale, 1935.

Brokensha, David, and Peter Little, eds. *Anthropology of Development and Change in East Africa.* Boulder, CO: Westview, 1988.

Brokensha, David, and Marian Pearsall, eds. *The Anthropology of Development in Sub-Saharan Africa.* Lexington: University Press of Kentucky, 1969.

Bunn, David. "The Insistence of Theory: Three Questions for Megan Vaughan." *Social Dynamics* 20.2 (1994): 24–34.

Butler, Judith. "Contingent Foundations: Feminism and the Question of 'Postmodernism.'" In *Feminists Theorize the Political,* ed. Judith Butler and Joan W. Scott. New York: Routledge, 1992.

Carnoy, Martin. *Education as Cultural Imperialism.* New York: David McKay, 1974.

Casely-Hayford, Adelaide. "A Girl's School in West Africa." *Southern Workman* (October 1926): 449–55.

Clarke, F. "The Double Mind in African Education." *Africa* (1932): 158–68.

Clarke, J. D. *Omu: An African Experiment in Education.* London: Longman, 1936.

Clifford, James. "On Ethnographic Self-Fashioning: Conrad and Malinowski." In *The Predicament of Culture: Twentieth Century Ethnography, Literature, and Art.* Cambridge, MA: Harvard University Press, 1988.

———, and George Marcus, eds. *Writing Culture: The Poetics and Politics of Ethnography.* Berkeley: University of California Press, 1986.

Cohen, David William, and E. S. Atieno Odhiambo. *Burying SM: The Politics of Knowledge and the Sociology of Power in Africa.* Portsmouth, NH: Heinemann, 1992.

Comaroff, Jean. *Body of Power, Spirit of Resistance: The Culture History of a South African People.* Chicago: University of Chicago Press, 1985.

———, and John Comaroff. *Of Revelation and Revolution: Christianity, Colonialism, and Consciousness in South Africa.* Vol. 1. Chicago: University of Chicago Press, 1991.

———, eds. *Modernity and Its Malcontents: Ritual and Power in Postcolonial Africa.* Chicago: University of Chicago Press, 1993.

Cooper, Frederick, and Ann Laura Stoler, eds. *Tensions of Empire: Colonial Cultures in a Bourgeois World.* Berkeley: University of California Press, 1997.

Crowder, Michael, ed. *West African Resistance.* London: Hutchinson, 1971.

Cureau, Adolphe Louis. *Savage Man in Central Africa: A Study of Primitive Races in the French Congo.* London: T. F. Unwin, 1915.

Curtin, Philip. *The Image of Africa: British Ideas and Action, 1730–1850.* Madison: University of Wisconsin Press, 1964.

Cutrufelli, Maria Rosa. *Women of Africa: Roots of Oppression.* London: Zed Press, 1983.

Davidson, A. B. "African Resistance and Rebellion against the Imposition of Colonial Rule." In *Emerging Themes of African History,* ed. T. O. Ranger. Nairobi: East African Publishing House, 1968.

Davidson, Basil. *The Lost Cities of Africa.* Boston: Little, Brown, 1959.

———. *Old Africa Rediscovered.* London: Gollancz, 1959.

Davis R. Hunt, Jr. "Charles T. Loram and an American Model for African Education in South Africa." *African Studies Review* 19.2 (September 1976): 87–99.

de Certeau, Michel. *The Practice of Everyday Life.* Trans. Steven Rendall. Berkeley: University of California Press, 1984.

———. *The Writing of History.* New York: Columbia University Press, 1988.

Derrida, Jacques. *Of Grammatology.* Trans. Gayatri Chakravorty Spivak. Baltimore: Johns Hopkins University Press, 1976.

———. ". . . That Dangerous Supplement . . . " In *Of Grammatology.* Trans. Gayatri Chakravorty Spivak. Baltimore: Johns Hopkins University Press, 1976.

———. "Différance." In *Margins of Philosophy,* trans. Alan Bass. Chicago: University of Chicago Press, 1982.

———. "The Principle of Reason: The University in the Eyes of Its Pupils." *Diacritics* (fall 1983): 3–20.

Diop, Chiekh Anta. *The African Origin of Civilization: Myth or Reality.* New York: L. Hill, 1974.

———. *Civilization or Barbarism: An Authentic Anthropology.* New York: L. Hill, 1991.

Dorward, David Craig. "The Development of the British Colonial Administration among the Tiv, 1900–1949." *African Affairs* 68.273 (1969): 316–33.

———. "Ethnography and Administration: A Study of Anglo-Tiv 'Working Misunderstanding.'" *Journal of African History* 15.3 (1974): 457–77.

Dougall, James W. C. "Characteristics of African Thought." *Africa* 5.3 (July 1932): 249–65.

Dover, Cedric. *Half Caste.* London: Martin Secker and Warburg, 1937.

Driberg, J. H. *The Savage As He Really Is.* London: Routledge, 1929.

Dubow, Saul. *Scientific Racism in Modern South Africa.* Cambridge: Cambridge University Press, 1995.

Earthy, E. Dora. *Valenge Women.* Oxford: Oxford University Press, 1933.

East, Rupert. "A First Essay in Imaginative African Literature." *Africa* (1936): 350–57.

Edwards, Adrian C. "Seeing, Believing, Doing: The Tiv Understanding of Power." *Anthropos,* 78.3–4 (1983): 459–80.

Ekpo, Denis. "Towards a Post-Africanism: Contemporary African Thought and Postmodernism." *Textual Practice* 9.1 (1995): 121–35.

Emecheta, Buchi. *Joys of Motherhood.* New York: G. Braziller, 1979.

Evans-Pritchard, E. E. *Witchcraft, Oracles, and Magic among the Azande.* 1937. Rpt., London: Oxford University Press, 1976.

———. *History of Anthropological Thought.* Boston: Faber and Faber, 1981.

Fabian, Johannes, and Kalundi Mango, eds. *History from Below: The "Vocabulary of Elizabethville" by Andre Yav—Text, Translation, and Interpretive Essay.* Philadelphia: John Benjamins, 1990.

Fancher, Raymond E. "Francis Galton's African Ethnography and Its Role in the Development of His Psychology." *British Journal for the History of Science* 15 (March 1983): 67–79.

Fanon, Frantz. *The Wretched of the Earth.* Trans. Constance Farrington. Preface by Jean-Paul Sartre. New York: Grove Press, 1965.

———. *Black Skin, White Masks.* 1952. Rpt., New York: Grove Press, 1966.

Fardon, Richard. "Sisters, Wives, Wards, and Daughters: A Transformational Analysis of the Political Organization of the Tiv and Their Neighbours. Part 1: The Tiv." *Africa* 54.4 (1984): 2–21.

———. "Malinowski's Precedent: The Imagination of Equality." *Man* 25.4 (December 1990): 569–87.

Fick, Laurence. *The Educability of the South African Native.* Pretoria: South African Council for Educational and Social Research, 1939.

Firth, Raymond, ed. *Man and Culture: An Evaluation of the Work of Bronislaw Malinowski.* New York: Routledge, 1957.

——. "The Sceptical Anthropologist: Social Anthropology and Marxist Views on Society." *Proceedings of the British Academy* 58 (1972): 177–213.

——. "Malinowski in the History of Social Anthropology." In *Malinowski between Two Worlds: The Polish Roots of an Anthropological Tradition,* ed. Ray Ellen, Ernest Gellner, Graznya Kubica, and Janusz Mucha. Cambridge: Cambridge University Press, 1988.

Fish, Stanley. "No Bias, No Merit: The Case against Blind Submission." In *Doing What Comes Naturally.* Durham: Duke University Press, 1989.

——. "With the Compliments of the Author: Reflections on Austin and Derrida." In *Doing What Comes Naturally.* Durham: Duke University Press, 1989.

——. "The Law Wishes to Have a Formal Existence." In *The Fate of Law,* ed. Austin Sarat and Thomas Kearns. Ann Arbor: University of Michigan Press, 1991.

Fisher, Donald. "American Philanthropy and the Social Sciences: The Reproduction of a Conservative Ideology." In *Philanthropy and Cultural Imperialism,* ed. Robert F. Arnove. Boston: G. K. Hall, 1980.

Fortes, Meyer. Review of "The African as Suckling and Adult." *Africa* (1945): 166–67.

Foucault, Michel. *The Order of Things.* New York: Vintage, 1973.

——. "Discourse on Language." In *The Archaeology of Language,* trans. A. M. Sheridan. New York: Harper and Row, 1976.

Freshfield, Mark. *The Stormy Dawn.* London: Faber and Faber, 1946.

Fyfe, Christopher. "Race, Empire, and the Historians." *Race and Class* 33.4 (1992): 15–30.

Galton, Francis. *Hereditary Genius.* London: Macmillan, 1892.

Geertz, Clifford. *Local Knowledge: Further Essays in Interpretive Anthropology.* New York: Basic Books, 1983.

Gikandi, Simon. "On Language, Power, and National Identity: The Project of African Literature." Paper presented at the Language and Identity in Africa Symposium, Program of African Studies, Northwestern University, 1989.

——. *Maps of Englishness: Writing Identity in the Culture of Colonialism.* New York: Columbia University Press, 1996.

Gilman, Sander. "Sexology, Psychoanalysis, and Degeneration." In *Difference and Pathology.* Ithaca: Cornell University Press, 1985.

Gjessing, Gutorm. "The Social Responsibility of the Social Scientist." *Current Anthropology* 9.5 (December 1968): 397–402.

Gluckman, Max. "Malinowski's 'Functional' Analysis of Social Change." *Africa* (1947): 103–21.

Goddard, David. "Limits of British Anthropology." *New Left Review* 58 (1969): 79–89.

Gollock, Georgina A. *Sons of Africa.* New York: Friendship Press, 1928.

Goody, Jack. *The Expansive Moment in Africa: Anthropology in Britain and Africa, 1918–1970.* New York: Cambridge University Press, 1995.

Gordon, H. L. "Amentia in the East African." *Eugenics Review* 25 (1934): 223–35.

———. "An Inquiry into the Correlation of Civilization and Mental Disorder in the Kenya Native." *East African Medical Journal* 12 (1935–36): 327–35.

———. "Is War Eugenic or Dysgenic?: That Is Does War Improve or Impair the Physical or Mental Qualities of Future Generations?" *East African Medical Journal* 19 (1942): 86–96.

Gough, Kathleen. "New Proposals for Anthropologists." *Current Anthropology* 9.5 (December 1968): 403–7.

Gould, Stephen Jay. *The Mismeasure of Man.* New York: Vintage, 1981.

Gouldner, Alvin. *The Two Marxisms: Contradictions and Anomalies in the Development of Theory.* New York: Seabury Press, 1980.

Gregg, Dorothy, and Elgin Williams. "The Dismal Science of Functionalism." *American Anthropologist* 50.4, pt. 1 (October–December, 1948): 594–611.

Guha, Ranajit. "The Prose of Counter-Insurgency." In *Culture/Power/History: A Reader in Contemporary Social Theory,* ed. Nicholas B. Dirks, Geoff, and Sherry B. Ortner. Princeton: Princeton University Press, 1994.

Gutman, Bruno. "The African Standpoint." *Africa* 8.1 (1935): 1–17.

Hamacher, Werner, Neil Hertz, and Thomas Keenan, eds. *Responses: On Paul de Man's Wartime Journalism.* Lincoln: University of Nebraska Press, 1989.

Hammond, Dorothy, and Alta Jablow. *The Africa That Never Was.* Prospect Heights, IL: Waveland Press, 1970.

Harpham, Geoffrey Galt. *One of Us: The Mastery of Joseph Conrad.* Chicago: University of Chicago Press, 1997.

Herskovits, Melville. *Acculturation: The Study of Culture Contacts.* New York: J. J. Augustin Publishers, 1938.

Heyman, Richard. "The Initial Years of the Jeanes School in Kenya, 1924–1931." In *Essays in the History of African Education,* ed. Vincent M. Battle and Charles H. Lyons. New York: Teachers College Press, 1970.

Hobsbawm, Eric, and Terence Ranger, eds. *The Invention of Tradition.* Cambridge: Cambridge University Press, 1983.

Hodgson, Frederick. "Hodgson to Chamberlain, The Fort, Kumasi, 16 April 1900." In *Great Britain and Ghana: Documents of Ghana History, 1807–1957,* ed. G. E. Hetcalfe. Accra: University of Ghana, 1964.

Hoernle, R. F. Alfred. *Race and Reason.* Johannesburg: Witwatersrand University Press, 1945.

Hollis, Martin, and Steven Lukes, eds. *Rationality and Relativism.* Oxford: Blackwell, 1982.

Hooker, James R. "The Anthropologist's Frontier: The Last Phase of African Exploitation." *Journal of Modern African Studies* 1.4 (1963): 455–59.

Hopkins, Terence, et al., eds. *World-Systems Analysis: Theory and Methodology.* Beverly Hills: Sage Publications, 1982.

Horton, Robin, and Ruth Finnegan, eds. *Modes of Thought: Essays on Thinking in Western and Non-Western Societies.* London: Faber, 1973.

Hunt, Nancy Rose. "'Le Bebe en Brousse': European Women, African Birth Spacing, and Colonial Intervention in Breast Feeding in the Belgian Congo." *International Journal of African Historical Studies* 21.3 (1988): 401–32.

Irele, Abiola. "Dimensions of African Discourse." In *Order and Partialities: Theory, Pedagogy, and the "Postcolonial,"* ed. Kostas Myrsiades and Jerry McGuire. Albany: State University of New York Press, 1995.

Jacoby, Russell, and Naomi Glauberman, eds. *The Bell Curve Debate: History, Documents, Opinions.* New York: Random House, 1995.

James, C. L. R. "The Voice of Africa." *International African Opinion* 1.2 (August 1938): 3.

James, Wendy. "The Anthropologist as Reluctant Imperialist." in *Anthropology and the Colonial Encounter,* ed. Talal Asad. Atlantic Heights, NJ: Humanities Press, 1973.

Jerschina, Jan. "Polish Culture of Modernism and Malinowski's Personality." In *Malinowski between Two Worlds: The Polish Roots of an Anthropological Tradition,* ed. Roy Ellen, Ernest Gellner, Graznya Kubica, and Janusz Mucha. Cambridge: Cambridge University Press, 1988.

Johnson, Samuel. *A History of the Yoruba.* 1897. Rpt., London, 1921.

Jones, Thomas Jesse. *Education in Africa: Report by Thomas Jesse Jones.* New York: Phelps-Stokes Commission, 1921.

Kakembo, R. H. *An African Soldier Speaks.* London: Livingstone Press, 1947.

Kaplan, Martha. "Meaning, Agency, and Colonial History: Navosavakadua and the *Tuka* movement in Fiji." *American Ethnologist* 17 (February 1990): 3–22.

Kayamba, H. M. T. "The Modern Life of the East African Native." *Africa* (1932): 50–59.

Kenyatta, Jomo. *Kenya: The Land of Conflict.* London: Panaf Service, 1946.

——. *Facing Mount Kenya.* 1938. Rpt., New York: Vintage, 1965.

Kimble, David. *A Political History of Ghana: The Rise of Gold Coast Nationalism, 1850–1928.* London: Oxford University Press, 1963.

Kuklick, Henrika. *The Savage Within: The Social History of British Anthropology, 1895–1945.* New York: Cambridge University Press, 1991.

Kurczewski, Jacek. "Power and Wisdom: The Expert as Mediating Figure in Contemporary Polish History." In *The Political Responsibility of Intellectuals,* ed. Ian Maclean, Alan Montefiore, and Peter Winch. Cambridge: Cambridge University Press, 1990.

Laudan, Larry. *Progress and Its Problems: Toward a Theory of Scientific Growth.* Berkeley: University of California Press, 1977.

Leith-Ross, Sylvia. *African Women.* New York: Praeger, 1965.

Lévi-Strauss, Claude. "Anthropology: Its Achievement and Future." *Current Anthropology* 7.2 (1966): 124–27.

——. *Tristes Tropiques*. New York: Atheneum, 1981.

Lewis, Diane. "Anthropology and Colonialism." *Current Anthropology* 14.5 (1973): 581–99.

Lloyd, Alan. *The Drums of Kumasi: The Story of the Ashanti Wars*. London: Longman, 1964.

Loram, Charles Templeman. *The Education of the South African Native*. London: Longmans Green, 1917.

——. Foreword to *The Bantu are Coming*, by Ray E. Phillips. New York: Richard R. Smith, 1930.

Lugard, Frederick. "The International Institute of African Languages and Cultures." *Africa* 1.1 (1928): 1–12.

——. *The Dual Mandate in British Tropical Africa*. 1922. Rpt., London: Frank Cass, 1965.

Lyons, Charles. *To Wash an Aethiop White: British Ideas about Black African Educability, 1530–1960*. New York: Teachers College Press, 1975.

Mafeje, Archie. "The Problem of Anthropology in Historical Perspective: An Inquiry into the Growth of the Social Sciences." *Canadian Journal of African Studies* 10.2 (1976): 307–33.

Magubane, Bernard. "A Critical Look at Indices Used in the Study of Social Change in Colonial Africa." *Current Anthropology* 12.4–5 (1971): 419–31.

Malinowski, Bronislaw. "Practical Anthropology." *Africa* (1929): 22–38.

——. "The Rationalization of Anthropology and Administration." *Africa* 3.4 (1930): 405–29.

——. "Native Education and Culture Contact." *International Review of Missions* 25 (1936): 480–515.

——. "The Present State of Studies in Culture Contact: Some Comments on an American Approach." *Africa* (1939): 27–47.

——. *Magic, Science, and Religion and Other Essays*. Boston: Beacon Press, 1948.

——. *The Dynamics of Culture Change in Africa: An Inquiry into Race Relations*. Ed. Phyllis M. Kabery. New Haven: Yale University Press, 1961.

——. Introduction to *Facing Mount Kenya*, by Jomo Kenyatta. New York: Vintage, 1965.

——. *A Diary in the Strict Sense of the Term*. New York: Harcourt, Brace and World, 1967.

Manicom, Linzi. "Ruling Relations: Rethinking State and Gender in South African History." *Journal of African History* 33 (1992): 441–65.

Mannoni, Octave. *Prospero and Caliban: The Psychology of Colonization*. 2d ed. New York: Praeger, 1964.

Maquet, Jacques. "Objectivity in Anthropology." *Current Anthropology* 5 (February 1964): 47–55.

Marcus, George, and Michael M. J. Fischer. *Anthropology as Cultural Critique: An Ex-*

perimental Moment in the Human Sciences. Chicago: University of Chicago Press, 1986.

Masolo, D. A. *African Philosophy in Search of an Identity.* Bloomington: Indiana University Press, 1994.

———. "African Philosophy and the Postcolonial: Some Misleading Abstractions about "Identity." In *Postcolonial African Philosophy: A Critical Reader,* ed. Emmanuel Eze. Cambridge, MA: Blackwell, 1997.

Mason, John, and Mari Clark, eds. *New Directions in U.S. Foreign Assistance and New Roles for Anthropologists.* Williamsburg, VA: Department of Anthropology, College of William and Mary, 1991.

Maxwell, W. E. Letter to the Marquis of Ripon, 9 May 1895. In *Great Britain and Ghana: Documents of Ghana History, 1807–1957,* ed. G. E. Metcalfe. Acera: University of Ghana, 1964.

McCullogh, Jock. *Colonial Psychiatry and "the African Mind."* Cambridge: Cambridge University Press, 1995.

Memmi, Albert. *The Colonizer and the Colonized.* Trans. Howard Greenfield. Introduction by Jean-Paul Sartre. Boston: Beacon Press, 1969.

Mitchell, P. E. "The Anthropologist and the Practical Man—A Reply and a Question." *Africa* 3 (1930): 217–23.

Mohanty, Chandra Talpade. "Under Western Eyes: Feminist Scholarship and Colonial Discourses." In *Third World Women and the Politics of Feminism,* ed. Chandra Talpade Mohanty, Ann Russo, and Lourdes Torres. Bloomington: Indiana University Press, 1991.

Molema, S. M. *The Bantu: Past and Present.* Edinburgh: W. Green and Son, 1920.

Montagu, Ashley. *Man's Most Dangerous Myth: The Fallacy of Race.* New York: Columbia University Press, 1942.

Moore, John. "Perspective for a Partisan Anthropology." *Liberation* 16.6 (1971): 34–43.

Moore, Sally Falk. *Anthropology and Africa: Changing Perspectives on a Changing Scene.* Charlottesville: University Press of Virginia, 1994.

Mouffe, Chantal. "Feminism, Citizenship, and Radical Democratic Politics." In *Feminists Theorize the Political,* ed. Judith Butler and Joan W. Scott. New York: Routledge, 1992.

Mudimbe, V. Y. *The Invention of Africa: Gnosis, Philosophy, and the Order of Knowledge.* Bloomington: Indiana University Press, 1988.

———, and Kwame Anthony Appiah. "The Impact of African Studies on Philosophy." In *Africa and the Disciplines: The Contributions of Research in Africa to the Social Sciences and the Humanities,* ed. Robert Bates, V. Y. Mudimbe, and Jean O'Barr. Chicago: University of Chicago Press, 1993.

Mumford, W. B., and C. E. Smith. "Racial Comparisons and Intelligence Testing. *Journal of the Royal African Society* 37 (1938): 46–57.

Murray-Brown, Jeremy. *Kenyatta.* New York: E. P. Dutton, 1973.

Musgrove, F. "A Ugandan Secondary School as a Field of Cultural Change." *Africa* 22.3 (1952): 234–49.

Ngũgĩ wa Thiong'o. *Decolonising the Mind: The Politics of Language in African Literature.* London: J. Currey, 1986.

Nietzsche, Friedrich. "On Truth and Lie in a Nonmoral Sense." In *Philosophy and Truth: Selections from Nietzsche's Notebooks of the Early 1870's*, ed. and trans. Daniel Breazeale. Highland, NJ: Humanities Press, 1979.

Ntara, Samuel Josia. *Man of Africa.* Trans. and ed. T. Cullen Young. London: United Society for Christian Literature, 1934.

———. *Headman's Enterprise.* Trans. T. Cullen Young. London: Lutterworth Press, 1949.

———. *History of the Chewa.* Wiesbaden: Franz Steiner Verlag, 1973.

Oliver, R. A. C. *General Intelligence Tests for Africans: Manual for Directions.* Nairobi: Government Printers Kenya, 1932.

———. "Mental Tests in the Study of the African." *Africa* (1934): 40–46.

———. "Mental Tests for Primitive Races." *Year Book of Education* (1935): 560–70.

Ouologuem, Yambo. *Bound to Violence.* Trans. Ralph Manheim. London: Heinemann, 1971.

Parpart, Jane L., and Kathleen Staudt, eds. *Women and State in Africa.* Boulder, CO: Lynne Rienner, 1989.

Philip, H. R. A. *Kikuyu News,* September 1938, 175–76. In *The Myth of "Mau Mau": Nationalism in Kenya,* ed. Carl G. Rosberg Jr. and John Nottingham. New York: Meridian Books, 1966.

Phiri, Kings M. "African History: An Assessment and an Agenda for Future Research." *African Studies Review* 30.2 (June 1987): 35–74.

Piaget, J. "Need and Significance of Cross-Cultural Studies in Genetic Psychology." *International Journal of Psychology* 1 (1996): 3–13.

Pieterse, Jan Nederveen. *White on Black: Images of Africa and Blacks in Western Popular Culture.* New Haven: Yale University Press, 1992.

Polanyi, Karl. *Primitive, Archaic, and Modern Economics: Essays of Karl Polanyi.* Ed. George Dalton. Boston: Beacon Press, 1968.

Porteus, Stanley, and Marjorie Babcock. *Temperament and Race.* Boston: R. G. Badger, 1926.

Prakash, Gyan. "Writing Post-Orientalist Histories of the Third World: Indian Historiography Is Good to Think." In *Colonialism and Culture,* ed. Nicholas Dirks. Ann Arbor: University of Michigan Press, 1992.

———. "Postcolonial Criticism and Indian Historiography." *Social Text,* 31–32 (1992): 8–19.

———, ed. *After Colonialism: Imperial Histories and Postcolonial Displacements.* Princeton: Princeton University Press, 1995.

Quayson, Ato. *Strategic Transformations of Nigerian Writing.* Bloomington: Indiana University Press, 1997.

Quick, Griffith. "Review of *General Intelligence Test for Africans: Manual of Directions.*" 7.2 (1934): 249.

Radhakrishnan, R. "Postcoloniality and the Boundaries of Identity." *Callaloo* 16.4 (fall 1993): 750–71.

Radin, Paul. *Primitive Man as Philosopher.* New York: Dover, 1957.

Raglan, Lord. "The Future of Social Anthropology." *Man* (May–June 1943): 58–60.

———. "Anthropology and the Future of Civilization." *Rationalist Annual* (1946): 39–44.

Ranger, Terence. "From Humanism to the Science of Man: Colonialism in Africa and the Understanding of Alien Societies." *Transactions of the Royal Historical Society,* 5th ser., 26 (1976): 115–41.

———. *The Invention of Tribalism in Zimbabwe.* Gweru, Zimbabwe: Mambo, 1985.

Ritchie, J. F. "The African as Suckling and Adult: A Psychological Study." Rhodes Livingstone Papers, no. 9 (1943).

Robbins, Bruce. *Secular Vocations: Intellectuals, Professionalism, Culture.* London: Verso, 1993.

———, ed. *Intellectuals: Aesthetics, Politics, Academics.* Minneapolis: University of Minnesota Press, 1990.

Rubin, Gayle. "The Traffic in Women: Notes on the Political Economy of Sex." In *Toward an Anthropology of Women,* ed. Rayna Reiter. New York: Monthly Review Press, 1975.

Rushton, J. Philippe. "Evolutionary Biology and Heritable Traits." *Psychological Reports* 71.3 (December 1992): 811–23.

Ruxton, F. H. "An Anthropological No-Man's Land." *Africa* 3.1 (1930): 1–11.

Sachs, Wulf. *Black Hamlet.* New introduction by Saul Dubow and Jacqueline Rose. Baltimore: Johns Hopkins University Press, 1996.

Sai, Akiga. *Akiga's Story: The Tiv Tribe as Seen by One of Its Members.* Edited and translated by Rupert East. London: Oxford University Press, 1939.

———. "The 'Descent' of Tiv from Ibenda Hill." *Africa* 24.4 (1954): 295–310.

Said, Edward. *Orientalism.* New York: Pantheon, 1978.

———. "Representing the Colonized: Anthropology's Interlocutors." *Critical Inquiry* 15 (1989): 205–25.

———. *Culture and Imperialism.* New York: Vintage, 1993.

———. *Representations of the Intellectual.* New York, Vintage, 1994.

Sartre, Jean-Paul. *Black Orpheus.* Translated by S. W. Allen. Paris: Presence Africaine, 1976.

Scott, James. *Weapons of the Weak.* New Haven: Yale University Press, 1985.

————. *Domination and the Arts of Resistance*. New Haven: Yale University Press, 1990.

Scott, Joan W. *Gender and the Politics of History*. New York: Columbia University Press, 1988.

————. "Experience." In *Feminists Theorize the Political*, ed. Judith Butler and Joan W. Scott. New York: Routledge, 1992.

Shaw, Carolyn Martin. *Colonial Inscriptions: Race, Sex, and Class in Kenya*. Minneapolis: University of Minnesota Press, 1995.

Slater, Montagu. *The Trial of Jomo Kenyatta*. London: Secker and Warburg, 1955.

Slaymaker, William. "Agents and Actors in African Antifoundationalist Aesthetics: Theory and Narrative in Appiah and Mudimbe." *Research in African Literatures* 27 (spring 1996), 119–28.

Smith, Barbara Herrnstein. *Contingencies of Value*. Cambridge, MA: Harvard University Press, 1988.

Smith, Edwin. *The Golden Stool: Some Aspects of the Conflict of Cultures in Africa*. 2d ed. London: Holborn Publishing House, 1927.

————. "Anthropology and the Practical Man." *Journal of the Royal Anthropological Institute of Great Britain and Ireland* 64 (1934): xiii–xxxvii.

————. *African Beliefs and Christian Faith*. London: Society for Christian Literature, 1936.

————. *The Blessed Missionaries*. London: Oxford University Press, 1950.

Smith, M. *Baba of Karo*. London: Faber and Faber, 1954.

Spivak, Gayatri Chakravorty. "Can the Subaltern Speak?" In *Marxism and the Interpretation of Cultures*, ed. Cary Nelson and Lawrence Grossberg. Urbana: University of Illinois Press, 1988.

————. "Subaltern Studies: Deconstructing Historiography." In *Selected Subaltern Studies*, ed. Ranajit Guha and Gayatri Chakravorty Spivak. Oxford: Oxford University Press, 1988.

Spurr, David. *The Rhetoric of Empire*. Durham: Duke University Press, 1993.

Staudt, Kathleen. "Women's Politics, the State, and Capitalist Transformation in Africa." in *Studies in Power and Class in Africa*, ed. Irving L. Markovitz. Oxford: Oxford University Press, 1987.

Stichter, Sharon B., and Jane L. Parpart, eds. *Patriarchy and Class: African Women in the Home and the Workforce*. Boulder, CO: Westview Press, 1988.

Stocking, George. "Maclay, Kubary, Malinowski: Archetypes from the Dreamtime of Anthropology." In *Colonial Situations: Essays on the Contextualization of Ethnographic Knowledge*, ed. George Stocking. Madison: University of Wisconsin Press, 1991.

Stoler, Ann Laura. "Carnal Knowledge and Imperial Power: Gender, Race, and Morality in Colonial Asia." In *Gender at the Crossroads of Knowledge*, ed. Micaela di Leonardo. Berkeley: University of California Press, 1991.

————. "Rethinking Colonial Categories: European Communities and the Boundaries of Rule." In *Colonialism and Culture,* ed. Nicholas Dirks. Ann Arbor: University of Michigan Press, 1992.

———. *Race and the Education of Desire.* Durham: Duke University Press, 1995.

Summers, Carol. "Intimate Colonialism: The Imperial Production of Reproduction in Uganda, 1907–1925." *Signs* 16.4 (1991): 787–807.

Tammy, Martin, and K. D. Irani, eds. *Rationality in Thought and Action.* New York: Greenwood, 1986

Thomas, Nicholas. *Colonialism's Culture: Anthropology, Travel, and Government.* Princeton: Princeton University Press, 1994.

Torgovnick, Marianna. *Gone Primitive: Savage Intellects, Modern Lives.* Chicago: University of Chicago Press, 1990.

Unwin, Joseph Daniel. *Sex and Culture.* London: Humphrey Milford, 1934.

Vansina, Jan. "Is Elegance Proof? Structuralism and African History." *History in Africa* 10 (1983): 307–48.

———. *Oral Tradition as History.* London: James Currey, 1985.

———. *Living with Africa.* Madison: University of Wisconsin Press, 1994.

Vaughan, Megan. *Curing Their Ills.* Stanford: Stanford University Press, 1991.

———. "Colonial Discourse Theory and African History, or Has Postmodernism Passed Us By?" *Social Dynamics* 20.2 (summer 1994): 1–23.

Vint, F. W. "A Preliminary Note on the Cell Content of the Prefrontal Cortex of the East African Native." *East African Medical Journal* 9 (1932–33): 30–55.

———. "The Brain of the Kenyan Native." *Journal of Anatomy* 68 (1934): 216–23.

Wallerstein, Immanuel. *The Modern World System.* New York: Academic Press, 1974.

Ward, W. E. F. *A History of Ghana.* London: Allen and Unwin, 1958.

Warminski, Andrzej. *Readings in Interpretation: Hölderlin, Hegel, Heidegger.* Minneapolis: University of Minnesota Press, 1987.

Wayne, Helena. Foreword to *Malinowski Between Two Worlds: The Polish Roots of an Anthropological Tradition,* ed. Roy Ellen, Ernest Gellner, Graznya Kubica, and Janusz Mucha. Cambridge: Cambridge University Press, 1988.

———, ed. *The Story of a Marriage: The Letters of Bronislaw Malinowski and Elsie Masson.* 2 vols. New York: Routledge, 1992.

White, Hayden. *Metahistory: The Historical Imagination in Nineteenth Century Europe.* Baltimore: Johns Hopkins University Press, 1973.

Whitehead, Clive. "British Colonial Policy: A Synonym for Cultural Imperialism?" In *Benefits Bestowed?* ed. I. A. Mangam. Manchester: Manchester University Press, 1988.

Williams, Raymond. *Keywords.* London: Oxford University Press, 1976.

———. *Marxism and Literature.* New York: Oxford University Press, 1977.

Willoughby, W. C. *The Soul of the Bantu: A Sympathetic Study of the Magico-Religious Practices and Beliefs of the Bantu Tribes of Africa.* London: Student Christian Movement, 1928.

Wilson, Bryan, ed. *Rationality*. Oxford: Blackwell, 1970.

Winniett, W. "Journal of Lieutenant Governor Winniett's Visit to the King of Ashantee." In *British Parliamentary Papers, 1949,* 230–36.

Winterbottom, J. W. "Can We Measure the African's Intelligence?" *Rhodes-Livingston Journal* 6.6 (1948): 53–59.

Wolf, Eric. *Europe and the People without History*. Berkeley: University of California, 1982.

Women in Nigeria, eds. *Women in Nigeria Today*. London: Zed Press, 1985.

Worsley, Peter. "The End of Anthropology." *Transactions of the Sixth World Congress of Sociology* (1970): 121–29.

Young, Robert. *White Mythologies: Writing History and the West*. New York: Routledge, 1990.

Index

Gordon, L. H., 30
Gough, Kathleen, 65–67, 98
Gould, Stephen Jay, 27, 34 n.43
Gouldner, Alvin, 70 n.26
Gregg, Dorothy, 97
Griaule, Marcel, 63
Guha, Ranajit, 141
Gutmann, Bruno, 157–58

Haakaa, 133–39
Habitus. *See* Bourdieu, Pierre
Heidegger, Martin, 77–78
Herskovits, Melville, 65, 97–98
Historian, 19, 130–31, 161
History, 16, 120, 124, 130–31, 161–66, 172
Hodgson, Frederick, 2, 80, 82
Hoernle, R. F. Alfred, 41 n.63
Hooker, James, 63–64
Human sacrifice, 1–3
Humanism, 80–86, 93–94, 170
Hunt, Nancy Rose, 153 n.82

Interests, 35, 49–58, 59–61, 64, 85–86, 93–96
International Institute of African Languages and Cultures, 80, 118
Invention, 7, 15, 107, 115, 138–39
Irele, Abiola, 8

James, Wendy, 105 n.110
Jameson, Fredric, 133 n.34
Jeanes School, 50
Jerschina, Jan, 100
Johnson, Samuel, 163
Jones, Thomas Hesse, 37 n.54, 38

Kakembo, R. H., 13
Kayamba, H. M. T., 145 n.65
Kenyatta, Jomo, 5, 10, 58, 79, 92, 106–16, 169, 172
Kikuyu Central Association, 106

Knowledge: local, 165; and objectivity, 46, 64–65, 125–39, 172; outsideness as a factor of, 171; and partial truths, 65, 124, 130; politics of, 41, 49–50, 52, 59–61, 62–80, 71–73; 75–77, 91–99, 117–18, 169, 176–77; and relativism, 65, 68; validity of, 132. *See also* Critical (mis)-understanding; Interests; Relevance; Writing

Labouret, Henri, 118
Laudan, Larry, 32 n.39
Leith-Ross, Sylvia, 49 n.77
Lévi-Strauss, Claude, 51 n.8, 67–69, 105, 159
Lévy-Bruhl, Lucien, 23–25, 29, 59
Literary studies: and the canon, 13, 79; and criticism, 14–18
Loram, Charles, 5, 35–40, 50
Lugard, Frederick, 2, 52, 118–19
Lyons, Charles, 40 n.59

Mafeje, Archie, 70–73, 75
Magubane, Bernard, 70–73
Malinowski, Bronislaw, 5, 52, 58, 79, 80, 86–105, 107, 109, 110, 116, 170, 177
Mall, F. P., 30
Mannoni, Octave, 27, 46–49
Maquet, Jacques, 64–65
Marfleet, Philip, 69
Masolo, D. A., 23–24 n.13, 176–77
Materialism, 5, 47–48, 50–52, 60
Mathari Mental Hospital, 32
Mau Mau, 110
McCullogh, Jock, 31, 32 n.38
Memmi, Albert, 47 n.73
Mentality: amentia and, 30; arrested development and, 27–30, 36, 59; brain and, 30–32; dependency complex and, 46–49; environmental characteristics and, 30, 36; eugenics and, 26, 31, 32–41,

Gaurav Desai is Assistant Professor of English and Co-Director of the African
and African Diaspora Studies Program at Tulane University.

Library of Congress Cataloging-in-Publication Data
Desai, Gaurav.
Subject to colonialism : African self-fashioning and the colonial library /
by Gaurav Desai.
p.   cm.
Includes bibliographical references and index.
ISBN 0–8223–2635–3 (hardcover : alk. paper)
ISBN 0–8223–2641–8 (pbk. : alk. paper)
1. Anthropology—Africa—Bibliography.   2. Africa—Colonial influence.
3. Africans—Ethnic identity.   4. Ethnology—Africa—History.   I. Title.
Z5113 .D47 2001
[GN645]
301'.096—dc21   00–010753